DISEWORTH
THE STORY OF A VILLAGE

To the people of Diseworth,
past, present and to come.

DISEWORTH
THE STORY OF A VILLAGE

SD Brompton and PN Hening

First published in 2000 by Diseworth Publications
supported by the Heritage Lottery Fund through the Awards For All Scheme.

Design: Brilliant

Typeset in Goudy Roman 10/12pt

Printed by Russell Press Ltd,
Russell House,
Bulwell Lane,
Basford,
Nottingham, NG6 0BT

ISBN: 0-9539565-0-4

British Library Cataloguing in Publication Data.
A record for this book is available from the British Library.

PREFACE

There is an idyllic dimension to Diseworth. Situated in an apparently sleepy hollow it is an oasis of tranquillity where a splendid steeple overlooks the sheep scattered slopes.

Travellers negotiating the burgeoning commercial conurbations along the busy A 453 could be forgiven for thinking that this is a village where nothing has ever happened.

Still waters run deep! A trawl through the county archives and the muniments room at Christ's College in Cambridge has netted a catch of rich and fascinating variety. A few red herrings have thrown us off course and there have been some fishy stories, but the story of Diseworth has proved to be surprisingly complex.

It has been - indeed still is - a community of no little importance.

FOREWORD

It is appropriate to recall, in this millennium year 2000, that the connection between Diseworth and Christ's College, Cambridge goes back almost half a millennium. In 1505 the Lady Margaret Beaufort, Countess of Richmond and Derby and mother of Henry VII refounded Christ's College. (It was originally established in 1448 under the name God's House). Among her generous benefactions to the new foundation were lands in Ditesworth (as it was then called), as well as in Kegworth, Hathern and Walton. Though these properties were sold in 1920, happily the College still has a connection with the area since it retains the advowson or right of appointment to the living of the parish of Kegworth.

Through the centuries the College has housed a large quantity of original deeds and documents relating to Diseworth, and it is pleasing to see that these have been utilized to good effect by the authors of this commemorative volume. We wish it every success.

AJ Munro
Master of Christ's College

CONTENTS

INTRODUCTION

The village of Diseworth has evoked interest from landowners and settlers throughout its history. Diseworth has had many variations of its name, but almost always with the suffix *worth* meaning enclosed settlement. From those who owned the land and derived their income from the people who farmed it, to those who used the revenue of the workforce to maintain their lifestyle and to finance the education of young men in the pursuit of academic and clerical studies. For all the people who purchased the land for their own advantage, Diseworth, with its population of never more than 1000 souls, has been an important feature of the landscape. With its interesting geographical position in Leicestershire, research has involved visiting record offices in three counties, as well as the visits to the Muniment Room at Christ's College. Certainly, it is the people and their stories that have made their mark on Diseworth Town.

The story takes shape with the priory of Langley, now a private home. In the four hundred years of its existence, Langley Priory exercised considerable control over the parish church and the villagers who worked for the nuns. Benefactors who donated land to the priory often chose land in Diseworth. Shortly before the Dissolution of the priory, along with other religious properties and land in England, Margaret Beaufort, mother of Henry VII, purchased a considerable part of the village to found what became Christ's College, Cambridge. The next five hundred years saw the villagers paying rents to either the Reverend Gentlemen at Christ's or the new owners of Langley, first the Grays, then the Cheslyns and then the Shakespears. The college sold their interest in Diseworth in 1920, but there remain a few farms and houses still owned by landlords.

The parish church that has stood through most of the centuries still stands as the central feature of the village with the four roads stretching out from its base. In the 18th century, the rise of the non-conformist churches was marked in the village with two churches, each with their own important history. The village survived the plagues that affected the country so badly through the 1500s and the 1600s. It also coped with being situated in one of the main areas of the Civil War in the middle of the 1600s and the collapse of national finances through the South Sea Bubble in the 1700s. At the same time the Industrial Revolution and the huge growth of towns and industry in the Midlands obviously affected the inhabitants as they moved away from the land to the promises offered by the new factories. The education of the young people, originally restricted to a few, became Education for All, and the village boasted a school in 1862.

The accounts of the owners and the occupants with their hopes and ambitions through the years make Diseworth a place of much interest, and the revelations of the twentieth century villagers show a village that has been occupied by many generations of families. We have traced those many names and others whose influence on Diseworth have made it such a special village.

EARLY DAYS

Diseworth has been home to people for very many years, evidence showing nearer two thousand years than one. We have evidence of Roman occupation, of Saxon and Viking occupation and at the time of the Norman Conquest Diseworth was sufficiently important to be allocated as reward to Norman Knights. Villages were normally built around a central spot, usually a well or around running water and Diseworth was no different. The brook has been of major importance throughout the history of the village. In the early days the villagers would have lived in homes that were half timbered and this was popular for centuries, as wood was plentiful. The trees would have been well cared for and saplings fenced in to inhibit damage from animals. The animals also would have had enclosures for protection. Horses were very important for work, transport and possibly food. Archaeological evidence has indicated that a Roman farmstead and possibly a Roman road existed in Diseworth.

'One cool evening in September 1998 there was a knock at the door. Once opened it revealed two metal detectorists, looking very serious who said they wanted to show us something special. Lying on a velvet cloth were a number of Roman silver Denarii coins in excellent condition. It seems the coins had lain in the field for 1800 years' From an account by Liz Jarrom, Diseworth Dialogue.

The Romans left in 5AD, and other settlers moved into Diseworth. The Angles, Saxons and the Jutes raided the country during the next few hundred years, each leaving their mark in some way or another. Our four Gates are from Viking times, though it is unlikely they were given their specific names as we know them today.

When the Domesday Book was recorded twenty years after the Battle of Hastings, there appeared to be just one owner in Diseworth a William Loveth, who held three caracutes of land (approximately 360 acres). This was land for three ploughs and six villeins (feudal serfs) and six bordars (smallholding cottagers - of lesser status than villeins). The arrangements under William the Conqueror were as they had been in Normandy, land in return for helping William to win battles. This land to be held in trust and when required, the fortunate knight would be called upon to assist William in battle. He could in turn let his land, for either cash rent called fines, or kind, depending what the land was used for, and how much was rented. It would seem William Loveth did not hold on to Diseworth for long and chronicles tell us of a variety of owners and also a considerable number of different claims.

'Easter 1357. Walter de Mauney and his wife Margaret demand a third part of the manor of Diseworth against Robert Bertram, chevalier, and his wife Blanche. Robert and Blanche dispute this saying the premises were given to Blanche by charter, to hold for life for the rent of one rose flower annually on the feast of St. John the Baptist.'

By the time of the Leicestershire survey of 1124/29, the amount of land, which went by the different spellings of the name Diseworth had increased considerably. The Earl of Leicester held 420 acres, the Earl of Chester 720 acres and Robert de Ferrers 720 acres. Property was held on a feudal system, based on the acquisition of land in return for services to the king. At the head of this hierarchy were the barons and the Church who were tenants in chief. In return for holding the land, they were expected to pay taxes to the king and also to provide him with knights to help fight his battles. The next in line were the yeomen or farmers and at the bottom end of the scale were the peasants - or cottars. Land in Diseworth changed hands frequently during the next 250 years with various fees, rents and dowers being paid accompanied by the occasional dispute.

In 1215 Thomas Overton and his wife Isabella were summoned to justify to Stephen de Segrave 240 acres of land in Diseworth that he held of them. Eight years later Reginald Bassett granted all this land to Stephen. For this, de Segrave promised to pay Reginald £10 a year until his death whereupon Stephen and his heirs would be absolved of the payment forever.

CORAM REGE ROLL 1358 William de Overton, parson of Kegworth Church v. John de Bredon of Dyseworth and Juliana his wife, Adam Tebbe and William Tebbe of Dyseworth, Ralph, prior of Repyngdon and Robert Tebbe, canon of the same priory in a plea wherefore they carried off from Kegworth, John, son and heir of Reginald de Gurmundley, under age being, whose marriage belongs to William de Overton, against William's wish and against the peace. The sheriff is ordered diligently to enquire where the said heir is, and to have the defendants in court in the octave of St. Martin.

The ownership of Diseworth was hotly disputed in the next fifty years with many court cases being brought. The land passed in 1461 to John Mowbray, Duke of Norfolk. His son, John, died in 1475 leaving one infant child, Anne, just three years old. She was married to Richard, Duke of York in 1478 but died childless. Her heirs were William Berkeley, created Earl of Nottingham and Marquess of Berkeley, and John Howard, created Duke of Norfolk in 1483. Howard was killed at the Battle of Bosworth in 1485 and the rights to the estate died with him.

In 1487 the estate was declared the property of Sir Henry Colet. It was from Sir Henry that the Lady Margaret Beaufort subsequently purchased the manor and estate of Diseworth which was presented to the Master, Fellows and Scholars of Christ's College, Cambridge as a useful source of revenue.

During these centuries the history of Diseworth has been dominated by two great landowners, those at Langley Priory and those at Christ's College Cambridge.

The first five hundred years indicate some control by Langley Priory, increasing with many gifts of land in Diseworth. After the Dissolution of the monasteries by Henry VIII, ownership for the Langley Estate was by the Lords of the Manor at Langley and for the Diseworth Estate by the Master, Fellows and Scholars of Christ's College in Cambridge.

It is only in the 20th Century that Diseworth has become independent of such strong control, and it was in that century that it has grown in its own right.

PART ONE
LANGLEY PRIORY

CHAPTER ONE THE NUNNERY AND THE NUNS

William Pantulf

One person, William Pantulf, was to arrive, who did not want the land for himself, but to found a nunnery near the village. Nuns need a Church and land to provide employment as well as constant prayers for the founders. William Pantulf and his wife Burgia founded Langley Priory about 1150 for a Benedictine order of nuns. In such times, it was their families rather than vocational calling that put nuns in convents. Men often went off to war, and as many did not come home the young women needed to be provided for. Here the girls would have a home and, if they were lucky, an education.

I desire by this notice that all people who are now living and be hereafter to understand that I, William Pantulf, a soldier renowned in arms, and Lady Burgia, my wife, have handed over to God and the Blessed Virgin Mary our estate at Langley as a mark of respect for her piety, and all our plumed helmets and all the other things in our possession which formerly by the ancient law were held to be marks of distinction. (The origin of Langley Priory.)

Who was this William Pantulf? Records indicate he was the great grandson of William Pantulf, who came over at, or immediately after the 1066 Conquest. William the Conqueror had long encouraged his supporters to help to develop monasteries and he gave generously himself. The older Pantulf followed suit, as did his descendants. After the accession of Henry 1st in 1100, there was a rebellion of noblemen and Pantulf was sufficiently regarded by the King to be given the governorship of Stafford Castle. William Pantulf's son Robert succeeded to his English estates.

Robert's son Ivo sired five children, three by his first wife and two by his second wife. The second wife was Alice de Verdun and their children were Norman and William and it is this son William Pantulf who founded Langley Priory. The de Verdun name was known in Diseworth, as Norman de Verdun, the father of Alice, was a landowner in the village.

Both the Pantulfs and the de Verduns were described as important people in Staffordshire. The de Verduns themselves were related by marriage to the de Ferrers, Earls of Derby, and much of the land given to the Priory: Somerby, Little Dalby and Tonge, were each part owned by de Ferrers, as was Diseworth. William's wife Burgia, is described as co-founder, and she also gave land and tithes to the Priory.

Thus the new Priory was given, together with two churches, the land that went with them, the whole of Langley Wood and the water mill at Tonge.

The Nuns Arrive

The nuns came from a mother-house in Staffordshire, Farewell Priory. In the book 'Holy Women of the Twelfth Century', by Sharon Elkins, it is suggested that Langley is the only nunnery with another nunnery as a mother-house. The reason may have been that the Bishop of Lichfield, who was the founder of Farewell Priory was related to William Pantulf through his grandmother. For a while they enjoyed the privileges of the Cistercian order which meant they were exempt from tithes, a matter which was reversed soon after when it was realised that they were not of that order.

It seems that the nuns soon became known in the village. Benedict of Diseworth, who was Lord of the Manor in Diseworth in the early thirteenth century, gave the patronage of the Parish Church of St. Michael and All Angels to the nuns at Langley Priory. The village had been divided between three parishes; part belonged to Lockington, part to Breedon and the rest to Diseworth. This was important when it came to paying tithes. And though it has been suggested that the nuns had sole use of the Church, this would have included all those who worked for them both in the Priory and on the land. The history of the Church indicates that much extra building took place in the Church in the thirteenth century, namely the construction of the south aisle. The generous Lord of the Manor or the Patrons of the Priory presumably, on the instructions of the Prioress funded this with income from numerous gifts of land. In fact, by 1291 the Priory was said to be worth £20 0s 9d, a fair sum in those days.

In the 13th century the nuns of the Priory benefited from endowments from various parts of the country. One of these included the gift of 500 eels from the fishery of Lady Basilia de Holmia.

Links with Wartoft Grange
Part of Wartoft Grange, on the edge of Diseworth, was linked to Langley Priory very many years ago when it was part of Norton Priory in Cheshire. William FitzNigel, Constable of Chester and his son Robert were benefactors to the canons of Norton. William Pate gave four acres of land 'between Wavertoft and the Priory mill' to the nuns at Langley.

'Extract from Burton's Leicestershire 1622
Wartoft neere Castle Donington, in the Hundred of West Goscote. This was sometimes a Grange, belonging to the Priory of Norton in Cheshire. It is now in the inheritance of Edward Lord Monticute, Baron of Beughton in Northamptonshire. It is in the Parish of Donington. '

The above note was received from Mr. John Bird, who has lived in Wartoft Grange for the past thirty-six years. Mr. Bird was told that the monks lived in the house and cooked meals and administered the farm. Farm workers also lived in the house. There is evidence of a priest hole, now boarded up, used for hiding priests during Cromwellian times.

Trouble at Langley
The Priory however, was not without its disputes. No doubt this was because, within such a short time of its commencement, Langley was so very well endowed by

benefactors who wished the nuns to pray for them and their souls thereafter, that the nuns became very affluent. The first dispute was with the Mother House, Farewell Priory. Whilst it may at first appear so, the arguments were not just about power and income. A Mother House could be reprimanded by the Bishop for failure to keep adequate control over the various and potentially ungodly activities of its offshoot. Farewell Priory in Staffordshire appeared to want to have some say in the election of prioresses at Langley and so give them some vestige of control over the running of Langley. The Prioress would always have much power in the Convent and the properties and land, and Langley disputed any involvement from Farewell. Unfortunately, Farewell Priory was proved right many years later, when Langley was very badly managed and it seems the current Prioress was at fault. It was agreed in the early 1200's that the Prioress of Farewell had the right to participate in the election of Prioresses of Langley, but all other claims must be renounced. The quarrel was resumed a few years later and resolved with money when Langley agreed to pay the sum of four marks to the mother house. The problems had reached the Pope, Alexander III or at least his envoy, for he ordered an inquiry as to whether the nuns of Langley had paid certain tithes for 30 years previously. It is unlikely that the Priory had even been in existence for that long but it raised the question that the nuns had claimed to be of the Cistercian Order and had claimed exemption from tithes as such.

The Priory of Breedon disputed this mainly because Langley held land in Breedon. After various enquiries and counter decisions, the nuns of Langley agreed to pay tithes to Breedon Priory for the land they held and cultivated there. In 1229 they agreed to give Breedon Priory a 'toft,' an acre of land and 7 marks in money in return for exemption from tithes for all the land they held in Breedon Parish. In proceeding years the nuns had to pay further tithes, so in the end they gave up their claims to Cistercian privileges and were known as a Benedictine House. Throughout that time the Priory still held the advowson (the right to appoint the priest) of Diseworth and held the rectory, so until the Dissolution of the Monasteries in 1536 they received the tithes from one third of the village.

Having responsibility for the churches was not without problems. One such occurred as early as 1209, at the church of Little Dalby, whose advowson was given to Langley by William Pantulf himself.

'The prioress presented one Robert de Leth to the Officials in Lincoln to be given charge of Little Dalby as parson provided he first dismissed his concubine with the added penalty that he would lose the job if she returned'

It seems Robert de Leth argued the point, though whether it was the appointment to Little Dalby, and the jurisdiction of the Prioress or whether he should dismiss the woman is not certain. However the Bishop insisted he dispose of the concubine and the Archdeacon was directed to see that he did so!

The Other Nun's grass!

In 1371 the villagers of Diseworth together with the men of Belton claimed pasture rights on certain fields where the boundaries of the two townships joined. John de Gormundeleye of Diseworth and many other villagers were summoned by the Prioress of Gracedieu for dispasturing her herbage on Ascension Day until the feast of the Holy Trinity.

The problems arose for the nuns in ensuing years through mostly errant tenancies and poor husbandry. Langley owned land in Belgrave near Leicester. In 1467 John Belgrave and others were summoned to answer Margaret Bellars, the Prioress in a plea wherefore they broke the close belonging to the Prioress at Belgrave, and trod and consumed her herbage to the value of £10. The defendants argued that John Belgrave had inherited the lands from his father. But in a subsequent suit the prioress recovered 5 marks against the said John Belgrave for damage done to her close at Belgrave. The prioress was on shaky ground because some years earlier in 1441 when Margery Pole was Prioress of Langley, she stated in an account to the Bishop that she had not received the 40 shillings a year due from Belgrave and did not even know where the land lay from which it was collected. However, either through bad management or diseased crops the finances of the Priory dropped considerably in the ensuing years.

The Involvement with Diseworth

As the religious houses were also the principal sheep farmers and Langley was no exception it is possible that much of Diseworth had sheep grazing around it. Records show that for miles around in Leicestershire sheep farming was prevalent. Launde and Langley Priories were each expected to produce yields of 5 sacks a year in the early fourteenth century. Considering that each sack contained 250 fleeces this implies 1250 fleeces, no small flock. How many villagers were employed as shepherds and sheep shearers? However, in a record in 1485 it states ...*'134 acres of Langley's demesnes consisted of arable lying in the open fields which provided much corn for the house. Another thirty acres were pasture for the exclusive use of the prioress...mainly from the said cross of Diseworth to a row of trees towards Langley...being accounted her chief pasture of comen for her sheep.'* From an account of the Priory circa 1300.

The flock was sufficiently large to demand the full time attention of a shepherd and numbered probably about two hundred.

It is interesting to note that the Cross at Diseworth has its name going back some five hundred years, and also confirms the naming of Ladygate as the route from the Church to Langley, albeit a shepherd's path.

When the tenants of Diseworth made their annual procession to mark the boundaries of the Parish, they made alterations to the route which were not in the best interests of the Prioress of Langley. She arrived hot foot to berate the vicar of Diseworth and then afterwards sent her steward to negotiate.

Hardship in Langley and the Bishop's Visitations

The first record that can be found concerning Bishop's Visitations was in 1354 when Bishop Gynewell arrived at Langley. He reported that he found the house in good order and occupied by twelve nuns, but the lands were barren for lack of cultivation, probably owing to the pestilence. (Plague was rampant at this time).

A mixture of poverty and laxity: Langley Priory, according to Bishop Alnwick's visitation. 1440.

The Prioress was Dame Margery Pole who was somewhat lacking in literacy and it was perhaps this that had caused the finances to be slack. For a start she could not produce her certificate of confirmation of position in the Priory. She claimed she knew when she had received the mandate as it was on the feast of St. Denys, but she had been unable to understand the certificate, nor could her chaplain to whom she had shown it. When the original mandate was read to her, not in Latin, she was asked if she understood it, she replied that she had and she had executed it for herself and her sister nuns. When asked for the Foundation Charter the only answer that she could give was that William Pantulf was the Founder but as the nuns were '*unversed in letters they could not understand the writings*'. This was not that they could neither read nor write, rather that they could not use the Latin tongue. The prioress confessed that she had not rendered her accounts yearly to her sisters but she would account to the Bishop. There followed the sad news that the Priory was in a poor state financially. The rents of the house were only £20. Amongst other falling income the prioress announced that income from Diseworth which used to be a hundred shillings was now only twenty-four and the house was in debt to the amount of £50.There appeared quite a number of boarders, one of whom, Lady Audeley, paid forty shillings a year for her stay which kept the house in repair. However this Lady Audeley unfortunately had a large number of dogs, which followed her into the church and the noise of twelve dogs frightened and upset the nuns at prayer.

After a few more details concerning the problems which beset them the other nuns gave evidence. These ladies whose names indicate their 'gentle birth' admitted other misdemeanours:- Dame Joan Etone (probably from Long Eaton) the sub prioress, said that the previous Prioress had permitted much dilapidation of the outbuildings and inner buildings had also suffered defects in their roofing. Dame Joan Groby (possibly from Groby) said that certain of the nuns wore silk veils, obviously frowned upon. Dame Margaret Montgomery blamed the prioress for not holding chapters and keeping to a private lodging rather than sleep in the dorter where they do and that secular children were accommodated in the dorter at night. Dame Elisabeth Bonyngton from part of what is now Sutton Bonington, made the serious comment that the sale of the timber, without the consent of the convent, took place twice and that the nuns did not receive the underwood from it. They were thus without fuel to cook food, also that when the trees were felled they were not fenced and the resulting sprouts of trees were trampled and eaten by the animals.

The Bishop Rules

The Bishop had to deal with all this and left a set of instructions for the nuns and in particular for the Prioress.

No more silk veils.
Veils down to their eyebrows.
The married couple who live in the priory to be removed altogether.
No secular folk to sleep in the dorter.
The woods not to be sold again without permission.
The woods to be enclosed again after felling.
No more nuns to be admitted than can be maintained by the house.
Every nun to have yearly, a cartload of fuel at the cost of the house.
No more letters or gifts or mutual tokens to be sent or received.
The Prioress to attend the chapters and also sleep sometimes in the dorter.
Lady Audeley to be warned to keep her dogs away from the church and the choir.

Langley was not really very different to other religious houses of the time, which seemed to lack good husbandry. The Bishop's Secretary recorded 'certain faults' at Langley but in fact the Bishop went on the following day to Grace Dieu where he found 'certain and notable defaults'. The Langley Prioress carried on a further seven years after the Bishop's visit and sadly, one assumes the House and the nuns suffered as a result.

Pure virginity and rare chastity

Some of the nuns may have been lax but there is evidence that one at least fulfilled her vocational role:

'There was many years ago, a nun of this house, as it goeth by current tradition, called Hawise of Colville, of so pure virginity and rare chastity, that was so free from sin of any kind, as that her thoughts were free from any such passions, and whole face did discover so much by a shining radiance and brightness thereof.'

Dissolution

The dissolution of the monasteries in England was a dramatic action on the part of the King. But the story of the suppression of the Church should be seen in a wider context of fast moving and religious change in the years 1530 to 1540. These moves not only strengthened the control of Henry V111 over the Church but also considerably improved his finances.

Valor Ecclesiasticus (general ecclesiastical survey)
The annual incomes of the monasteries and nunneries at the time of the Dissolution in 1535 is provided by the Valor Ecclesiasticus

Convents and monasteries being places of prayer and contemplation, it is easy to understand why the occupants did not always manage a successful economy, and unfortunately Langley was no different to others in this respect. However they usually employed a lay person to act as steward and who handled much of the day to day business of the house and lands. In return the steward generally lived on farms leasehold to the Priory and often lived in some style. John Villiers was the Langley steward and he managed to lease two valuable farms at Little Dalby. His assistant was John Davy who was bailiff at Diseworth and Langley, and who was probably a local man. They did not do too badly at the Dissolution, Villiers receiving £1 and Davy £1 6s 8d.

It must have been a frightening experience for the prioress and sisters to learn that they were to be expelled from their home. They were not young and had probably not travelled very far during their lifetime at Langley. Doctors Leigh and Layton visited the Priory to estimate its value. The assessors recorded that the patroness was the wife of Sir Francis Bigot, and the yearly income of the house stood at £36, though they were in debt for 20 marks.

The report in 1536 noted that
'The Priory dedicated to God and the Blessed Virgin, contained six nuns besides the Prioress, who was very old and impotent. All the nuns desired to continue in religion, and all were virtuous, though one was over eighty and another feeble minded. There was a priest attached to the nunnery, and the lay servants consisted of ten men and four women'.

On the 24th June 1536 the process of the Dissolution began which took three months. Plate and Jewels were taken and forthwith despatched to the Treasury. It is recorded that the Prioress Dulcosa Bothe, was obliged, during the weary time of waiting, to sell some silver in order to maintain the hospitality and alms of the house. Vestments and movables of the convent were sold for more than £81 while the lead of the roof and gutters and two small bells realised another £34. Once the dissolution was completed the nuns were expelled and 34s 8d was distributed amongst them. Sadly there is evidence of only one reference to a sister receiving a pension.

Some four hundred years after William Pantulf had established Langley Priory, it took only a short time to be dissolved. In addition to the many prayers for its founders and benefactors the Priory had provided much local employment. It had benefited from good times as well as bad and we have a fine inventory of its contents in 1485, said to be unique in an account of the contents of a convent made before the Dissolution of the monasteries.

The inventory includes mass books, chalices, cloths for the altars, vestments for the priests, numerous towels of different materials and quality, ornaments and banners, jewels and relics, and crosses and silver plate. In addition are mentioned from 'the Priory Chambers' feather beds and mattresses, sheets, coverlets, curtains, bolsters, blankets, pillows, towels, basins, cushions and such. Any item which is embroidered has full details of the embroidery given. They may have taken vows of poverty and obedience, but there were times when the sisters lived in affluence.

The Prioresses of Langley

Whether the Farewell Mother House had influence or not in the election of the Prioresses at Langley, the earlier ones were well connected either through the founder or benefactors of the Priory or through distinguished names of the time.

There is some evidence of their names, either when they were professed or elected or when they died, but documents vary as to names and dates. However these ladies must have had certain influence on Diseworth and deserve being recorded.

Roseia and Burgia	were the first Prioresses recorded from 1229 and 1230. Their appointments were witnessed by Mathias, Abbot of Leicester and confirmed by the Prior of Nostell
Isabel of Leicester	elected 1229
Juliane of Winchester	appointed 1269, and
Christine of Winchester	who resigned in 1294, were connected by marriage to the de Ferrars family, who had strong links with Langley Priory, and gave land and funds to the nuns
Alicia of Tatysrsal	who died in 1275, was possibly from the Tatersal family who became patrons of the Priory in the 13th century
Margaret of Leicester	1278
Amice de Burgh	confirmed in 1295 and who died in 1302 was related to the Verdons (who were related to the Pantulf family)

Alice Gifford	elected 1302
Elizabeth of Caldwell	elected 1306 until 1332
Joan of Outheby	elected 1333 until 1336, probably came from the Oadby family
Margaret de Sulveye	elected 1335 to 1374
Margaret Salhowe	is named as Prioress in 1429 and could have been related to the above Margaret
Margery Pole	was Prioress in 1440 at the Bishop's Visitation.
Margaret Bellers	took over from Margery Pole from 1447 to 1485
Dulcosa Bothe	was Prioress in 1536 at the Dissolution

Langley Priory becomes Langley Hall

When the king sent his commissioners to the religious houses to value everything prior to the dissolution, a great task was placed before them. In a short time, usually a few days, the entire contents of the priory had to be listed and valued, as well as the properties and farms, leases and woods. Some of this was inevitably left to the clerks or perhaps the lay stewards employed by the house. Sybil Jack in 'The Last Days of the Smaller Monasteries in England' states that the commissioners, if they so chose, were certainly in an excellent position to acquire small or not so small perquisites in this way. The religious community would surely not have put any barriers in their way, when the leniency with which they themselves were treated depended so much on the goodwill of those same commissioners. The same may have been true for recommendation of the possible new owner of the property.

In 1536, at the time of the Dissolution, Langley had a tenant, Thomas Gray, and it was to this gentleman that King Henry VIII subsequently sold the Priory.

'The nunnery of Langley was returned by the Commissioners to be worth, in spiritualities and temporalities, according to one commissioner, £29 7s 4½d.; according to another, £34 6s 2d yet herein were maintained eight nuns. The site and demesne lands of Langley nunnery were at the dissolution, of the yearly value of £7 5s 4½d; and they were demised, at the same rent, to Thomas Gray.'

'Letters Patent: Henry VIII
Thomas Gray Esq.
The King grants the following property: Property of the former Priory of Langley. The site of precinct of the former Priory of Langley with all its appurtenances and the mill within the site.'

The Gray family came from Castle Donington and were to own Langley for 120 years. Whether any of the family actually ever lived there is not certain. There is evidence that in 1550 Thomas Gray leased the 'capital messuage in Langley with certain lands to one John Bozon for a term of 51 years with the proviso that in the event of the deaths of the Grays before that time, the lease would become void'.

However Parish Registers from the Church in Diseworth mention the Gray's of Langley.

Extracts from the Register of Diseworth

Thomas Gray of Langley	**died**	**March 1662**
Ann Gray widow of above	**died**	**June 1662**
William Gray son of William Gray	**born**	**1664**
Mary, Daughter of George and Sarah Gray	**born**	**1673**
John Gray married Hannah Kniveton		**1673**
John Gray of Castle Donington married Mary Mee of Diseworth		**1680**

Certainly the Priory required much renovation. The lead on the roof and the guttering had been sold and the nuns would not have spent their much-needed money on a property that was about to be taken from them.

A document quoted in the Leicestershire Archaeological Society relating to lands at Langley Priory suggests that much of the refurbishment was undertaken using stone from the castle at Donington.

'Castle at Donington dilapidated and fallen down…

As for the stone of the said castle and broken walls, it is not of any great value nor much to be made thereof and is little worth as we think but to such persons as have building in hand near thereunto…

Mr Gray for his building now in hand at his house at Langley within two miles, is content to pay yearly for the one, old square tower, three shillings to the Queen's Majesty's use, so that he may have free egress and regress from time to time to carry away the loose stones and occupy the same site within the Castle and without the castle to enclose the ditch.

A commission repaired to the Queen's Mylnes of Donington (now Kings Mills) - in reasonable state of repair and ought to be at the said farmer's charges repaired and maintained during his time. Repairs done by Thomas Gray (said farmer).

Timber for piles, crabtree for cornmills, maple for the malt milne, sallow for the park pales, all felled and taken of the said Gray within his manor of Langley these three years now last past to the value of £14 8s 0d being so valued by the testimony of saying of several honest persons that felled and carried the wood. The same justified before us to have taken within the said woods, for there was not like to be had within the Queen's Majesty's woods.'

And thus Langley was built up again. Probably the 'appurtenances' included the land in the area, parts of Diseworth, as well as the productive woods, these possibly employing the local workforce.

Four generations of Grays owned Langley, and these included the years of the Civil War, when Castle Donington and presumably the Gray family were much involved.

An affluent family, the Thomas Gray who was born at the end of the sixteenth century sired four sons and proceeded to purchase property and land for them, in Sutton Bonington and in Repton. However his eldest son must have upset him very much when he married against his father's consent, because he was disowned to the material benefit of his brothers. This may have been the deciding factor in the ownership of Langley for in 1686, four years after the death of the father, Langley was sold.

IT'S WHO YOU KNOW

There were far fewer surnames three hundred years ago than today, so it is worth mentioning a few links.

1536 Sir John **Villiers** was the Langley Priory steward who had managed to lease for himself two of the most valuable farms around the time of the Dissolution.

1550 approx. Thomas **Gray** who acquired the Priory was married to Cecilia **Villiers**.

1600 approx. The granddaughter of this Thomas **Gray**, Dorothy, married a John **Bainbrigge** of Lockington.

Elizabeth **Bainbrigge**, daughter of above, married John St. Andrew, had a daughter Mary.

1603 Death of John **Hawford,** Grand Tenant of Diseworth, and brother of Edward **Hawford,** Master of Christ's College and Rector of Kegworth, whose daughter Margaret was married to Gervase **Pigott.**

1610 Gervase **Pigott,** marries Mary St. Andrew, granddaughter of John **Bainbrigge** and Dorothy **Gray.**

1662 Thomas **Bainbrigge** was Master of Christ's College

1722 Luke Abbott assigned to **Mary Bainbrigge**, widow of John **Bainbrigge** of Lockington, a cottage and land at Diseworth in consideration of £350.

1724 William **Bainbrigge** of Lockington, administrator of Mary **Bainbrigge**, assigned the remainder of the above lease to Peter Harvey.

1770 approx. The grandson of Richard **Cheslyn** who purchased Langley married Katharine **Bainbrigge**, widow of Philip Bainbrigge of Lockington.

1818 A Richard **Cheslyn** was rusticated from Christ's College for 'sending a challenge to Wetherby races'.

CHAPTER TWO THE CHESLYNS OF LANGLEY

Langley Hall as it became known was purchased by Richard Cheslyn in 1686 for £7,769 17s 6d. Richard Cheslyn was noted as an important person, an eminent founder who had set up the Whitechapel Waterworks in London.

The Cheslyn family were to own and occupy Langley through five generations for over one hundred and fifty years. During that time they became land and property owners in Diseworth and the Cheslyn name was prominent in many aspects in the life of the village. The field containing the cricket pitch in Diseworth is still known to senior residents as 'Cheslyns' and the pulpit in the Church bears the initials RC 1713.

However from the beginning of the sixteenth century Diseworth had another Lord of the Manor, Christ's College in Cambridge, and over the following two centuries the two major landlords of Diseworth became inextricably linked.

Soon after purchasing Langley, Richard Cheslyn set about obtaining land in Diseworth. A document dated October 1693 indicates that he took over the remainder of a 21year lease of 1½ yardlands in Diseworth when Robert Lilly was the lessee of Christ's College. At the same time Richard Cheslyn purchased a messuage, cottages and lands in the village.

He had four wives, two of whom provided him with five sons between them, and it was the fifth son, Robert, who inherited Langley in 1717. Robert was married to Cave King, niece of Sir John Cave of Clifton, and this good woman bore her husband five sons and ten daughters.

Langley declared extra parochial

Robert Cheslyn also acquired leases for properties and lands in Diseworth owned by Christ's College, paying rents amounting to almost £2 10s per annum. This same Robert was one of forty signatories to a letter signed by the farmers in Diseworth, in 1744, to the 'Reverend Gentlemen' at Christ's College pleading against the rise in rents being imposed by the Grand Tenant, Charles Barwell (see More Trouble at Diseworth). He was considered sufficiently important by his fellow farmers to be named as the recipient to whom the answer was to be addressed.

Robert Cheslyn was a popular member of the village. A story tells of a court case at Leicester assizes in 1717 when Robert was tried for non payment of the poor levy. The verdict was given against him, but a new trial was immediately set into motion, and before a special jury the new verdict was given for plaintiff Cheslyn. In March 1720 the vicar and twenty-four inhabitants of Diseworth signed a document acknowledging Langley to be extra parochial and stating it not to be liable to be assessed for poor rates.

Cheslyn as Grand Tenant

The eldest son of Robert, Richard, who inherited in 1750, was a barrister of the Middle Temple and also was keen to purchase leases and property in Diseworth as they became available.

A unique opportunity arose some years later when Leonard Fosbrooke became the Grand Tenant for Christ's College with responsibility for handling all the leases and collecting all the rents. Some prior discussion must have taken place as within nine days Richard Cheslyn had drawn up articles of agreement whereby Fosbrooke assigned 'the manor and Grand College Lease' to him in consideration of £1130. Unfortunately Cheslyn took a while to pay up and some two years later Fosbrooke applied to the Court for payments of debts amounting to £740.

Indenture

Witnesseth that the said Master, Fellows and Scholars with one assent and consent as well as for and in consideration of the sum of £3640 of lawful money of Great Britain to them paid by the said Richard Cheslyn as and for a Fine for the renewal of a lease of the Lands and Hereditaments hereinafter demised also for and in consideration of the…

All that the manor or Lordship of Diseworth in the county of Leicester, Langley Lands, Walton Leys and appurtenances…

And all lands, tenements, house buildings, barns, stables, edifices, meadows, feedings pastures, inclosures, moors, fishing, fowling, hearths, fold courses with liberty of fold and profits of Courts, rents, fines, forfeitures, amerciaments, waifs, strays, felons, goods, wards, marriages etc. to the said manor or lordship and the game therein.

Also mentioned are Kegworth, Hathern Isley Walton, Hemington, Belton and Castle Donington.

Expansion and Improvement at the Hall

About this time Richard Cheslyn married Katharine Bainbrigge, a rich widow, which must have helped matters. However he made much use of his wife's fortune to expand and improve Langley spending £5000 on plantations, gardens and pleasure grounds, as well as purchasing lands in Diseworth and Castle Donington. (Whether Katharine Bainbrigge approved of her new husband's expensive life style is not known, but when she died five years after Richard, she was buried beside her first husband at Lockington).

The Cheslyn family were to hold the title of Grand Tenant for almost seventy years. Richard Cheslyn died in 1787, and his named executors held the role until his nephew, Richard, the eldest son of his brother Thomas took over the leases. An elaborate will had been drawn up by his uncle, who had no children from his marriage, by which the nephew and then his eldest son inherited Langley. Many documents record the details of the leases which this nephew made with the tenants of Diseworth. But his own financial matters were giving him cause for concern.

Hardship at Langley

The family fortune, which his uncle had built up, together with the many properties purchased, afforded the Cheslyns a life of relative luxury, but a mining speculation proved disastrous, and the family had to face losing their home and property. The son Richard came of age in 1818 with many high family expectations which unfortunately came to nothing. With the decline in fortune came a decline in the attention to the property, especially the property belonging to Christ's College. The evaluation of the College in 1837 showed the buildings in a bad state of repair and their occupants in much need. The timber plantations which were the main stay, not only of the College, but also of the tenants for repair and fuel, had not been cared for and new plantations not set out. However, it was noted that while the tenants complained about their hardships, not one complained about the Grand Tenant!

The Grand Tenant had sufficient problems of his own and in 1837 he conveyed a considerable amount of his properties, with the exception of Langley and its appurtenances, but including the coal wharf and colliery, to John Mammatt and John Johnson, both of Ashby de la Zouch, with power to sell or mortgage, in order to settle his debts. It is recorded that Richard Cheslyn remained cheerful throughout his ordeals, helped by his many friends, but unfortunately by 1840 Langley had to be sold.

The Sale of Langley Priory

The Famed Langley Priory Estate, as the agents described it, was to be sold by Auction in July 1843 at the Auction mart in London. Described as a most important freehold property with small part leasehold, the agents spared nothing in their eloquent writings concerning the property. Eighteen hundred acres of *'choice land'* and *'the village of Diseworth in the centre of, and forms a portion of, the Priory Estate'*. Thanks to the earlier efforts of Robert Cheslyn, the agents extolled the virtues of the property being: *'extra parochial, and exonerated from tithe, two points which are rarely centred in one Property'*.

Shooting, Hunting and Fishing was also offered to the successful purchaser, and the interesting addition that

'it may not be out of place to remind those who may desire to economise, that coals are in this vicinity at a cost of 6s 8d a Ton only, and provisions of every sort obtained reasonably'.

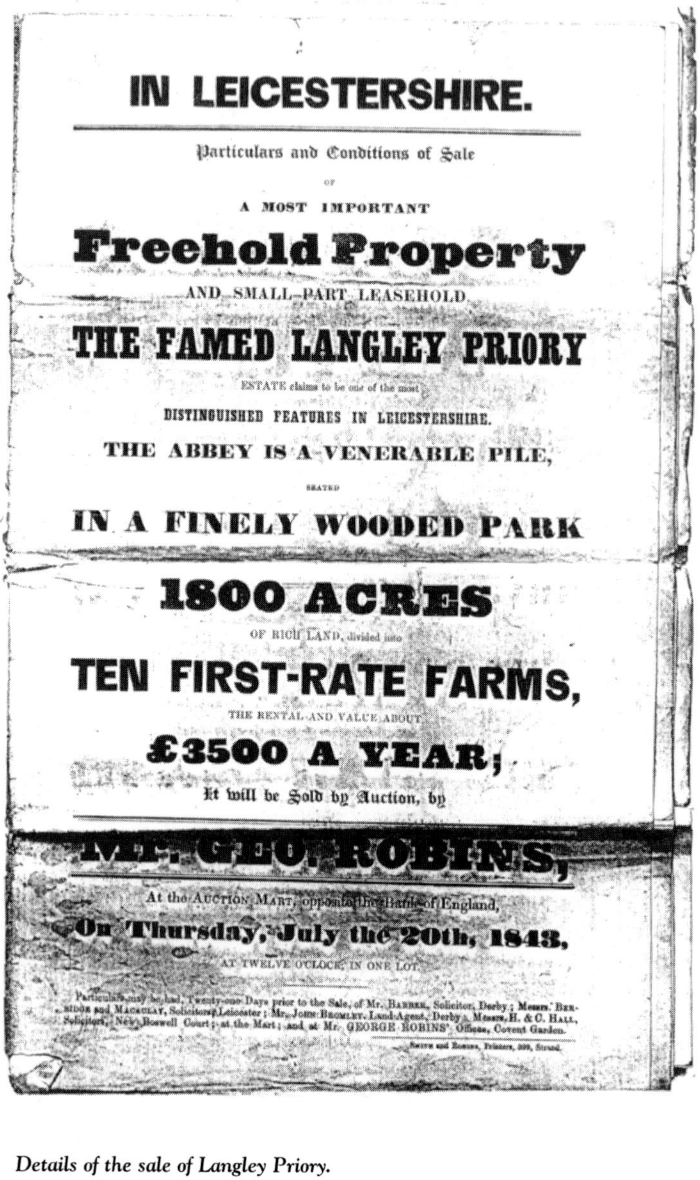

IN LEICESTERSHIRE.

Particulars and Conditions of Sale

OF

A MOST IMPORTANT

Freehold Property

AND SMALL PART LEASEHOLD.

THE FAMED LANGLEY PRIORY

ESTATE claims to be one of the most

DISTINGUISHED FEATURES IN LEICESTERSHIRE.

THE ABBEY IS A VENERABLE PILE,

SEATED

IN A FINELY WOODED PARK

1800 ACRES

OF RICH LAND, divided into

TEN FIRST-RATE FARMS,

THE RENTAL AND VALUE ABOUT

£3500 A YEAR;

It will be Sold by Auction, by

MR. GEO. ROBINS,

At the AUCTION MART, opposite the Bank of England,

On Thursday, July the 20th, 1843,

AT TWELVE O'CLOCK, IN ONE LOT.

Particulars may be had, Twenty-one Days prior to the Sale, of Mr. BARBER, Solicitor, Derby; Messrs. BERRIDGE and MACAULAY, Solicitors, Leicester; Mr. JOHN BROMLEY, Land Agent, Derby; Messrs. H. & C. HALL, Solicitors, New Boswell Court; at the Mart; and at Mr. GEORGE ROBINS' Offices, Covent Garden.

Smith and Robins, Printers, 399, Strand.

Details of the sale of Langley Priory.

In the third millennium we hear descriptions of properties in Diseworth as being close to East Midlands Airport, near the M1 motorway, close to Derby, Leicester, Nottingham etc, but in the mid 1800's the account is far more relaxed:

'Derby is only a short ride of one hour; and London within reach in six short hours; with Nottingham, Leicester and Loughborough within a pleasant morning lounge'.

The Sale Particulars comprised fourteen pages of which ten were devoted to the specific properties and land concerned. These pages afforded a detailed account of the freehold properties and their occupants, and those which were leased to Christ's College, together with their occupants. Field names and measurements are also included, as were the estimated rents.

In the **Grand Summary** included are all the properties in and around Langley:

		Acres	Roods	Perches
LANGLEY PRIORY	Extra Parochial Freehold and Tithe Free	558	2	12
BREEDON	" "	13	2	17
CASTLE DONINGTON	" "	466	0	18
DISEWORTH	" "	242	0	30
DISEWORTH	Leasehold and Tithe Free	447	2	24
ISLEY WALTON	" "	63	0	7

Thus the entire sale covered over 1791 acres. The reserved rent on the Leasehold Estate, payable to Christ's College is noted as £227, and estimate particulars conclude with the statement: *'The Presumed Annual Value, under a sound course of management, has been estimated at about £3500 a year.'*

Diseworth in 1843

From the above can be calculated how much of the village was owned by the College and how much by the Cheslyns. Other properties existed, either owned by the Churches, or the Parish, or privately. Some of the properties mentioned, which currently are considered as part of Diseworth, are listed in the Sale Particulars as being in Castle Donington or Isley Walton.

An example of this is Wartoft grange, described as *'A most excellent and capacious FARM HOUSE called 'Whartop Grange', brick built and in first-rate order, with newly erected Barn, stabling for Twelve Horses, extensive Cow Sheds, with all the other requisite Outbuildings, and the following closes of land...'*

Of the properties in Diseworth, eighteen are listed as freehold and tithe free, presumably those belonging to the Priory estate, and twenty-three are marked as leasehold to Christ's College. There would have been other leasehold properties where the leases had been sold. Some were freehold, but the land was leasehold, which may have caused some problems when rents were due. However after the sale of Langley, John Sherwin of Bramcote Hills in Nottingham and Edward Bouchier Hartopp of Dalby House in Leicestershire handled the tenancies of Christ's College with effect from 1850.

Despite all the style and description, Langley Priory did not sell at the Auction in London. It was then offered for auction at the Bull's Head in Loughborough but with the same result. It was to be ten years before one John Shakespear purchased the property in 1853 for £77,500. It could not have been an easy time for the Cheslyn family, particularly as Richard Cheslyn had died in 1843. However, the Cheslyn name was still respected in Diseworth and a memorial erected in the chancel of the Parish Church reads:

'In memory of Richard Cheslyn Esq. Late of Langley Priory, Leicestershire who died February 16th 1843 aged 73 years. This tablet is erected by Anne, his eldest daughter and sole survivor of this generation of an ancient family'.

Almost forty years later Anne herself died and is also remembered in the Church.

'In memory of Anne Cheslyn, eldest daughter of the late Richard Cheslyn Esq. of Langley Priory, Leicestershire who died July 4th 1882 aged 87 years. This tablet was erected to the memory of their aunt by Sophie Mary Gough and Admiral Frederick William Gough CB.'

Richard Cheslyn Esq. &
his trustees and Mortgagees
to
John Shakespear Esq.

Conveyance & Assignment
of the Freehold and Leasehold
Manors of Langley and Diseworth
and of divers farms and lands in
Langley, Diseworth, Castle Donington, Breedon
and Isley Walton in the County of Leicester

And so the estate, which was valued at £7 at the Dissolution in 1536, sold to Richard Cheslyn for £7,769 in 1686, was sold again for £77,500 in 1853.

CHAPTER THREE THE SHAKESPEARS OF LANGLEY

The story of the cowherd who found fame and fortune is worthy of any romantic writer. This event took place towards the end of the eighteenth century. The kind hearted benefactor was Lord Moira, Master of Donington Hall, a gallant soldier and Governor General of India. The lowly peasant was John Shakespear, who lived in a humble dwelling in Tonge. He was the eldest of six sons of John and Martha Shakespear, all of whom are buried in Breedon Churchyard. John sometimes tended the gardens of Langley Priory, perhaps often looking up at the fine house and wondering about the life of luxury within. But most of his time was spent tending the cows in the lanes.

The setting was a large tree during a great storm, where boy and benefactor took shelter. Conversation commenced, and the gentleman was so impressed with the seeming intelligence of the lad, that he instructed him to call at Donington Hall the very next day. The boy in his turn, assumed he had been talking to one of the senior servants at the Hall, and possibly, imagining that a job may be found for him which would not entail standing in storms, duly presented himself as requested.

Whatever John's reaction when confronted with Lord Moira, it did not dampen his Lordship's conviction that the lad should be sent to school and educated. John was thus sent to an educational establishment where he displayed an aptitude for languages and progressed to become eventually Professor of Oriental Languages at Addiscombe College. Through his work and his writings he amassed a considerable fortune, living in London at India House. At the age of eighty years, John Shakespear came back to his humble roots, but this time to Langley Priory.

Unfortunately he did not live long at Langley, and died in 1858 at the age of eighty-three years.

A stone and brass tablet in the chancel of Diseworth Parish Church commemorates him.

'John Shakespear died 1858
Late Professor of Oriental Languages at Marlow and Addiscombe and author of several publications most useful to students of Hindustani, but more especially he was compiler of a Dictionary of this language, which from its great accuracy and the vast amount of labour necessary to complete it is a most valuable and remarkable work. He was the eldest son of John and Martha Shakespear, late of Lount. He was born on the 14th August 1774 and died in perfect peace at Langley Priory on 10th June 1858 in the 84th year of his age'

John Shakespear was buried at Breedon on 17th June 1858

The Langley estate was left to Charles Bowles, a nephew and professor colleague, who took the name of Shakespear. Charles and his wife Elizabeth lived at Langley and raised their family at the Priory, but held a strong allegiance to Diseworth Church.

Langley Priory, late 19th century.

The 1881 census shows the Langley estate well occupied.

Charles Shakespear		**Head**
Elizabeth Shakespear		**Wife**
Martha	"	**Daughter**
Constance	"	"
Emily	"	"
Gertrude	"	"
Selina	"	"
Sarah Schultz		**Governess**

Also occupying the house were four housemaids and a young farm servant.

In two cottages on the estate lived two families. The Adcocks, where William was an agricultural labourer, and his wife Sarah a dairy and poultry woman; and the Hanfords, where John was the coachman, his wife Anne, four sons and a daughter.

Ten years later in the 1891 census Charles Shakespear the twenty year old son is mentioned, presumably returned from his education, (the elder son, John, having died in 1886, aged 17 years) and three of the five daughters. Six house servants are named, and

Langley Priory, late 20th century.

the coachman and his wife still occupying one of the cottages. The other occupancy has changed to a Joseph Adlington and his wife.

Links with Diseworth School

The Shakespear family took great interest in Diseworth School with regular visits.
From the school log books
'Feb. 2nd 1899 Mrs Shakespear of Langley Priory visited the School today'
'April 21st 1899 Mrs Shakespear distributed the prizes on Wednesday afternoon'

There was also a school holiday for a special event:
'June 1st 1899 Holidays this afternoon on the occasion of the marriage of Miss G Shakespear of Langley Priory.'

After the death of his father, the new head of Langley, Charles Bowles Shakespear, also took an interest.
'Nov 20th 1901 CB Shakespear Esq. called at the school at about 3.30pm'

Mr. Shakespear and his mother continued to visit the school regularly, and in 1903 Mr Shakespear is noted as being present at a meeting of the new managers.

'June 2nd. 1908, CB Shakespear (treasurer of the Schools) is married today in London at 2pm. Mr Shakespear is the squire of Diseworth'

It seems Mrs Shakespear senior did not stay on at Langley, after the wedding.
'Mrs Shakespear, (late of Langley Priory), visited the school, and was presented by the teachers and scholars to a silver water jug and toast rack'

However she continued to visit the school, and this is recorded in 1909 when she was accompanied by one of her daughters. In one report it is noted that she now lives at Sutton Fields.

Mr Shakespear and his new wife also visit, and Mr Shakespear is noted as Treasurer, manager and correspondent at various times by the Headteacher in the log book.

'15th Nov.1915, Mrs Shakespear of Langley Priory visited the school and examined the girl's sewing and knitting.

Mrs Elizabeth Shakespear, who had regularly visited the school for a considerable number of years, died at the age of 85. The school did not forget her.

18th Dec. 1916, Mrs Shakespear, late of Langley Priory and a visitor of the School died at Sutton Fields, Kegworth yesterday. Dec 17th (The children's friend)

In 1919 the Headteacher resigned after twenty-five years at the school, and the log books record that Mr Shakespear visited the school regularly and was involved with the appointment of the new Head Teacher. There were a number of changes at this level in the school over the next few years, and each time Charles Bowles Shakespear came to the school presumably to express interest and concern. After a fire in the school, the log book records:

'8th Feb.1926, CB Shakespear Esq. and Mr Edwards, (Managers) also visited to inspect damage done to the floor by fire on Sunday 7th Feb. The cement which protected the boards having worn away a live cinder had rolled beneath the protecting iron sheet and set alight to the very dry boards'

With the changes in headship at the school, there is no further evidence of the Shakespear links, though there may well have been. Newspaper cuttings show that the family continued to be very involved with Diseworth village.

Langley Priory in 1999.

From the local newspapers of the time:

July 1939. Mr CB Shakespear welcomed all at the fete at Langley, and said it was the first public event outside of the church at which the public had the opportunity to meet the new vicar. He expressed the general desire that the vicar and Mrs Hacker would quickly feel at home in the parish.

April 1942. The funeral of Mrs Mary Jane Shakespear, wife of Mr CB Shakespear, JP of Langley Priory was conducted in the Parish Church by the vicar, the Rev. PB Hacker. The mourners were Mr CB Shakespear, Miss Shakespear, Sir Lambert and Lady Ward and Miss Ward; also members of the household staff. The bearers were Messrs S Barnett, T Edwards, A Marshall, A White, all tenants on the estate.

Miss Roseia Shakespear is mentioned many times at meetings of the Women's Institute, and functions were held at Langley Priory. However she became ill possibly at the same time as her mother, and died one year later, in April 1943, at the age of 31 years.

Charles Shakespear died in 1959.

February 1959. The death occurred at Langley Priory of Mr Charles Bowles Shakespear, who had been a Justice of the Peace for many years. Mr Shakespear was 88 years of age and trustee of Harley's Charity. He had been a keen follower and supporter of the Quorn Hounds and a Commissioner of Income Tax. Mr Shakespear leaves a son, Mr John Hornby Shakespear.
John Hornby Shakespear never married and on his death the estate was split, and the Priory sections were sold.

Langley Priory is now privately owned by a family who has maintained the residence as it was in the time of the Shakespear family.

The chancel of the Parish Church exhibits the love and respect of the Shakespear family at the end of the 19th Century.

Carved in the wood of the reredos screen are the words:
'To the Glory of God in loving memory of our mother Elizabeth Shakespear 1916'

The window above the altar bears the inscription:
'To the Glory of god in loving memory of Charles Shakespear of Langley Priory Esq. who died on 25th day of April 1899. This window is erected by Elisabeth Shakespear'

The windows to the right of the altar commemorate two of the children of Charles and Elizabeth Shakespear.

'To the Glory of God, in loving memory of John Shakespear, born November 15th 1868 died September 6th 1886'

'To the Glory of God, in loving memory of Emily Shakespear, born June 8th 1863 died April 14th 1898'.

PART TWO
CHRIST'S COLLEGE

CHAPTER FOUR THE LADY MARGARET BEAUFORT

Lady Margaret Beaufort and Christ's College in Cambridge have played a very powerful role in the history of Diseworth and it is fascinating to see how the connections with the good lady, the university of Cambridge and important milestones in British history have affected the fortunes of this small village.

Margaret was born in 1443, daughter of John Beaufort, Duke of Somerset who died shortly after her birth. Her family connections with the house of Lancaster (her great grandfather was John of Gaunt) made her a political pawn, and she was married at the age of twelve to Edmund Tudor, Earl of Richmond and half-brother of Henry VI. She became pregnant very quickly but Edmund succumbed to the plague and died three months before her baby was born. In January 1457, still only thirteen and after a long and difficult confinement, which almost cost both their lives, her son Henry Tudor was born.

Margaret's brother-in-law was an incompetent king. Deeply religious, he spent more time at prayer than politics and his inadequacy incited hostility with the house of York. The weakness of government under Henry VI and the breakdown of law and order led ultimately to the Wars of the Roses, the thirty year civil war between the Yorkists and the Lancastrians. Her ancestral links with the red rose of Lancaster placed Lady Margaret in a perilous position and she needed to be protected. When she was still only 14 she was married to her distant cousin, Sir Henry Stafford. The Lancastrians suffered heavy defeats in following years and many were deprived of their lands. Edward IV had gained the throne and although the Lady Margaret and her husband were allowed to keep their properties, custody of her young son was given to the Yorkists.

In 1470, Margaret and her son were re-united for a short time when Henry VI regained the throne. This was all too brief a reign for in the following year, his son Edward died at the battle of Tewkesbury and King Henry was murdered in the Tower of London. The young Henry Tudor was now tipped to become the head of the house of Lancaster and therefore posed a threat to the Yorkist faction. With his uncle, Jasper Tudor, he fled the country and sought sanctuary in Brittany.

The death of Lady Margaret's second husband coincided with her son's exile and added considerably to the tragedy in her life. Less than a year later she married for the third time. Her husband was Thomas Lord Stanley, a wealthy widower and a steward in the household of Edward IV. When Richard III became king in 1483, Lord Stanley kept his position and Lady Margaret was given many privileges by the new monarch.

Even as she enjoyed these favours she plotted the king's downfall. All the time that her son was in exile, she had never lost her desire to see him crowned and managed to supply him with enough funds to enable him to return from France. When her actions were dis-

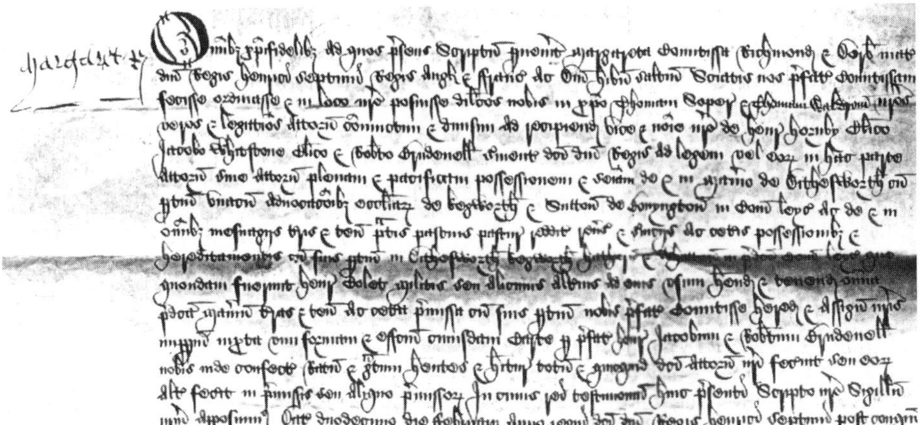

Signature of the Lady Margaret, Countess of Derby and Richmond in a letter of Attorney to receive Diseworth and other properties from her Chancellor Henry Hornby, 21st of Henry VII, 1506.

covered she found herself in extreme danger, convicted of high treason and deprived of her assets and title. Her life was spared only due to her husband's pleas for leniency and his promise to keep her locked up to prevent any further communication with her son.

In 1485, her patience was rewarded. Henry launched an invasion of England and marched, unchallenged to the heart of England. The Wars of the Roses reached their climax at the Battle of Bosworth when Henry defeated Richard III, the last English monarch to die on the battlefield. Lady Margaret's ambition was realised and her son became King Henry VII of England. When Henry married Elizabeth of York, the white rose of York and the red rose of Lancaster were combined to form the Tudor rose.

The Founding of Christ's College

With her son now securely established upon the throne, Lady Margaret enjoyed a position of great privilege. She had considerable influence with Henry, enjoyed equal status with her daughter-in-law Elizabeth and exercised a certain amount of control over her grandchildren. The queen had little concern with state affairs, devoting herself to her four children, born in rapid succession. It was the Lady Margaret who had the king's ear and few at court dared to challenge or ignore her.

A woman of substance before, she now became one of the wealthiest women in the kingdom and proceeded to acquire a vast amount of land. She took her role as a landowner very seriously, carrying out repairs and improvements at great cost to herself. Strict with her tenants, she ruthlessly pursued those who were late paying their rents or

Lady Margaret's apartment at Christ's College.

debts - no matter how small. She did however fall into the 'strict but fair' category, compassionate to the poor and the poorly, often caring for the sick herself and providing them with food, clothing and shelter. Always pious, she now took a vow of chastity, devoting yet more time to her prayers and spending many painful hours on her knees.

During this period, the University of Cambridge was growing rapidly but despite this, there was a distinct lack of spirituality. The church had gone into serious decline during the Middle Ages. It was the desire of Lady Margaret Beaufort and John Fisher, (Bishop of Rochester and Vice-Chancellor of the University) to create a new centre of learning, an environment in which young men could achieve the knowledge and piety required to preach in the parishes of England. This establishment was to be called Christ's College.

God's House, as the college was originally known, was founded in 1448 by Henry VI and subsequently re-founded in 1505 by Lady Margaret. Endowment of the college came chiefly from four counties: Norfolk, Cambridge, Essex and Leicestershire. The Lady Margaret bought Diseworth (formerly known as Ditesworth) together with lands in

Kegworth, Hathern and Isley Walton and presented them to the college as a valuable source of income. This was a huge property, 1600 acres in all and was purchased from Sir Henry Colet. Diseworth represented the largest part of the estate, both in size and value.

Villages Sell For £740

This indenture made between Master Henry Hornby clerk chancellor to the right excellent Margaret, Countess of Richmond and Derby and mother to our Sovereign Lord the King on the one partie and Sir Henry Colet Knight on the other partie. Witnesseth that the land of Henry Colet hath freely bargained and sold and by these presents freely bargaineth and selleth on to the saide as after Henry Hornby the Manor of Dythesworth and the appurtenances in the county of Leicester and the advowson of the Churches of Sutton Bonyngton in the saide County of Leicester and all other landes, tenements, pastures, rents, reversions and fines, possessions and hereditaments with appointments which the said Sir Henry or any other person or persons to his hath or in Dythesworth, Kegworth, Hathern and Walton in the saide County of Leicester. To have all the saide Manor, lands and tenements and other premises. Forthwithe the Manor, landes, tenements and other premises, the said Master Henry Hornby granteth to content and pay unto the saide Sir Henry Colet seven hundred and fourty pounds of lawful money of England.

The manors and lands endowed, which included Kegworth, Hathern and Isley Walton, enabled the college to support one Master, twelve Fellows and forty seven Scholars. Lady Margaret stipulated that the Master should ideally be a doctor of divinity and he would be given an annual stipend of £6 13s 4d. The allowance for his commons (meals eaten in college) was to be one shilling a week. The Master's clothing allowance was £1 a year.

Fellows were required to take holy orders within one year of appointment and were forbidden '*to play at dice or cards except in the hall for recreation at Christmas*'.

Building continued at Christ's College until 1511, with wood from Lady Margaret's estates around England being sent to Cambridge to complete the construction. The timber plantations in Diseworth were to continue to play a vital role in the upkeep of the college for the next 400 years.

CHAPTER FIVE THE CAMBRIDGE CONNECTION

Christ's College was the patron of many livings, some of which were given to 'God's House' as a training ground, others were to *'provide adequately for the cure of souls'*. At a later date, the college either received or bought advowsons (the right to present to a benefice) so that those who had acquired theological qualifications at Christ's would have a parish to serve. The advowsons of Kegworth and Sutton Bonington should have been included with the Diseworth purchase but these were both disputed.

'The Rectory of Sutton Bonington was bought by the Lady Margaret, Foundress of Christ's College and truly made over as a gift to the college. In 1579 they presented Edmund Barwell as rector. The College seems to have lost it by the two following mistakes:

By misnaming the county in its presentation.

By next calling it an appendage to the manor of Diseworth.

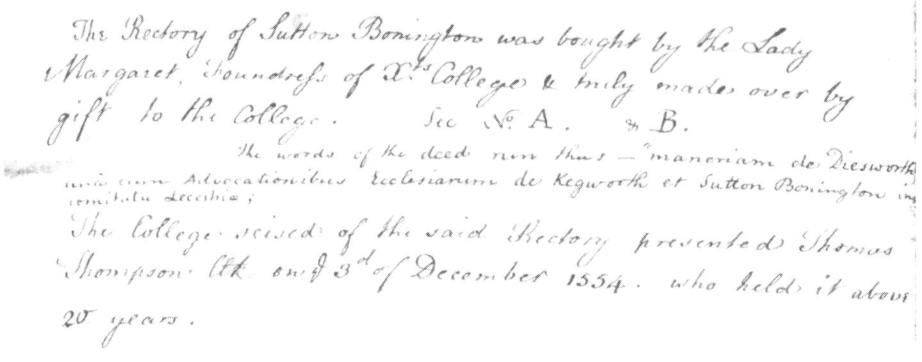

The Rectory of Sutton Bonington was bought by the Lady Margaret, Foundress of Xts College & truly made over by gift to the College. See No A. & B.

The words of the deed run thus – "manerium de Dieswortht una cum Advocationibus Ecclesiarum de Kegworth et Sutton Bonington in comitatu Leicestriae;

The College seized of the said Rectory presented Thomas Thompson Clk on ye 3d of December 1554. who held it above 20 years.

The gift of the Rectory of Sutton Bonington to Christ's College.
(Transcribed from a 16th century document)

Throughout the ownership of Diseworth by Cambridge, there are many references to the Master, Fellows and Scholars of Christ's College. Of the twelve Fellows, six were required to belong to the nine counties north of the river Trent. A desire was held to encourage learning throughout the north of England and Christ's had a close connection with certain northern schools although no more than three undergraduates could be taken from any one county. In 1531, Henry Lockwood was appointed Master of the college. Before his appointment, he had apparently been on good terms with Thomas Cromwell, later to become chief minister and Vicar-General to Henry VIII. Although Lockwood was recognised as being astute in the area of business, the account books showed the college's finances to be in an unhappy state and it is possible that Cromwell had some influence in this matter as Lockwood had written to Cromwell saying that he was 'indebted to him'. Cromwell's son Gregory was a charge of Lockwood and several letters were exchanged in 1532 about the welfare of Gregory. In 1535 a grant was made by the college to Mr Secretary Cromwell and his son Gregory in survivorship, of a rent of 10 marks from the manor of Diseworth.

In this year alone, the expenses of the Master and of Mr Wyatt, a Fellow of the college, exceeded the stipends of all the Fellows for six months and Lockwood was subject to attacks from the Fellows who accused him of releasing college lands without security.

The Master's despondency over finances increased over the years and was exacerbated no doubt by the plague prevalent during his Mastership. More than 120 scholars succumbed to the sickness in the years between 1531 and 1544, and the epidemic during this thirteen year period meant the evacuation of the college to its sanatorium at Malton no less than five times.

The expense incurred was considerable. Dates of the University's term had to be altered and some domestic staff were allotted up to twice their normal wages for attending to laundry, nailing up doors and windows and for kitchen duties. In addition, those Fellows who remained were granted extra allowances, as were those who rode to the sanatorium to prepare the house. There was no doubt that Lockwood had seriously impoverished the college during his time as Master and he was compelled to spend about 70 days a year in London attempting, apparently without success, to sort the matter out.

Following the death of Henry VIII there were changes at the top in the college and several senior Fellows were ejected. In 1554 one senior Fellow, Henry Bovill was sent to Kegworth, receiving on his departure '*20s for pains taken for the College*'. During this time, rent payments from the estates were irregular and many bills were left unpaid by the Fellows. In 1554 they wrote off a debt of £65 13s 3d as '*one without all hope of recovery.*'

Edward Hawford became Master in 1559 and played a leading part in University matters, restoring the finances of Christ's College and greatly increasing the number of residents. Dr Hawford remained in this position until 1582 when he retired to become Rector of Kegworth. It was shortly after this that Rev Edward Hawford's brother, John was installed as the Grand Tenant of the Diseworth estate.

A FISHY STORY FROM THE FENS

When Dr Hawford died in 1585 it became necessary to appoint a new Rector at Kegworth but this was rather a complicated process. The advowson of Kegworth church had been purchased from the Segrave family of Diseworth and transferred through several families before being acquired by the Earl of Berkeley. A requirement of selection was that two candidates should be nominated by the College and interviewed personally by Lord Berkeley.

The Rev John Ireton was a senior Fellow of Christ's and the favoured successor to Hawford. A rather fervent Fellow, he was a believer in *possession by devils and the casting of them out by prayer.* The College proposed John Ireton and Martin Keye, another *sufficient clerk* for the position. On March 7th a copy of the nomination was *delivered and sett upon the Hawle dore of the Rt Hon Sir Henrie Berkelye at his howse at Calladon nere Coventrie.*

Sir Henry asked for both nominees to attend for interview. The College, keen to have Ireton appointed were not too happy about this and *contested the point with much excitement.* The Master, Edmund Barwell and Ireton rode to see the Bishop in Lincoln and the College lawyer, Mr Anger, became involved.

The whole business lasted for six months and involved many visits to Lincoln, with the college still refusing to allow the candidates to attend a personal interview. As a result, proceedings began at Hertfordshire Assizes in Michaelmas Term.

The college arranged for *a pyck and eeles* to be sent to the judge, Mr Justice Ayloffe, but to no avail. Despite the temptations of this gourmet gift, the judge decided that the College must send the two clerks personally so that Sir Henry could *make a better appointment.*

The College could have saved considerable time and expense. John Ireton *found favour in his eyes* and held the living at Kegworth until his death in 1606.

In 1576 an Act was passed by Sir Thomas Smith stating that one third of all the rents of college tenants must be paid in wheat or malt. The effects of this act began to appear by 1580 and in 1589, the *'Fellows' Corn Money'* rose to an exceptional £12 18s which was to seriously affect the fortunes of college tenants in Diseworth.

Edmund Barwell succeeded Edward Hawford as the tenth Master of Christ's College in 1582. As Christ's was possibly the most puritan of all the colleges in Cambridge, his election would have been a disappointment. Barwell was totally different to his energetic predecessor. Although a puritan, he was easy going, the prey of his relations and constantly lending money to his brothers, sisters and cousins. His private affairs appear in a rough copy of the college accounts but he is recorded as being weak, rather than corrupt, in allowing such extravagances. In Master Hawford's time, the weekly allowance for commons had risen from 1s 6d to 2s. Under Master Barwell it suddenly rose to 3s and there were no longer any savings available for the purchase of new estates. In 1586/87, new injunctions were delivered to halt the decline of college finances. One of these was that *'The Master and Fellows are no longer to divide among themselves the profits of the sale of timber, or the fines on renewal of leases'*. The rise of the Fellows' commons allowance was also mentioned and there was little doubt about the laxity in the College. Edmund Barwell was Master of Christ's College from 1582-1609. This record from his rough account book shows charges and expenses peculiar to those days:

'LAYD OUT FOR MY HORSEMAN INTO IRELAND' 22nd March 1595

Imprimis, a horse ...	...	£4	0s	0d
Item for the furniture of my horse	...		20s	7d
Item for apparelling my man	...		33s	7d
Item for botes and spurres	...		6s	2d
Item for my gun and things belonging to it	...		27s	0d
Item for sword dager and girdele	...		10s	0d
Item for his souldier coat...	...		30s	6d
Item for his souldier hate	...		6s	7d
Item for his curasse	...		20s	0d
Item money for his purse	...		26s	0d
Item conducion [i.e. travelling] money	...		32s	0d
Item reparacion money	...		16s	0d
Item laid out by Howell for him	...		5s	5d
Item paid that he borrowed coming home	...		5s	0d
Item lent to my man by Mr. Wood	...		7s	10d
Item paid more in money to my Lord of C....ter	...	£10	0s	0d

Trouble at Diseworth

The college records state that *'At our great estate at Diseworth there was no peace from 1588. Searches and suits go on for eleven years'*. The dispute appears to have been between the chief tenant of Diseworth and his undertenants. The chief tenant was John Hawford, brother of Edward Hawford, the late Master of Christ's College who had ended his days as Rector of Kegworth.

John Hawford had persuaded all of the copyhold tenants (between 40 and 50 in all) to convert their copyholds into leaseholds which would need to be renewed every 21 years. This arrangement was very convenient for Hawford. It would mean that he would have cash in hand from the lease renewals when the time came for him to renew his own fines (the sum of money paid by a tenant in consideration of rent). Yet another advantage of the arrangement was that the chief tenant could override the right which the undertenants had always claimed - that of renewing their tenancies at the same rent and for a certain fine.

John Hawford died in 1603 and was replaced as chief tenant by Gervase Pigot. Hawford was buried at Kegworth and it is interesting that his memorial plaque in Kegworth church also bears the name of his daughter Margaret who was the wife of Gervase Pigot. It is by no means certain that this was the same Gervase who succeeded John Hawford as chief tenant but it does appear to be a coincidence.

When Gervase Pigot took over from John Hawford, the tenants were in '*deep disquiet*'. They complained bitterly about the oppressive fines being levied upon them and humbly asked to have '*a true copie of the acts, deeds and statute of the benefactors, founders and well-willers*', of the college. They also wanted clarification of their '*sutes, services and dueties*'. In a subsequent petition they reminded the Society of the reasons why the Lady Margaret had left the manor of Diseworth to the College, '*not only to further yore godlie studies, but also that you might be charitablie and kindlie deale with the tennants of those lands and their succession, following that godlie and charitablie course that shee extendede towards you*'.

There was a deep sense of unease in the village. The people feared for the future, for their ability to make a living and to support their wives and children due to the crippling increase in rents imposed by Pigot. They continued to grumble, making their '*humble mone and relacion*', saying that Gervase Pigot was most presumptuous in taking '*new graunts of our poor tenements and states, demandinge of us such fynes and incombes for the same, which, if we should or could condiscend to give unto him, would be the utter undoing and impoverishinge of us, our wives and children, and the rooting out of all our children*'. They wanted to know once again the terms and conditions laid down by the Lady Margaret '*for the usinge and setting of the said lande*', and demanded to have a copy of the lease to John Hawford and now claimed by Gervase Pigot.

This second petition proved to be ineffectual to the '*inhabitants of Dyseworth*', so they boldly took their grievance right to the top and approached Her Majesty Queen Elizabeth I. They made the point once again that the manor of Diseworth did not exist solely for the benefit of Christ's College Cambridge but '*that the occupiers of these lands should be hable to mayntayne their severall families and to pay and performe their Rents and Services due for the same*'.

They requested that the Queen should issue instructions to the college to show the people of Diseworth the statutes setting out the intentions of the Lady Margaret Beaufort. It appears that the Queen considered the tenants' argument justified for she sent the petition down to the college where it lies with the others in the Diseworth drawer in the Muniments room. Unfortunately the dispute does not seem to have been resolved and life went on pretty much as it had before.

In 1640 the tenants surrendered their leases to Gervase Pigot *'Humbly signifying that we have yielded and surrendered up into the hands and custodie of Gervase Pigot of Trumpton and Robert Lillie of Diseworth'*. Among the signatures on the certificate were those of John Exon, Thomas Ragg, John Mee, Robert Mee, Robert Lilly, Robert Walton, George Sheffield, and a member of the Jarrom family. All names which were to play a significant role in the continuing story of the village of Diseworth.

THE CIVIL WAR

The year 1642 saw the outbreak of the Civil War, or as some people called it, the Great Rebellion and Leicestershire suffered considerably for the duration. Situated on the main routes to the North East and North West, it was an important line of defence for both Royalists and Parliamentarians at various points during the conflict. The county did not show particular allegiance to either side as the great families of Leicestershire were divided between the Royalists and the Parliamentarians.

Many battles took place in the vicinity of Diseworth but there is no evidence of fighting within the village boundaries. It is possible though that local men were recruited to fight in individual campaigns but there is no documentation, either from the archives of Christ's College, or from the records of the Jarrom family, of allegiance to either side.

Robert Lilly, (one of the original petitioners) took over the lease from Pigot and subsequently became grand tenant, a position he held until 1674 when the title passed to Rowland Lilly. He agreed the sum of £400 for 'The Manor and Lordship of Diseworth' with Ralph Cudworth, then Master of Christ's College. This agreement was believed to be sufficiently important to be signed, sealed and delivered in the presence of three witnesses: *James Abney, John Shawner and William Chilwell.*

The dispute over the raising of the fine by £100 was to continue for the next 70 years.

The Role of the Grand Tenant

The Master, Fellows and Scholars of Christ's College, Cambridge, leases the manor of Diseworth, Langley's Land, Walton Leys, and properties rights and profits belonging to the manor (including estovers but excluding Courts Leet and timber) in Diseworth, Kegworth, Hathern, Walton, Hemington and Donington.

The Grand Tenant covenants to keep the property in good repair; to provide lodging for the Master or his Deputy when he comes to keep the Courts; to deliver to the College one brawn at Christmas and one quarter of oats annually or their money equivalent; to pay all taxes etc., and to deliver to the College within three years, and at the end of every seven years, a terrier of the property.

The Master of Christ's College also covenants to make within 3 months new leases to the under-tenants and farmers of the manor, they paying a proportion of the fine paid by the Grand Tenant to the College for renewing the lease, and agreeing to pay the rents in their former leases, a proportion of the cost of conveying the fines to the College, and a proportion of any future fines for renewing the lease. The leases to the undertenants shall become void upon payment of 6d by the Grand Tenant when he renews his lease, and that if any undertenant endeavours to conceal, alienate or plough away any part of the land his lease shall become void.

If the Master or his deputy do not keep court in any one year, the Grand Tenant may do so in their name, delivering the Court Rolls to the College.

Rent: £29 17s; 20 quarters of wheat; 33 quarters 1 peck of malt; or the value of the wheat and malt in Cambridge market immediately before rent day.

The title to the estate of Diseworth was to be exchanged several times during the next 50 years with one Simon Barwell of Leicester acquiring control over the village tenants in 1719. One of the conditions written into his lease was '*Simon Barwell shall give unto the said Master, his deputy etc., money with lodging sufficient for him and his men for the space of two days and two nights when he or they shall come to keep their Court ... and charging him to attend*'. A condition he failed to fulfil as will be revealed later.

Simon Barwell died without leaving a will but he bequeathed a considerable number of legal and financial problems for Charles Barwell, also of Leicester who assumed guardianship of Simon's young daughter. Charles Barwell became trustee of Simon's estate and immediately ran into trouble. The college was insisting on a rise in rents but Charles apparently did not have the authority to comply with this and found it necessary to take legal advice to protect himself and his young charge.

In 1726 his lawyer, Mr Brown wrote to the college explaining that Simon Barwell had died intestate since the drawing up of the tenancy agreement, that he had one heir, an underage daughter and the administration of Simon's goods and chattels had been granted to Charles Barwell. He went on to say that Charles had only the royalty and a small part of the manor. The college was insisting on a rise of £100 to £400 for seven years fine but the undertenants were having none of this. They refused to pay as the sum had been £300 for '*time out of mind*' and Mr Brown felt the college's insistence on the rise would be a greater damage to the infant daughter than the value of her part of the estate.

He proceeded to enquire whether Mr Barwell could agree to the raise without the consent of the undertenants. He also asked whether, if he had the right to win without their consent, would he be subjecting himself to lawsuits and yet more hardship.

Mr Brown wrote: *'I have perused the copy of the last draft and am of the opinion Simon Barwell could only grant new drafts under this present agreement, and not future ones though it is possible a court of equity could compel them'*.

He recommended that Charles Barwell act as trustee for the infant and pay the extra without the consent of the undertenants. If they objected, then Charles should not *'venture to renew'* but allow the peoples leases to expire unless the college could accept the former fines of £300.

Charles Barwell also wrote to the Master under separate cover, saying that he had taken legal advice when last in London about his case with the college. He begged to point out what a hardship it would be to raise the fines as grand tenant as he had no power to raise that sum. He hoped the college would take further consideration on the matter and that when the lease was drafted it would be worded in such a manner as to force the undertenants to comply.

The Lawsuit

The sorry story of the rents came up again in 1728. A bill was brought in Trinity term by two of the undertenants, Robert Cheslyn and Leonard Fosbrooke. This was on behalf of themselves and the other tenants to force the college to renew the leases at the original fines. They claimed that the Lady Margaret had stipulated, in her original grant to the college, that the copyholders should always be able to renew at the same fine but the college had now increased the chief tenant's fine from £300 to £400. This fine had always been extracted from the undertenants as well as part of the rent. They accepted the original agreement as reasonable but objected to this increase and argued that the chief tenant had no right to agree to the rise without their consent.

The Master of the college, the Reverend B Towers, immediately engaged the services of an eminent lawyer in Grays Inn. This gentleman, Mr Joseph Nicoll, was successful in acting for the college, despite suffering poor health. Indeed he seems to have been something of a hypochondriac as the opening paragraph of his letter to the Master shows in May 1730. He apologised for not being able to meet the Rev Dr Towers when he was in London, explaining that: *'I was taken very ill and obliged to have a Physitian. I am much better, tho far from being well'*.

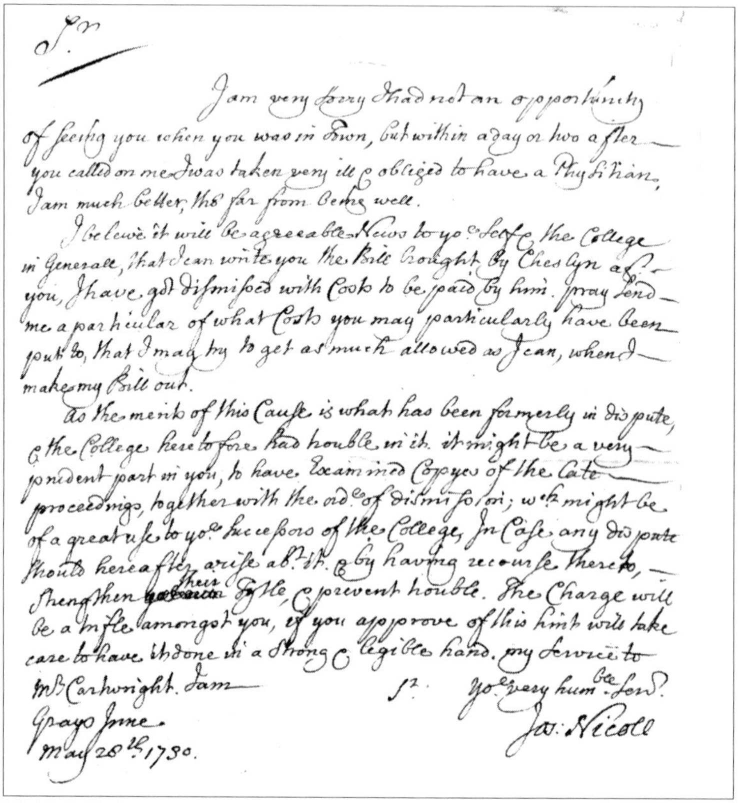

Sr

I am very sorry I had not an opportunity of seeing you when you was in Town, but within a day or two after you called on me I was taken very ill & obliged to have a Physitian, I am much better, tho' far from being well.

I believe it will be agreeable News to yor selfe & the College in Generall, that I can write you the Bill brought by Cheslyn agt you, I have got dismissed with Costs to be paid by him. pray send me a particular of what Costs you may particularly have been put to, that I may try to get as much allowed as I can, when I make my Bill out.

As the merits of this Cause is what has been formerly in dispute, & the College heretofore had trouble in it, it might be a very prudent part in you, to have Examined Copyes of the late proceedings, togther with the ordr of dismission; wch might be of a great use to yor Successors of the College, In Case any dispute should hereafter arise abt it. & by having recourse thereto, strengthen their title & prevent trouble. The Charge will be a trifle amongst you, if you approve of this hint will take care to have it done in a strong & legible hand. my service to Mr Cartwright. I am Sr. Yor very humble Servt

Jo: Nicoll

Grays Inne.
May 28th 1730.

Mr Nicholl's letter to the Master. Grays Inn 1730

He wrote with the agreeable news that he had got the bill dismissed with costs which were to be paid by Cheslyn. He then asked the Master to send particulars of any costs incurred by the college during the case so that he could claim as much against Mr Cheslyn as he was allowed.

Mr Nicoll recommended that the college would do well to study the proceedings of the case as the dispute had been going on for such a long time*. Indeed it would be useful for the Master's successors as it would strengthen their title and prevent further trouble should the problem arise again in the future. He went on to say: *'The charge will be a trifle amongst you, if you approve this sum I will take care to have it done in a strong and legible hand'*.

*(Whether this took place is not recorded but the problem certainly did not go away).

More Trouble at Diseworth

In 1744 there was, once more, high dudgeon in deepest Diseworth. A letter, dated September 15th and signed by 40 village tenants was sent to the Master, The Rev Dr Towers. This missive, worded in the strongest possible language, argued the case of the tenants against the rise of £100 in the annual fine. The grand tenant at this time was still Charles Barwell.

The tenants bemoaned what a hard time they were having, especially the farmers. Corn was too cheap and not fetching a reasonable price. Cattle were *'a mere drag'* and horses that formerly sold for between £12 & £14 were scarcely worth half that sum. They complained that taxes were exorbitant and that the community was burdened with very many poor people. Not only that, the cottages and farm buildings were in a terrible state of repair and the villagers, whose only source of income was from farming were *'hard put to it'* to maintain their dwellings despite *'the utmost frugality and industry'*. Farmers and smallholders who had small parcels of land were having to choose between borrowing money to do vital repairs or selling up, (which they would have to do at a much lower rate than usual due to the raising of the fines).

The college had put the reason for raising the fine on the increase in the price of land, which the tenants associated with the *Pernitious South Sea Time*.

> THE SOUTH SEA BUBBLE
>
> Many merchants and nobles of the day made their money by investing in British trade overseas: wool, slaves and other goods. Shares were bought in the 'South Sea Company ' which promised profits from all the trade they took over in the Pacific Ocean. Company shares were bought and sold for ten times their true value but the promises made were found to be false. The 1720 equivalent of the Wall Street Crash occurred and the so called South Sea Bubble was burst. The shares dropped dramatically in value and many thousands of people lost their savings.

As a result of the general depression of the rural economy, the tenants explained that farmers could not raise the annual rack rent (the maximum rent that a tenement can fetch in one year). They pointed to instances in Diseworth where livings formerly set at £29 p.a. had fallen to £20. Others had dropped from £23 to £15, a decrease in value of one third. The undertenants however were anxious that they might have gone too far in their entreaty. Not wishing to appear ungrateful for the college's benefaction of the new schoolhouse, they closed the letter with deference and the following plea:

We cannot but beg and hope your Goodness will prompt you to be compassionate of the hard case of us your tenants, and to take up with the old Fine; to which we humbly Intreat you would Vouchsafe an Answer, Directed to Mr Cheslyn at Langley, near Loughborough, Leicestershire.

In the meantime we cannot but with all Gratitude and Thankfulness acknowledge, and shall ever gratefully remember your great Generosity and Kindness to us towards building our School house for which by God's Blessing is finished to the great Satisaction, and we hope Happiness and Improvement of this Town; Thus willing continual Prosperity for the College and Heartily Praying for the Health and Happiness of your Self; and the present Members of it; We beg leave to Subscribe ourselves: Your ever Faithful and Obedient Servants and Tenants.

Richard Exon; John Boley; Gabriel Boley; John Boley; Sam Boley; Elizabeth Cumberland; John Aldershaw; Thomas Harriman; William Harriman; Ann Vale; John Harvey; Robert Mee; Joyce Sheffield; Ann Hayes; Robert Cheslyn; Edward Lawson; Thomas Bonsall; Thos Ragg Senr; Thos Sperey; John Knowles; Joseph Foster; Robert Lilley; Joseph Sharman; Robert Mugglestone; Daniel Bonsall; William Mee; John Mee; John Harris; James Hays; John Jerrome; William Jerrome; Joseph Harvey; George Garton; Joseph Atkins; John Shepherd; Wm Jarrom; Joseph Sheffield; William Houton; Robert Hall; Elizabeth Mee.

Diseworth September 15th1744.

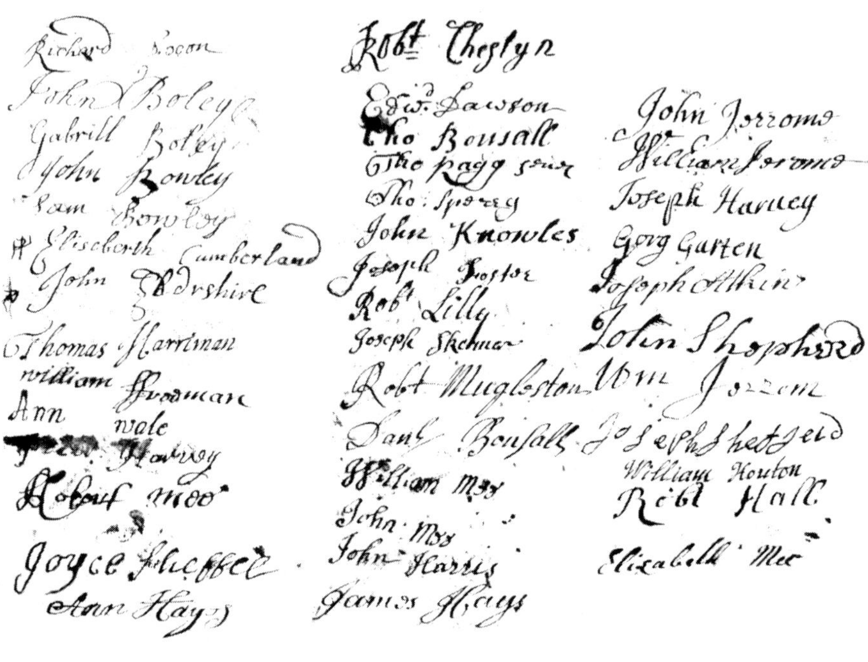

Signatures of the forty farmers, 1744.

The Grand Tenant Exploits His Position

Throughout Diseworth's varied and colourful history there has been an element of compassion. A sense of injustice on the behalf of those less fortunate and a desire to assist people who, through no fault of their own, are vulnerable or have been exploited.

One exception to this rule was Charles Barwell, a grand tenant of the Diseworth estate for some 27 years who appears to have spent a considerable amount of time and effort furthering his own interests.

Now it was required each year that a land agent from Cambridge should visit the village to carry out a valuation of the estate for the college. During the period of the civil war and at other times of unrest, journeys from Cambridge were somewhat hazardous and some annual inspections were dispensed with. Not surprisingly, when the visits resumed, several problems were discovered.

In 1766, Mr Case came to the Manor of Diseworth for his '*Yearly valuation thereof with some observations thereon*'. His suspicions were aroused soon after he began his survey. He noted that the area of the Hall Close was listed as only 14 roods in the Terrier when it actually amounted to upwards of 60 roods (approximately 15 acres), a fact that he found most extraordinary.

He discovered that a great deal of timber had been felled without permission from the college and felt that the wood could not possibly have been for repairs or for plow bote (the right to remove wood from common land to make or repair a plough). In addition, the remaining good oak trees had been heavily damaged by cutting the large side branches off. He remarked that a considerable amount of ash timber could be cut from a close called Dudley Hyzone which could be used for the benefit of the College. '*This without any detriment to the Estate as it is old and decaying*.' Mr Barwell was obviously no fool, as he was disposing of the good timber and leaving the inferior wood for Cambridge.

The further Mr Case looked, the more he discovered. He observed that there used to be a very good windmill in Diseworth which had blown down some years ago. The timbers from this mill, which were of considerable value, had been sold by Mr Barwell. Mr Case's report went on to say that the villagers were suffering great inconvenience without this windmill and he felt that if another were to be built, it would be worth £10.

Further evidence was piling up as Mr Case reported that Mr Barwell had disposed of nearly all his interest in the college leases and that although he had made a considerable sum of money from the deals, he had barely £60 a year left. Mr Case did not venture to speculate on the disposal of these monies. He did however report that the undertenants were not only doing their own repairs but were also paying the college rents and fines.

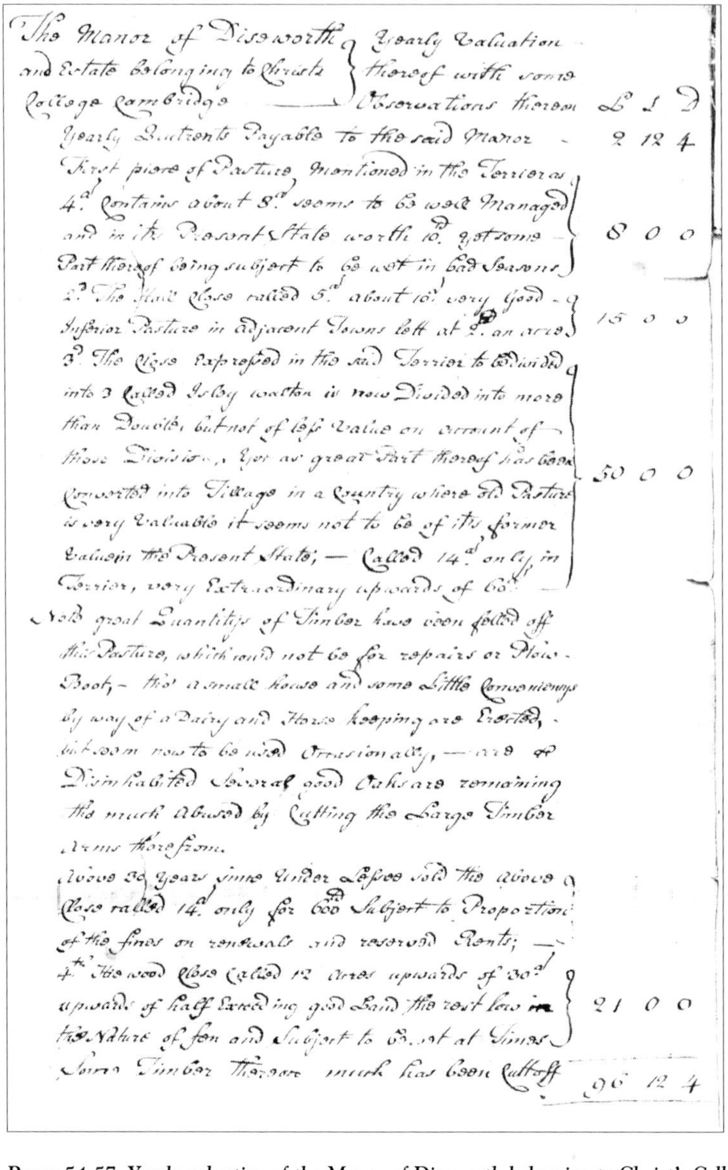

The Manor of Diseworth and Estate belonging to Christs College Cambridge — Yearly Valuation thereof with some Observations thereon | L. S. D.

Yearly Quitrents Payable to the said Manor — 2 12 4

First piece of Pasture mentioned in the Terrier as 4^d^ Contains about 8^a^ seems to be well Managed and in its Present State worth 10^s^ yet some Part thereof being subject to be wet in bad Seasons — 8 0 0

2^d^ The Hall Close called 5^d^ about 10^a^ very Good Inferior Pasture in adjacent Towns lett at 2^l^ an acre — 15 0 0

3^d^ The Close expressed in the said Terrier to be divided into 3 Called Isley walton is now Divided into more than Double, but not of less Value on account of those Divisions, Yet as great Part thereof has been Converted into Tillage in a Country where old Pasture is very Valuable it seems not to be of its former Value in the Present State; — Called 14^a^ only in Terrier, very Extraordinary upwards of 60^a^ — 50 0 0

Note great Quantitys of Timber have been felled off this Pasture, which could not be for repairs or Plow-Boot, — tho' a small house and some Little Conveniencys by way of a Dairy and Horse keeping are Erected, but seem now to be used Occasionally, — are as Disinhabited Several good Oaks are remaining tho much Abused by Cutting the Large Timber Arms therefrom.

Above 30 Years since Under Lessee sold the above Close called 14^a^ only for 600^l^ Subject to Proportions of the fines on renewals and reserved Rents; —

4th The wood Close Called 12 Acres upwards of 30^a^ upwards of half Exceeding good Land the rest low in the Nature of fen and Subject to be wet at Times — 21 0 0

Some Timber Thereon much has been Cut off — 96 12 4

Pages 54-57: Yearly valuation of the Manor of Diseworth belonging to Christ's College, 1766 by Mr Case.

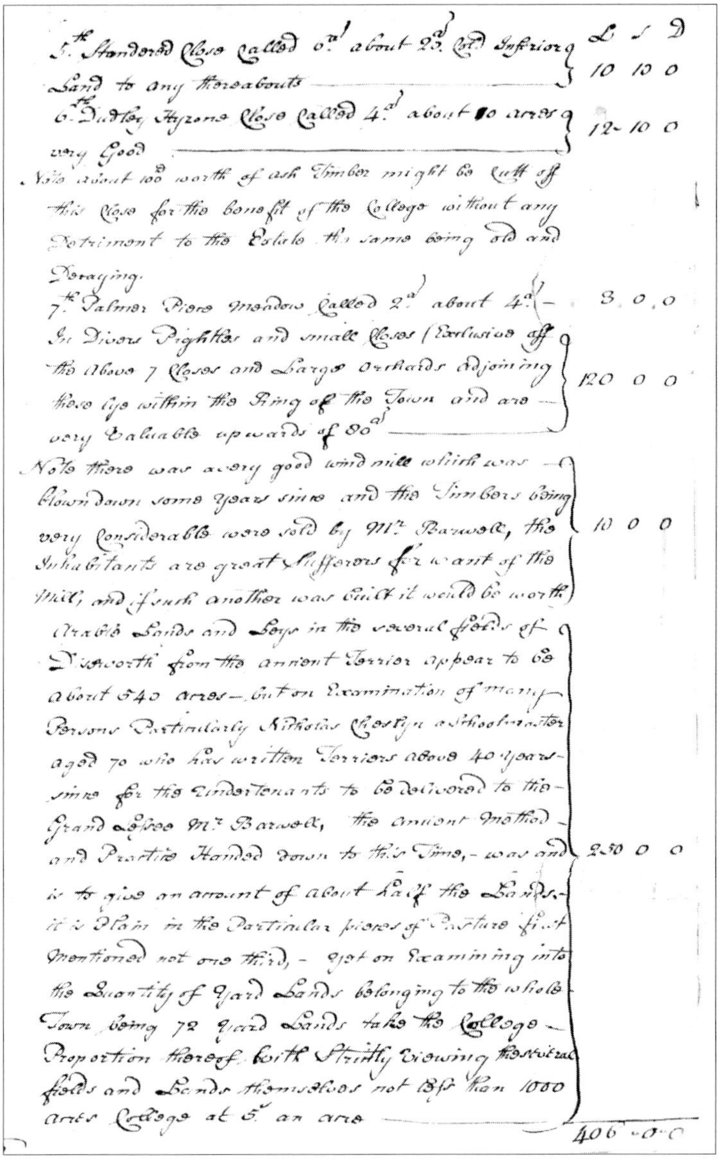

5.th Standerd Close Called 6.a about 2a. Cold Inferior } L s D
Land to any thereabouts ——— } 10 10 0
6.th Dudley Hyzons Close Called 4.a about 10 acres } 12-10 0
very Good ——— }
Note about 100 worth of ash Timber might be Cutt off
this Close for the benefit of the College without any
Detriment to the Estate the same being old and
Decaying.
7.th Palmer Piece Meadow Called 2.a about 4.a — 3.0.0
In Divers Pightles and small Closes (Exclusive off }
the Above 7 Closes and Large Orchards adjoining }
these lye within the Ring of the Town and are — } 120 0 0
very Valuable upwards of 80.a ——— }
Note there was a very good wind mill which was — }
blown down some years since and the Timbers being }
very Considerable were sold by Mr. Barwell, the } 10 0 0
Inhabitants are great Sufferers for want of the }
Mill, and if such another was Built it would be worth }
Arable Lands and Leys in the several fields of }
Disworth from the antient Terrier appear to be }
about 540 acres — but on Examination of many }
Persons Particularly Nicholas Chesty a Schoolmaster }
aged 70 who has written Terriers above 40 years }
since for the Undertenants to be delivered to the }
Grand Lessee Mr. Barwell, the antient Method }
and Practice Handed down to this Time, — was and } 250 0 0
is to give an account of about half the Lands. }
it is Plain in the Particular pieces of Pasture first }
Mentioned not one third, — yet on Examining into }
the Quantity of Yard Lands belonging to the whole }
Town being 72 Yard Lands take the College }
Proportion thereof with Strictly viewing the several }
fields and Lands themselves not less than 1000 }
acres College at 5.s an acre ——— }
406 - 0 - 0

	£	s	D
Messuages in Disworth 21 allow Seven of the Capitals with the Homestalls which are Considerable and more than are in part used for the Occupying the above Premises by way of farm houses — nothing 14 remain many of which with Orchards etc upwards of 10^d a year are made allowing for the repairs call them only 5^d each	70	0	0
Tenements 14 (besides 5 built on the waste) — Many of which are actually lett at above 5^d a year say 3^d each for the 14. Exclusive of the 5 that may be of benefit to the farms, to put poor Persons into	42	0	0
Cottages 9 at 1^d each	9	0	0

The right of Sheep going Large not half the Quantity now kept that in right may be tho: about 1000 Sheep may now be going there. — Horses and beasts to each Yard Land 15 over the — Commons and Sheepwalks etc One fine piece of Common called by one of the principal Lessees by way of Deceiving only 40 acres Contains 100 acres — these rights are Considered in the above — Valuation.

It is said that Mr Barwell and his Predecessors have disposed of near the whole of his Interest in the College Lease and have made a Considerable Sum of Money thereof, has not above 50^d a year left — The several under tenants repair and pay the College Rents and fines, — Several of the Barns and Buildings are much out of Repair, — The Timbers of a good barn belonging to the widow Jerrold were about 2 years since taken down and sold by a Mortgagee in Order to raise the Interest of Mortgage,

	£	s	D
	121	0	0
first side	96	12	4
second side	406	0	0
	623	12	4

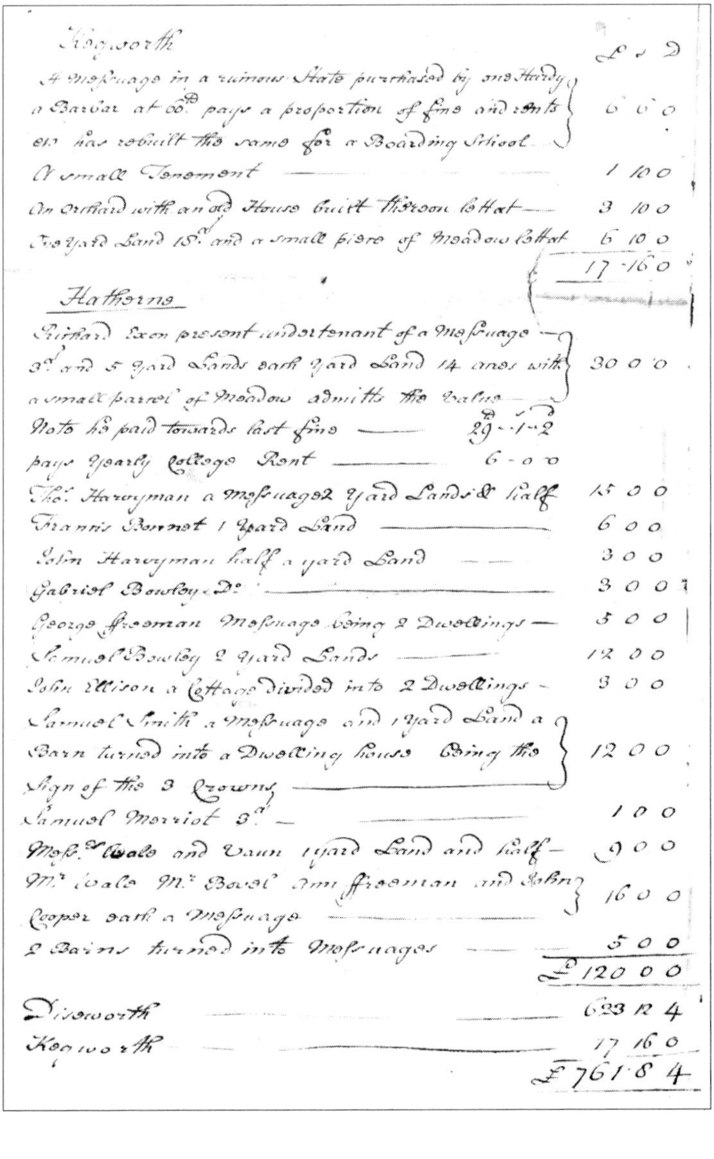

	£ s D
Kegworth	
A Messuage in a ruinous State purchased by one Hardy a Barber at 60£ pays a proportion of fine and rents etc has rebuilt the same for a Boarding School	6 6 0
A small Tenement	1 10 0
An Orchard with an old House built thereon lett at	3 10 0
Two Yard Land 18 a and a small piece of Meadow lett at	6 10 0
	17 16 0
Hathorne	
Richard Exon present undertenant of a Messuage 3 d and 5 Yard Lands each Yard Land 14 acres with a small parcel of Meadow admitts the value	30 0 0
Note he paid towards last fine — 29 – 1 – 2	
pays Yearly College Rent — 6 – 0 0	
Thos. Harryman a Messuage 2 Yard Lands & half	15 0 0
Francis Bennet 1 Yard Land	6 0 0
John Harryman half a yard Land	3 0 0
Gabriel Bowley Do.	3 0 0
George ffreeman Messuage being 2 Dwellings	5 0 0
Samuel Bowley 2 Yard Lands	12 0 0
John Ellison a Cottage divided into 2 Dwellings	3 0 0
Samuel Smith a Messuage and 1 Yard Land a Barn turned into a Dwelling house being the Sign of the 3 Crowns	12 0 0
Samuel Morriot 3 d	1 0 0
Messrs Wale and Vaun 1 yard Land and half	9 0 0
Mr Wale Mr Bowel Ann ffreeman and John Cooper each a Messuage	16 0 0
2 Barns turned into Messuages	5 0 0
	£120 0 0
Disworth	623 12 4
Kegworth	17 16 0
	£761 8 4

Even so, several of the barns and outbuildings were much out of repair and the timbers of a good barn belonging to a widow lady, had been removed two years previously and sold by a mortgagee to raise the interest on the mortgage.

There is unfortunately, no documentation available to show the outcome of this damning report, or whether Mr Barwell was ever made to make reparation although this seems unlikely. However the mercenary behaviour of the grand tenant had a profound effect on one villager who found it difficult to stand by and ignore the consequences.

The Sorry Affair of the Windmill - A Villager's Conscience is Pricked

Living in Diseworth at this time was a young man called Joseph Exton. Joseph was a highly respected member of the community and son of the late Joseph Exton - weaver of this parish. He lived in a cottage known as Exton's house which boasted an orchard and a considerable number of trees, timber which was no doubt of great value for repairs at the college and which presumably the grand tenant had not been able to appropriate.

In 1767, one year after the report on the windmill Joseph wrote to the *Reverend Gentlemen* in Cambridge regarding Mr Case's visit. He began his letter with great deference to the Master and confessed that the inhabitants of Diseworth had attempted to keep things from the gentlemen of the college and that some of the villagers had behaved indecently, particularly Charles Barwell in whom they all had such great confidence...'*But when you hear of his behaviour both to you and them...You will easily and very clearly apprehend every thing in the clearest light*'. Joseph promised to give a true and just account concerning the windmill. Charles Barwell had said that the windmill had fallen down before his family had got the grant lease. This, said Joseph, was blatantly untrue as old Simon Barwell had paid the fine on the windmill in 1709 when it was '*up and grindable*'. He went on to say that in March 1715 there was a great storm with gale force winds. Known locally as 'Birds Wind', the gusts blew one sail off the windmill completely and badly damaged another, removing a large part of it.

The mill was repaired and it continued grinding until 1717 when there was yet another storm. Despite the efforts of William Slater the miller, who had set it down during the storm, one horizontal beam and both pairs of grinding stones fell down. The black stones were undamaged but the grey stones were broken. Nobody bothered to repair the damage this time and the remains of the windmill stood redundant, on props of wood, until even they were demolished.

The ruins remained undisturbed until 1728 when Charles Barwell, who was by now executor of Simon Barwell, sold the posts, spurs, shafts and black stones to Charles Freeman of Sheepshead Mill. Mr Freeman in turn sold them on to a miller in Long Clawson in the vale of Belvoir. The black stones in particular were reputed to be one of

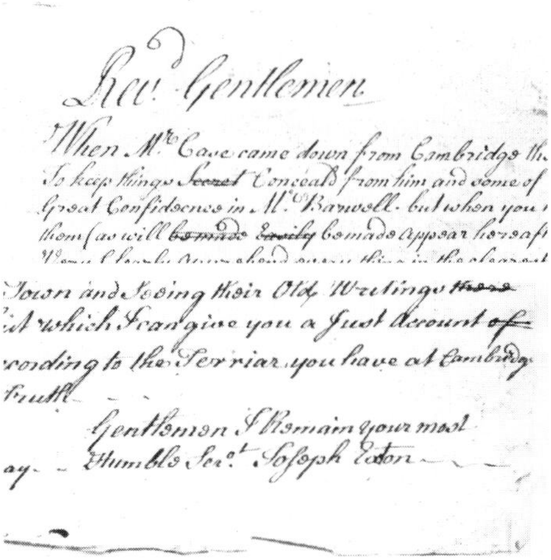
Rev.d Gentlemen
When Mr Cave came down from Cambridge th...
to keep things Secret Conceal'd from him and some of
Great Confidence in Mr Barwell. but when you
them (as will be made easily be made appear hereaft...
[illegible]
Town and Seeing their Old Writings
...at which I can give you a Just Account of
...ording to the Terriar you have at Cambridg
Truth
Gentlemen I Remain your most
...ay. Humble Ser.t Joseph Exton

the Ground may
Barwell for a Mill
last Judge your Selves how
...ten is the Real truth there is
...ood work of the said Mill when

Extracts from the letter to 'Reverend Gentlemen' from Joseph Exton of Diseworth, 1767. The detail above shows a sketch of the windmill standing stones which would have resembled the illustration (right).

the best pair of their kind in the country.

Joseph then asked the Master if he realised that the college had been liable for a windmill which had been ungrindable for upwards of 50 years and had now been sold. He felt that the Master and Fellows had had a raw deal and insisted that he was writing a true account of events as they had happened. He called upon John Darby, an inhabitant of Diseworth, to verify his story as Mr Darby had been one of those who had helped to load the timber from the mill when it was sold.

Furthermore, when Mr Barwell had gathered the fine from the undertenants, he collected somewhere in the region of £900. Regrettably, he had kept the tenants and those at Cambridge in the dark about his dealings. Many of the poorer people in Diseworth could barely afford to buy bread and clothing. They were living in dire circumstances but they had paid up in the mistaken belief that Mr Barwell had acted to prevent the college from suing the bond for breach of trust.

Joseph's embarrassment was very apparent at this stage of the letter. He went on to assure the Master of his integrity and insisted that he was telling the truth. He told how he had been born in the town of Diseworth, as were his ancestors and that he remembered when Mr Lilley had been chief tenant of the town. He had seen all the old records, knew them to be accurate and could tell exactly who had lived where and when for the past one hundred years.

Poor Joseph Exton left a postscript to his letter stating that there were seven messuages (dwelling houses with outbuildings) and cottages, plus other parcels of land which had been sold. The properties were as dear as if they were freehold *'with their own proper right of, and to and by inheritance'*. He went on to list various estates belonging to tenant farmers in the village including one belonging to Thomas Mee, a millwright.

The letter concluded: 'No man in Diseworth knows so much of Old affairs as I do concerning the Old things. Gentlemen, yours to serve you in all reasonable obligations. If you send to enquire of any more particulars, direct to Joseph to be left at the Flying Horse in Kegworth, near Diseworth.

Gentlemen, I remain your most humble servant

Joseph Exton. *Diseworth. February 10th 1767.*

Such was Joseph's embarrassment that he did not post the letter. It was discovered among his personal effects after his death in 1782 and only then was it forwarded to Cambridge by his son.

The Right to Vote in Parliamentary Elections

Extract from the Preface to the Leicestershire Poll Book, 1719:

'Among all the privileges of our Nation, there is none more considerable than that of being represented in Parliament. This is what Foreigners lament want of in their Constitutions, and what we look upon as the Happiness of our Own. But whatever Advantages we derive from this Representation, they are owing only to a Fair One; to a Freedom of Elections, which as it is essential to the Constitution of our Parliament, is necessary also to make them desirable. Take away this Freedom, and the very end of their Institution is destroyed; and they have been made the source of many Mysteries to the Nation, as they were originally designed to be of Blessings to it'.

The Oath of a Freeholder

'You shall swear, that you are a freeholder in the county of Leicester and have Freehold lands or Hereditaments lying or being at Diseworth in the County of Leicester of the yearly value of Forty shillings above all charges payable out of the same; and that such Freehold Estate hath not been Made or Granted to you Fraudulently, or purpose to Qualify you to give your Vote; and that the Place of your Abode is at Diseworth in the County of Leicester and that you have not been polled before at this Election'.

In the 1719 parliamentary elections the candidates were Lord William Manners and Frances Mundy Esq. The following freeholders of Diseworth were entitled to vote: Thomas Baxter; John Garner; John Hays; Mr Hickingbotham; William Jenkinson; George Knowles; Thomas Matthews; John Mee; Robert Mee; Robert Mee junr; William Mee; John Sheffield; John Swann Cleric; Robert Tomlinson; William Watts and Robert Cheslyn of Langley Priory.

The successful candidate was Lord William Manners.

CHAPTER SIX THE ENCLOSURE ACT

In 1794, the Act for enclosing the open fields, meadows, pastures and common grounds of Diseworth was passed. The Enclosure Act was created to increase the efficiency of farming and the medieval practice of open fields being farmed in strips by villagers was changed to a system of allocated ownership. There are, to this day, fields in Diseworth which retain the old ridge and furrow system.

Four acres were allotted to the Master Fellows and Scholars of Christ's College, the expense of enclosing to be defrayed by their tenants. The other lands held by the College had to be fenced in at the expense of the undertenants. As a result, many villagers lost their grazing rights, and a proportion of their income.

Between 1792 and 1794, in the run up to the Enclosure Act, Thomas Dalby of Castle Donington wrote copious letters to Doctor Barker, the Master of Christ's College, not only about the tenants agreements to the proportions of land, but what was planted on it at the time of the Enclosure Act and also prior to it.

One of these letters confirmed the unanimous view of the proprietors of lands within the Lordship of Diseworth that enclosure should take place. A Solicitor was nominated to settle the proportions of tithes as the owners had not been prepared to make any agreement at the last meeting.

A further letter named the Commissioners for Enclosure as:

Edward Dawson	Steward to the Earl of Moira.
Samuel Wyatt	Commissioner on behalf of Christ's College.
John Smith	Packington Surveyor.

Mr William Hale joined in this letter asking for a 'peculiar favour' from the College, granting a month longer than the fine originally appointed for the rent payments. He found that many of the inferior tenants were unable to raise their quota of it until they had sold some of their produce. If the indulgence could be dispensed, it would greatly accommodate the tenants.

The notes from the Enclosure plan stated: *whereas within the Lordship and Liberty of Diseworth in the county of Leicester are several Open Fields, Meadows, Common Pastures and Common Grounds to contain in the whole 1630 acres or thereabouts.*

On April 10th 1793, the commissioner Samuel Wyatt wrote to the Master and thanked him for his letter. He asked for the necessary information to estimate the yearly value of the Diseworth estate belonging to Christ's College. Mr Wyatt was obviously a very busy man. He promised to send an opinion within a fortnight but explained that as he had many engagements upon his hands, he could not promise to complete the information in less time than this.

Four weeks later, Mr Wyatt again wrote to the Master, apologising for the delay in sending the yearly estimate and hoped that the delay had not caused inconvenience to Doctor Barker. He considered the valuation to be the extent of what the estate would bear in an unenclosed state. The tenants would be taking upon themselves the repayment of tithes, land tax, poor rates and repairs to buildings. Upon completion of enclosure, which had been postponed, he felt that a considerable improvement could be made to the estate.

He went on to say that there were a great number of trees on the land which would take far more time to value than he had leisure for. He further explained that as he had little knowledge about trees he suggested that if the Master wished to know the value of the timber, Thomas Dalby of Castle Donington would send a person more qualified. However, if enclosure did take place, the trees would be of more value for fence posts and rails than for any other use.

Mr Wyatt's report on the 4th May 1793 estimated the total quantity of land at 1,258 acres, 3 chains 35 roods with a yearly value of £784 6s 8d. The elegantly handwritten valuation document began: *Particular and Estimate of the yearly value of the Estate in the Parish of Diseworth in the County of Leicester belonging to Christ's College:*

The report showed the number of properties in Diseworth as 34, with labourers occupying 20 small tenements at 20/- each, and that the cottages on the waste and inhabited by the poor people were of no advantage to the estate. It continued - *each yard land is entitled to 15 sheep commons but as they have no right upon the great common called Hadley and have only the fallow field and the other fields in open time, they are not meant to be included in the value put upon the field and meadow land.*

In January 1794, Samuel Wyatt again wrote to the Master regarding his appointment as Commissioner for the Enclosure Act and representing the College. He said that he would have liked to reply earlier but had been away from home. He stated once more that the trees were only suitable for fencing although some could be reserved for future repairs to buildings.

Particular and Estimate of the yearly Value of the Estate in the Parish of Diseworth in the County of Leicester belonging to Christ College.

Doct. Barker's Account	Parcels	Occupiers	Quantity A	R	P	Value p Acre s.	Yearly Value £	s	d
A Piece of Land containing	The Land Close	George Muggleston	7	.	6	25	9	4	4
about 8 Acres	Farm House thereon	Do.	.	.	.	.	2	.	.
The Hall Close	The Hall Close with House	Leonard Fosbrook Esqr.	10	.	.	28	14	.	.
Isley Walton Closes	Now in Eight Closes	Jonathan Bosworth	60	.	.	15	45	.	.
Highwood Close	Far High Wood	George Muggleston	7	.	23	21	7	10	.
	Butchers Nook	Do.	3	1	20	17	2	17	4
	Nether Highwood	Do.	10	3	33	9	4	18	7
	Upper Do.	Do.	10	2	4	22	11	11	6
Randand Close	Great Randand Close	Do.	11	.	.	17	8	10	.
	Lesser Do.	Do.	4	.	25	15	3	2	4
Dudley Iron	Dudley Iron in two parts	Mr. Dawson	10	.	.	16	8	.	.
Palmer Piece Meadow	Palmer Piece or Field Close	William Jerrom	4	.	.	20	4	.	.
Not in Doct. Barker's particular	Gelscoe Close	Upton	4	.	14	14	2	17	2
	Do.	Heffield	4	.	7	14	2	16	8
	Townend Close	William Dexter	1	1	23	23	1	12	.
	Moor Leys	George Sewter	1	.	.	25	1	5	.
	Langley Moor Close	Do.	1	.	.	25	1	5	.
	House and two Closes	Do.	3	.	.	.	5	.	.
	Moor Leys	Do.	1	1	..	25	1	11	3
	Two Mill Closes	Peter Jerrom	4	2	.	21	4	14	6
	Wad Croft	George Craven	2	2	.	30	3	15	.
	Long Croft	Robert Mee	1	2	.	30	2	5	.
Messuages	House Garden & Croft	John Jerrom	1	.	..	.	2	10	.
	Do.	Thomas Upton	1	1	.	.	6	.	.
	Do.	John Mee	1	.	.	.	4	.	.
	House and Garden	Joseph Sheaffeld	..	1	20	.	3	.	.
	House Garden and Croft	Thomas Sewter	2	.	.	6	6	.	.
	Farm House and Orchard	George Atkins	.	3	.	.	1	10	.
	Do.	John Bonsall	2	.	.	.	4	.	.
	Do. } Richd. Cheslyn Esqr.	Mr. Hall	1	.	.	.	1	10	.
	Do. } Richd. Cheslyn Esqr.	William Dexter	.	2	.	.	1	10	.
	Do. } Richd. Cheslyn Esqr.	George Sewter	1	.	.	.	1	10	.
	House and Croft	John Draper	1	.	.	.	4	10	.
	House and Croft	Baker	2	.	.	.	4	.	.
	Do.	George Hind	2	.	.	.	5	.	.
	Do.	Mr. Harris	2	.	.	.	4	.	.
	House and two Crofts	Robert Mee	1	2	.	.	4	10	.
	House and Croft	Robert Sewter	1	.	.	.	4	.	.
	Do.	George Craven	1	.	.	.	3	.	.
	Do.	Langley School	1	.	.	.	2	10	.
	Do.	Cox's School	1	.	.	.	2	.	.
	Do.	George Sperry	1	.	.	.	2	.	.
	Do. & Garden (a public house)	Thomas Ragg	.	2	.	.	8	.	.
	House and Garden	John Jacques	1	.	.	.	2	.	.
	House Garden and Orchard	Mary Atkins	1	.	.	.	1	15	.
Tenements occupied by Labourers	In all 20 small Tenements	at 20s. each	.	.	.	.	20	.	.
Nine Cottages	House and Orchard	Richd. Cheslyn Esqr.	.	1	20	.	3	.	.
	Do.	Wm. Hall	.	3	.	.	4	.	.
	Do.	Samuel Farmer	.	2	.	.	2	10	.
	Do.	Joseph Harvey	.	1	.	.	4	.	.
	House and Croft	William Jerrom	1	.	.	.	4	10	.
	House and Orchard	John Walton	.	2	.	.	2	.	.
	Do.	John Stevenson	.	3	.	.	3	5	.
	Do.	John Upton	.	2	.	.	3	.	.
	House and Croft	Joseph Preston	1	.	.	.	3	.	.
Cottages on the waste	Inhabited by poor people & of no advantage to the College								
In the open Fields 56 yard Lands	Each yard Land is computed to contain 18 Acres of arable and 1 Acre of Meadow in all		1064	.	.	9 6	505	8	.
Cottage Commons	of which there are nine, valued at 7s. each		.	.	.	.	3	3	.
	Total Quantity and Yearly Value		1258	3	35		£784	6	8

each yard Land is estimated thus	£. s. d.
Field Land 18 Acres at 12s.	10. 16. 0
Ploughland 1 acre [illegible]	1. 0. 0
Two Cow Commons & a Sheepwalk (a half)	0. 7. 0
Three Horse Commons	0. 7. 6
	12. 10. 6
Deduct Tithes	3. 10. 0
Net Rent of each yard Land	£9. 0. 6

Each yard Land is entitled to 4 Sheep Commons, but as they have no right upon the great Common called Hadley and have only the feed or shack over the Fallow Field & the other Fields at open time they are meant to be included in the value put upon the Field and Meadow Land.

Tenants exclusive of these Rents are supposed to pay Tithes, Land Tax, and Parish Rates

Sam: Wyatt

Burton 4th May 1793

Particulars and estimate of the estate of Diseworth by Samuel Wyatt, 1793.

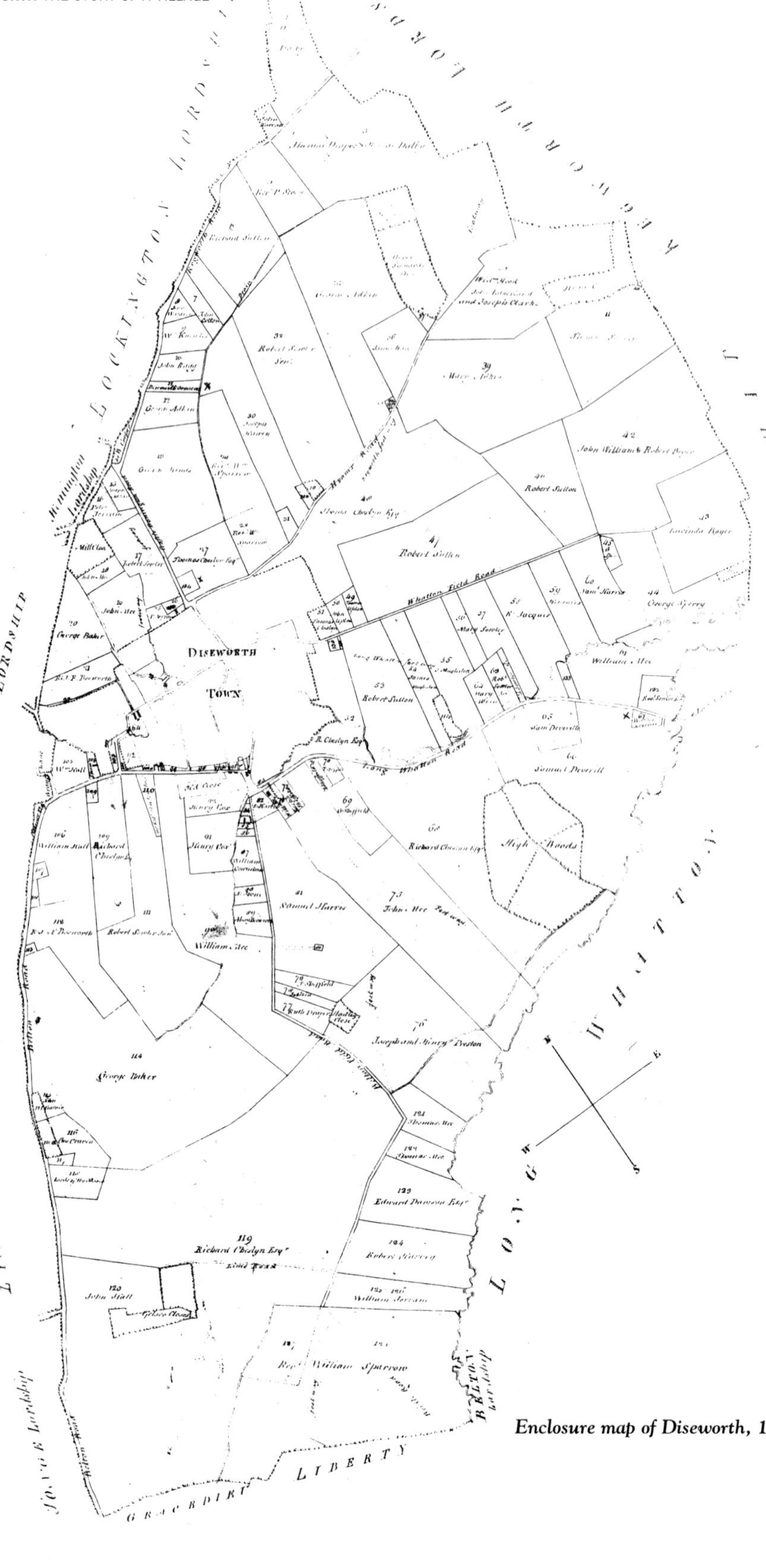

Enclosure map of Diseworth, 1794.

The Oath of The Commissioner for Enclosure
I do solemnly swear that I will faithfully, impartially and honestly, to the best of my skills and judgement execute the trust reposed in me as a surveyor by virtue of an Act for dividing and enclosing the open fields, meadows, common pastures and common grounds within the Lordship of Diseworth in the county of Leicester without favour or affection to any person whomsoever. So help me God.

Sworn at Diseworth aforesaid *John Smith.*
Witness *E Dawson.* 8.5.1794.

The names of the public foot-roads at the time of the Enclosure Act were:
Sheephead, Belton, Castle Donington, Cockthorn, Churchyard, Isley Walton, Wadcroft, Ladygate, Long Close, Sperrys, Long Whatton, Kegworth.

Public Carriage Roads.
Belton Road, Grange Road, Long Whatton Road, Ladygate Road, Castle Donington Road, Kegworth Road.

Private Carriage Roads.
Belton Fields Road and Public Bridle Road to Belton, Hyams Road, Whatton Field Road, Gent's Road, (H)Emery Lane, George Street, Road to the Windmill, Road to the Bates House, Road to the Mee's Lane, Road to the Smedley's House, Road to the Earl of Moira's House, Road to John Snee's Cockthorn Allotments.

The commissioner for enclosure received the following statement from the Master of Christ's College:

Diseworth Additional Christ's College 5th July 1794
The quantity of land within the lordship of Diseworth claimed by Christ's College amounts to 1,250 acres, 3 roods, 35 perches.

Witness my hand seal of office *J Barker.*

Valuations of the estate continued to be made at annual intervals by the land agents in Cambridge. As reported in Samuel Wyatt's letter in 1793, the value of Diseworth village was assessed at £784 6s 8d. This rose to an astonishing £1,457 6s 0d in 1795, double the price in two years. Another example of how valuable the village was to the college.

After the Enclosure Act, the College continued to lease the estate to its chief tenant in return for an annual rent and a specific quantity of wheat and malt, or its equivalent value at the market in Cambridge. The grand tenant in turn would make new leases on the property available to the existing undertenants. The rent was payable in cash and also in wheat and malt as set out in the original lease. In addition to the cereal, there

The account of the wood on the several farms at Diseworth, 1794.

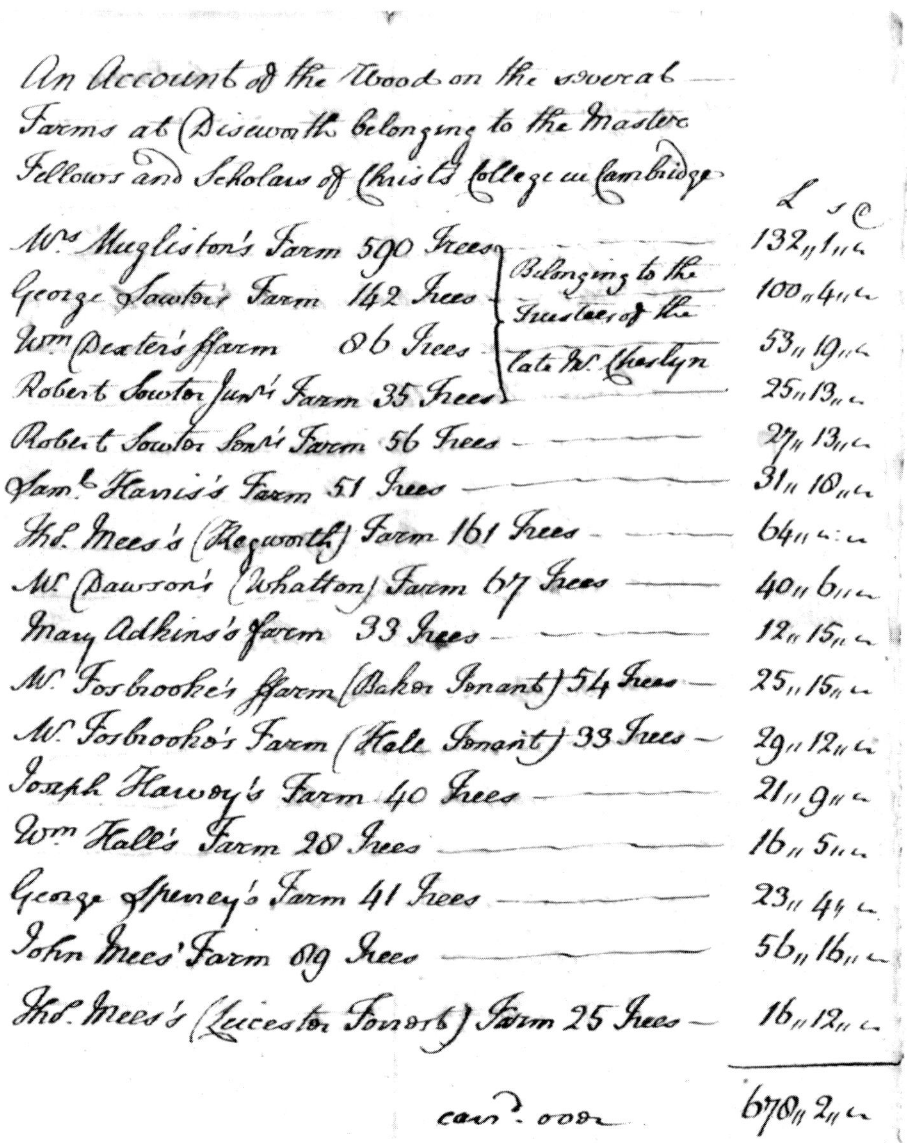

An Account of the Wood on the several Farms at Diseworth Belonging to the Master Fellows and Scholars of Christs College in Cambridge

		£ s d
Mrs Muggleston's Farm 590 Trees	Belonging to the Trustees of the late Mr Charlyn	132,,1,,–
George Sowter's Farm 142 Trees		100,,4,,–
Wm Dexter's Farm 86 Trees		53,,19,,–
Robert Sowter Junr's Farm 35 Trees		25,,13,,–
Robert Sowter Senr's Farm 56 Trees		27,,13,,–
Saml Harris's Farm 51 Trees		31,,10,,–
Thos Mees's (Kegworth) Farm 161 Trees		64,,–,,–
Mr Dawson's (Whatton) Farm 67 Trees		40,,6,,–
Mary Adkins's Farm 33 Trees		12,,15,,–
Mr Fosbrooke's Farm (Baker Tenant) 54 Trees		25,,15,,–
Mr Fosbrooke's Farm (Hale Tenant) 33 Trees		29,,12,,–
Joseph Harvey's Farm 40 Trees		21,,9,,–
Wm Hall's Farm 28 Trees		16,,5,,–
George Spencer's Farm 41 Trees		23,,4,,–
John Mees' Farm 89 Trees		56,,16,,–
Thos Mees's (Leicester Tenant) Farm 25 Trees		16,,12,,–
carrd. over		670,,2,,–

	£	s	d
Bro.t over	67	8	2
Mr. Devrill's Farm 10 Trees		6	9
George Heafield's Farm 12 Trees		5	6
John Adkin's Farm 4 Trees		1	7
James Hayes's Farm 5 Trees		4	8
Robert Gregory's Farm belonging to Mr. Chorlyn's Trustees 12 Trees		3	
Thos. Sowter's Farm 16 Trees		6	8
Wm Jerram's Farm 20 Trees		8	3
Robert Jacques's ffarm 15 Trees		9	6
John Exton Gent's ffarm 13 Trees		7	7
Mr. Hood's farm 30 Trees		21	16
John Stevenson's ffarm 2 Trees			12
Thos. Upton's ffarm 2 Trees		1	
Peter Jerram's Farm 33 Trees		13	8
Joseph Sowter's ffarm 3 Trees		1	
George Adkin's ffarm 25 Trees		14	19
Robert Harvey's ffarm 25 Trees		15	
George Hinds's ffarm 7 Trees		4	2
Robert Sutton's ffarm 39 Trees		9	15
Total £		811	8

was often an extra payment of a hen or capon. If poultry was not available, the grand tenant would accept a substitute payment of one shilling instead of a capon or sixpence for a hen.

Properties frequently changed hands and elaborate leases were drawn up. These were beautifully written on parchment and there were always two identical copies. These two documents would be placed together and then cut along the top in a wavy line. One copy was held by the tenant and the other by the undertenant. The individual cutting ensured that leases could not be altered or substituted and removed any possibility of fraud. A typical example of a lease from the college is detailed below.

From Wm Herrick esq & others to Mr Edward Ragg.
Lease of Collegehold houses, lands at Diseworth from Lady Day 1802.
House in Clements Gate, occupied by Robert Muggleston, undertenant of Edward Ragg. Cottage on the site of a Barn, Cowhouse and Coalhouse, heretofor leased by Richard Cheslyn. Rents to be paid in one Bushel of good sweet clean and well dressed wheat and one Bushel one peck and three quarts of the best Malt at Michaelmas and Lady Day by equal portions or instead of the said wheat & malt, paying yearly at the feast aforesaid such sum of money as would have been valued and sold for (bona fide) in Cambridge market, the market day next before said rents become due.
From time to time, repair and maintain cottages, tenements, all outbuildings belonging, all hedges, mounds, fences, walls, gates and stiles and scour and cleanse all the ditches, brookes and watercourses.
During the last four years of the said twenty years, cultivate the lands according to the usual course of husbandry.

Christ's College Takes Account

Martin Nockolds & Son took over the valuations in the early 1800's, carrying out exhaustive surveys and sending detailed reports back to the Master of the College. The state of the properties was commented upon by Mr Nockold in 1827. He wrote that many buildings and outbuildings, including the manor house, were in a very bad state of repair. His report is reproduced here:

Particulars of the estate situate at Diseworth, in the county of Leicester. The property of the Master and Fellows of Christ's College, Cambridge under lease to Richard Cheslyn Esq.

	Farmhouse converted into two cottages and occupied by two labourers in moderate repair.
John Adkins	**Farmhouse, barn, piggery, wagon shed, cowsheds & stables in moderate repair.**
John Adkins	**Dwelling house & blacksmith's shop. All in good repair.**

Mary Adkins	**House, cowshed, wheelwright's shop. House in good repair, all other buildings in bad repair**
Chas Harris	**Farmhouse, stable, cowsheds, wagon hovel. In good repair.**
Mary Harris	**House, shop, barn, brewhouse & piggery. Thatch of brewhouse in bad repair, house, shop & barn in good repair, piggery down to be rebuilt.**
John Hynds	**Weavers shop and 4 tenements, roof of tenements in bad repair, stable and cowsheds in very bad repair.**
Wm Jarrom	**Farmhouse and offices in good repair.**
Muggleston	**Dwelling house and shop, bakehouse, stable, warehouse and wash-house. All in good repair.**
J & W Shaw	**Cottage and stocking shops, cowhouse and barn. Cottage in good repair, barn new.**
Sarah Upton	**Three tenements and shop. Thatch in bad repair**
Sarah Upton	**Public House, The Old Plough, thatched stable, barn, piggery. All in good repair. Except thatch of house which is trifling.**
Thos Upton	**Public house and offices adjoining called the Bulls Head . All in good repair.**
Thos Upton	**Wheelwright's shop & sawpit shed in good repair**
Two labourers and a baker	**House in 3 tenements (lessee W Jarrom). Lean-to roof in bad repair, gable end and thatch want repair, detached bakehouse, roof wants repairing.**
John Wheatley	**Blacksmith's shop, brick & tiles in good repair.**
William Mee	**The Manor House, brick stone and plastered. ALL in bad repair. The tenant is paralysed and unable to get about but the wife promises to get the repairs done as soon as possible.**

His observations in the 1831 report were: '*The lands in Diseworth are very cold and wet generally and the parish altogether is in a very distressed state. The parish rates are set at between £4 and £5 per acre and except in a very few instances, the lands are in a shocking state of cultivation. The tenants do not stay for long, only two or three years*'.

The Grand Tenant Takes Advantage Once More

The Nockolds' report continued that the sub-lessees were very discontented, living in reduced circumstances and complaining about the heavy financial burdens thrust upon them at the time of renewals. The grand tenant, Richard Cheslyn, in turn complained that the land planted, all 29 acres, 3 rods and 30 poles, was in the hands of the college and should therefore not be valued. On the other hand, Mr Cheslyn felt that he still had the right to charge the sublessees for losing that land.

Mr Nockolds questioned this fact, saying that in his opinion this was not right. He was shocked by the extraordinary sums being charged by Cheslyn, especially as the amount of land allotted for manorial rights was less than 5 acres and he felt that the people had been misled. Cheslyn's counter-argument was that he had to pay annual rent on it and was entitled to pass on the charge.

Lease for 14 years:
(i) Richard Cheslyn of Langley Priory Esq.
(ii) Joseph Shaw of Stockport Lancs, cotton spinner.
A messuage and garden (2r 34p) and a piece of land (20 perches) in Diseworth which (i) holds of Christ's College.
Rent: one capon and a proportion of the rents. *1st February 1821*

A further revelation was that the grand tenant was charging the undertenants with their share of expenses for keeping the Courts in the village, even though no Courts had been held for more than thirty years. (It is interesting to note that this opinion was being voiced less than 90 years after the tenants had written to the Master complaining of similar problems with Mr Barwell. Clearly a case of history repeating itself!)

Mr Nockolds' son came to Diseworth in 1837. His remarks at the end of the valuation are thought-provoking, particularly his reference to the sub-tenants and their regard for the grand tenant. He commented on his father's report in 1831 and considered the property to have improved, both in the state of cultivation and in repairs to the buildings. He found evidence that the occupiers were generally in needy circumstances with a large number of buildings to maintain on small amounts of land and the added burden of high rents. He made a remark against each occupation where the buildings were in a bad state but felt that most were very old. He further noticed that three of Mr Cheslyn's cottages had gone since the previous valuation.

Nockold advised that the wooded areas of the village, both the Diseworth gorse plantations and the area known as Scaffacre, should be properly thinned during the next few years. These were full of thriving oaks, but in parts were so thick that when the ash stubs were cut they did not shoot again for want of air. He recommended that any timber felled should be used for repairs at the College but also that a fair proportion of it be used by the lessees for their own repairs. His closing remarks were about the grand tenant: 'Mr *Cheslyn claims an allowance at every renewal from all the sub-lessees in consequence of a portion of his land being planted. I am clearly of the opinion that he is not justified in taking it, as the land was not considered of any annual value to the Tenant at the last Renewal. The demand was fair for the first 14 years after the land was planted as Mr Cheslyn had an interest in the property for that time*'. Mr Nockolds completed his report with the following remark: '*I saw several of the sub-lessees but heard no complaints against* Mr *Cheslyn as to apportioning the Fine*.'

During the next seven years, many improvements were carried out to the collegehold properties. Where buildings had not been repaired, complaints were made to Mr Cheslyn's solicitor who promised to attend to the matter. The value of the estate had dropped by 10% to £2,435 0s 0d in this time. There were a total of 155 trees: 7 oak, 57 ash, 51 elm and it was recommended that a few trees should be planted each year in the hedgerows or corners of the fields to ensure the continuity of timber supplies.

The End Of An Era

There is indisputable evidence that Christ's College had a very powerful influence in the life of Diseworth, but it was a reciprocal arrangement. The account books in Cambridge show the farm rents paid to the college over a period of four years. At Michaelmas 1871, Diseworth paid £2,324 in a six month period. The nearest to this amount was Hathern at £554 15s with Kegworth coming in third at £70 10s. The sum paid by Diseworth continued to be in the region of four times that of Hathern for the remaining period.

Farm Rents - Michaelmas 1872	£	s	d
Diseworth	2,315	15	6
Hathern	554	15	0
Kegworth	74	0	0
Belton	20	0	0
Hemington	2	0	0
Isley Walton	100	0	0
Total:	£3,066	10	6

Michaelmas 1874	£	s	d
Diseworth	2,300	6	0
Hathern	542	5	0
Kegworth	76	0	0
Isley Walton	100	0	0
Belton	20	0	0
Hemington	2	0	0
Total:	3,040	0	0

The Russell family outside the Bull's Head. (Early 20th century)

There are two particularly interesting valuations in the archives at Cambridge for the year 1876.

George Hudson junr The Bull's Head Public House

'These premises are very old and considerably out of repair. The outbuildings are much larger than necessary and should be pulled down. It appears desirable that there should be one public house in the village. In this view of the case, the house should be put into good repair and some new stables and other buildings erected. To accomplish this, a considerable outlay will be necessary.'

Frederick Pountain The Plough Public House

'This is the second public house in the village. It is an inferior building, little better than a brick cottage. It is proposed to improve the Bull's Head Public House. It then becomes a question as to whether it would not be better to close this as a public house, leaving it as a cottage which the present tenant would, we think, continue to occupy as at present'.

There is no further documentation regarding the outcome of these recommendations and we can only assume that the plans to merge the two hostelries were abandoned. For this we can be thankful. Both inns provide, to this day, a welcome and hospitable environment where villagers can relax in a convivial atmosphere. It is here that the main business of village meetings is discussed, long after committee and general meetings have been brought to a close.

A survey of Diseworth was carried out in 1900 by the vicar, The Reverend Herbert Lock and his old friend Henry Orton, churchwarden, poet and musician. Their observations on the decline of properties in the village are enlightening:

The older residents may well remember when many houses stood which no longer exist, amongst which being the manor house. These few remarks will show the dilapidated state of the village of Diseworth within the space of fifty years. There have been 83 houses either pulled down or condemned as dwelling houses under several holdings.

The trade from the following has departed:
9 frameworth knitters (since many stockingers used to dwell in Diseworth).
6 public houses
4 malt houses
4 lacemakers shops
3 bakehouses
2 butchers shops (one being also one of the public houses)
1 blacksmith's shop (in addition to the present blacksmith's)
1 mechanic's shop

The Master, Fellows and Scholars of Christ's College Cambridge continued to be the landlords of Diseworth until 1920 when the estate was auctioned by the agents German & German. It is not clear why the College disposed of the village. The demolition of the above properties and the demise of local business may have been a contributory factor. The continuing rise in maintenance costs which outstripped the income from the property was another possibility. Whatever the reason, four hundred years of involvement with the Diseworth estate had finally come to an end.

Described as a '*Valuable Agricultural and Sporting Estate*' it was detailed in the schedule as '*extending to 1300 acres, comprising 10 Mixed Farms, 45 Cottages, Some Very Nice Small Holdings, Accommodation Land, 2 Licensed Houses and 30 acres of Woodland.*'

The land agents for the college were none other than Martin Nockolds & Sons of Cambridge who had carried out the valuations in the 18th and 19th centuries.

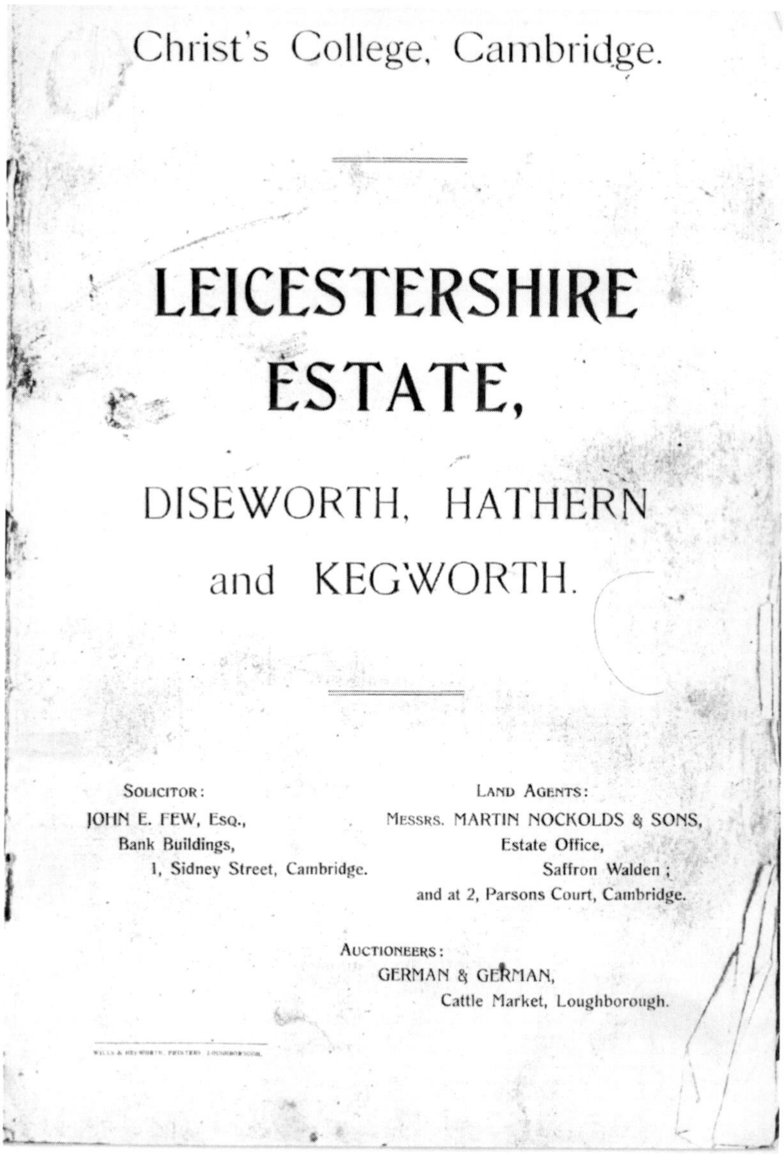

Christ's College, Cambridge.

LEICESTERSHIRE ESTATE,

DISEWORTH, HATHERN and KEGWORTH.

SOLICITOR:
JOHN E. FEW, ESQ.,
Bank Buildings,
1, Sidney Street, Cambridge.

LAND AGENTS:
MESSRS. MARTIN NOCKOLDS & SONS,
Estate Office,
Saffron Walden;
and at 2, Parsons Court, Cambridge.

AUCTIONEERS:
GERMAN & GERMAN,
Cattle Market, Loughborough.

Sale of the Leicestershire Estate by Christ's College, 1920.

The Grand Tenants of Diseworth and The Masters of Christ's College

	Grand Tenant	*Master*	
		Henry Lockwood	1531-1559
		Edward Hawford	1559-1582
1588	John Hawford	Edmund Barwell	1582-1609
1604	Gervase Pigot		
1617	Gervase Pigot	Valentine Carey	1609-1622
1638-48	Gervase Pigot	*Thomas Bainbridge	1622-1646
1648-67	Robert Lilley	Samuel Bolton	1646-1654
		Ralph Cudworth	1654-1688
1674-95	Rowland Lilley	John Covel	1688-1722
1695-1719	Edward Bigland		
1719-31	Simon Barwell	William Towers	1722-1745
1731-65	Charles Barwell	George Henry Rooke	1745-1754
1765-72	Leonard Fosbrooke	Hugh Thomas	1754-1780
1772-93	Richard Cheslyn	John Barker	1780-1808
1793-1820	John Stokes; Thos Fisher; William Herrick		
		Thomas Browne	1808-1814
1820-41	Richard Cheslyn (Langley)	John Kaye	1814-1830
1841-50	Lease surrendered to John Shakespear		
		John Graham	1830-1848
		** Joseph Shaw	1848-1849
		James Cartmell	1849-1881

*Thomas Bainbridge became Master in 1622 and remained there until his death in 1646. He is recorded as being so addicted to his kin that where they may have a benefit, there is no persuasion, whosoever has the injury.

**Joseph Shaw was a popular tutor. He had many students but not very many qualified. He could generally be seen at Newmarket on race days and many of his pupils followed him there. 1818 Cheslyn and Jackson rusticated for two years, the former for sending a challenge to Wetherby, the latter for being the bearer.

Shaw was appointed Master in 1849 but did not stay. He was sent to Kegworth in December 1852 but resigned three months later in February 1853 and returned to Christ's College. He was allowed to keep his Fellowship and spent the remainder of his days looking after the grass.

A CATALOGUE

OF THE

VALUABLE STOCK OF

NEAT CATTLE, SHEEP, HORSES,

AND

IMPLEMENTS OF HUSBANDRY,

the Property of

MR. BENLEY,

Of DISEWORTH, in the COUNTY of LEICESTER,

(WHO IS LEAVING HIS FARM,)

Which will be Sold by Auction,

By Mr. BOOTT,

ON THE PREMISES,

On MONDAY the [illegible] DAY of FEBRUARY, 1800,

At Ten o'Clock.

N. B. The Sale of Mr. BENLEY's Houſehold Furniture is poſtponed.

CONDITIONS OF SALE

I. THE Higheſt Bidder to be the Buyer, and if any Diſpute ariſe between two or more Bidders the Lot in diſpute to be put up again.

II. NO Perſon to advance leſs than Six-pence each Bidding; above a Pound, One Shilling; above Five Pounds Two Shillings and Six-pence; and ſo on in Proportion.

III. THE Purchaſers ſhall give in their Names, and Places of Abode; and, if required, ſhall pay down Five Shillings in the Pound in part of Payment of the Purchaſe-Money, in Default of which the Lot or Lots ſo purchaſed to be immediately put up again and reſold.

IV. THE Lots to be taken away, with all Faults, at the Buyer's expence, immediately after the Sale is ended; and the remainder of the Purchaſe-Money to be abſolutely paid on or before Delivery.

V. UPON Failure of complying with the above conditions the Money ſo depoſited in part of Payment ſhall be forfeited which together with the Lot or Lots ſo remaining ſhall become the Property of the Vender.

ADAMS, JUN. PRINTER, LOUGHBOROUGH.

Sale of Mr Benleys farm, 1800.

CHAPTER SEVEN TWO FAMILIES OF DISEWORTH

The One that got Away

The Lillys of Diseworth

There is just one property surviving in the village named after the family who lived there, Lilly's Cottage, although there is evidence of other houses, long since demolished, that were named after the occupants.

Lilly's Cottage is understandably linked with the William Lilly who lived from 1602 until 1681 though only for a few years in Diseworth. Yet, although much has been written about just him, many other members of the Lilly family resided in Diseworth both before and after his time. However William Lilly offers a great deal of information about his life in the village in his writings.

Unfortunately he did not think much of Diseworth, and complained that the farmers did not educate their sons. He was fortunate in that he was sent to the Grammar School in Ashby where he stayed until his father's fortunes collapsed and he was obliged to return home. William himself claimed that he had been well educated at the school, and he was the star pupil! *'For the last two years of my being at school I was of the highest form of the school, and chiefest of that form.'* He sadly states that all of his class went to Cambridge except for himself who lived 'miserably' in the country, (Diseworth), wasting his time and not likely to achieve anything. He writes that his father often informed him he could not work, drive the plough or endure country labour, and was therefore *'good for nothing'*.

The good for nothing lad left Diseworth at the age of eighteen years and there is no evidence to show that he ever came back. He obtained a post as secretary and general dogsbody to a gentleman and managed to make himself indispensable to his master in many ways, even to caring for his wife when she was ill and organising the funeral arrangements when she died. That he had a good command of English is shown by his writings; he describes the marriage of his master one Gilbert Wright and his affluent wife as uncomfortable, the woman being of a very jealous nature and always wishing to know where her husband was and with whom. However after her death he lived well as Gilbert Wright returned to Leicestershire and left him in charge of the house. The master returned shortly with a new wife, but by May 1627, she was a widow.

William Lilly married the widow and, it seems, lived happily ever after, or at least during her lifetime, as she was twenty-five years older than him. Certainly he had no financial worries and went on to study astrology and move in the highest circles. He married three times in all, and although he spent only his formative years in Diseworth, he leaves a good account of the origins of the village in his writings.

The position of Lilly's Cottage is confirmed as *'This town of Diseworth is divided into three parishes; one part belongs unto Lockington, in which part stands my father's house, over against the west side of the steeple, in which I was born'*. He also writes that his father and his ancestors were born and lived there and they had *'continued many ages in this town as yeomen'*

William Lilly gives his ancestors names as *'My father's name was William Lilly, son of Robert, the son of Rowland etc.'*

These names with others appear regularly through the years in Diseworth.

Although the earlier Lilly family claimed to own much land in Diseworth, Lilly's Cottage was owned by Christ's College, and the Lilly name features much in the many letters concerning the rents disputes and in the parish registers.

1583	**Rowland Lyllye married Anne Layce**
1584	**Thomas Lyllye, son of Rowland Lyllee christened**
1648-1674	**Robert Lilly, Grand Tenant of Diseworth for Christ's College.**
1674-1695	**Rowland Lilly taking over the lease as Grand Tenant and agreeing the sum of £400 for the manor and Lordship of Diseworth**
1682	**There is a lease which identifies one Robert Lilly of Austrey in Warwickshire, with a messuage and lands in Moorleys Close and Kegworth Hedge Close in Diseworth, with annual rent of 12s, wheat and malt, and two hens.**
1703	**Lease for 19 years (Christ's College) To Alice Lilly of Diseworth, spinster, the Townsend Close in Diseworth. Rent 1s per annum. This lease was mortgaged four years later for £16**
1736	**Lease for 15 years (Christ's College) To William Lilly and Rowland Lilly, both framework knitters of Leicester, a messuage and lands in Diseworth. Rent 7d wheat and malt, two capons.**
1744	**The long letter from the 'servants and tenants' complaining about the rents rise, bears the signature of forty tenants, one of them being Robert Lilly.**
1753	**Lease for 19 years (Christ's College) To Robert Lilly of Diseworth, framework knitter. A cottage and rights of common in Diseworth. Rent 2s 10½d, wheat and malt, and two hens.**
1766	**Robert Lilly has mortgaged his property in consideration of £9 9s.**
1767	**When Joseph Exton wrote his famous letter informing the Reverend Gentlemen that they were being treated dishonestly he mentions** *'My ancestors and Mr Lilleys in old times was the Chief in this town'*
1769	**Robert Lilly, framework knitter buried aged 79 years.**

The Lilly name does not appear in documents or leases after this time and it is assumed that the family connections moved away.

The Family that Stayed

From Viking Warrior to Village Farmer

Throughout any research of the last thousand years of Diseworth, the name Jarrom has surfaced in one form or another. In the 1100's when Stephen de Curzun exchanged with his brother Thomas *'one virgate of land'* he gave that land to the nuns of Langley. A detailed charter was drawn up with witnesses, one of whom was one Geraum. The name is of Viking origin, derived from two Norse words, Gejn meaning spear and Hrafn meaning raven. it is possible they came over with the Norse men and settled in Diseworth. Indeed the other names as witnesses on the document are those of the Normans, and perhaps they trusted each other through their common ancestry. These Norse or Normans were not so much the fierce warriors who plundered, rather a nation talented in building ships, but also in reality farmers from a harsh, barren, cold climate in search of land to settle in which to continue their farming

The Geraums were land holders or free tenants and they certainly held some land, which though rented was not considered part of an estate. In 1205 there was a trial before the Assizes over 125 acres of land in Diseworth which John Geraum claimed the right to farm. By 1327 the Geraums were being assessed for tax on their personal property, the substantial sum of 28s 4d. This is interesting in that money was not easy to come by, as most exchanges involved produce or livestock, one assumes that with so much land to farm there was some payment. Some of the land may well have belonged to Langley Priory as the nuns were never large in number and always needed farmers and shepherds. Indeed in later years a Walter Geraum was ordered to make repairs to a hole in the roof of a property he rented from the Lady Prioress and given a set time to have completed the task under threat of a fine equivalent of 16p. This did not appear to worry him as he failed to comply and was subsequently evicted!

However the Gerums thrived through two big events in the village. In 1506 the greater part of the village was purchased by Lady Margaret, the King's mother, and the rents from the properties and land went to Christ's College. The Dissolution of the Monasteries in 1536 also saw the handing over of Langley Priory to the Grey family. Suddenly the villagers had new landlords. The Jarroms' property belonged now to Christ's College, and the following years saw the constant cry from the villagers that the rents demanded from the Chief Tenant to be sent to the 'Reverend Gentlemen' at Cambridge were too high. In just about all the correspondence pleading for understanding over the cost of living there is a Jarrom. The name had a variety of spellings as before but with the G changed to a J. One of the interesting ways of finding out about the family in the Middle Ages was through their Family Wills. These were always written in some detail, and go some way to showing the family's wealth. In 1580, Rychard Jarrom bequeathed, among other items, *'one cowe betwixte sonne George and daughter Elizabeth'*. Another son and daughter got a cow between them as well as a colt. In addition brass pots and pans are mentioned, as well as *'my best cupboard'*, tables and pieces of land. In some cases inventories are also included. However all the wills, as was common in those times, began with bequeathing one's soul to God. Of course this was the time when the Reformation was taking place and there was considerable fervour in the church. The next century saw some great happenings that must have had some effect on this family, namely, the Civil War and the Plague. Diseworth is not mentioned in any of the documentation concerning the Civil War in these parts. Battles ranged as close as Zouch, Cotes and Ashby and there were garrisons at Castle Donington. Presumably there was some activity, whether housing or hiding troops, feeding them, holding weapons or actually going out to fight and it is possible the Jarroms, like others in the village, became involved. One of the advantages of the War is that the rent collectors from Cambridge did not care to come travelling in this direction, and the accounts written in Cambridge at the time was that their income fell considerably as a result. The Plague also hit the wider area, but there is no evidence that the village or any of its families was stricken.

Jerrome or Jarrom, the family continued and the first mention of the family Christian name of William of Diseworth appears as early as 1600's. The inventory of his son William at the end of that century is extensive. Six cows, two heifers, two colts, six mares and foals, swine, lambs and sheep, carts and wagons and such. The names of his witnesses are village names, Hoyland, Mee, and Wootton. Indeed as the wills and inventories of the family are revealed the names of people in the village who feature in other research come to light. Robert Lilley, Samuel Barwell, Adkin, and later Nathaniel Gayton, the village schoolmaster in the first part of the nineteenth century. The first name William continues as does the other family name Peter to this day.

In the late 18th Century, in Diseworth a Baptist Church was built, and the Jarrom family joined it. The Baptist Minute books show that the Jarrom brethren as they were called played a prominent role in the Baptist Church. With the disposal of the Christ's College properties in 1921, the family purchased their farms and continued with the family tradition of husbandry, one they have been able to trace back through the past millennium.

That they have always put their farming first was well illustrated in the Diseworth School Log books which show for the early part of the 20th century, *'the Jarrom brothers were absent again today, owing to the harvest!'*

There are numerous references to the Jarrom in the Cheslyn Manuscripts

Lease for 14 years
1 Charles Barwell of Leicester, gent.
2 William Jerrom of Diseworth shoemaker
A messuage and lands etc. in Diseworth, which 1 holds of Christ's College.
Rent: 4s 6d wheat and malt and two hens. 7th November 1737

Mortgage (assignment of lease)
1 William Jerrom of Diseworth, cordwainer
2 John Orton of Rearsby, clerk
1 assigns to 2 the remainder of his lease for 14 years of a messuage, half a yardland or nine acres of land, one rood of meadow and rights of common in Diseworth (held by 1) of Charles Barwell who holds them of Christ's College, unless principal and interest are repaid.
Consideration £40 9th November 1737

Assignment of Mortgage
1 John Orton of Rearsby, clerk
2 William Jerrome of Diseworth, cordwainer
3 Grace Boss of Woodthorpe, widow
1 assigns to 3 subject to redemption by 2 the remainder of a lease for 14 years on the lands etc. (not the messuage), which Charles Barwell holds of Christ's College and leased to 2 and which 2 mortgaged to 1.
Consideration £40 16th June 1741

Lease for 17 years
1 Charles Barwell of Leicester gent.
2 William Jerrom of Diseworth, yeoman
3 Grace Bosse of Woodthorpe, widow
By direction of 2, 1 leases to 3 lands etc. in Diseworth (details given) which 1 holds of Christ's College.
Rent: 1s 9d wheat and malt 26th September 1741

Assignment of Lease

1 Grace Boss of Woodthorpe, widow

2 William Jerrome of Diseworth, cordwainer

3 Robert Hall of Tonge Mill in Breedon, miller

1 and 2 assign to 3 the remainder of leases for 14 and 17 years of ½ yardland, I rood of meadow and rights of common in Diseworth, which Charles Barwell holds from Christ's College and leased to 1 to whom 2 had mortgaged the property.

Consideration £44 16s to 1 £4 4s to 2 21st April 1743

Assignment of Lease

1 Peter Jerram of Diseworth, labourer

2 William Ford of Diseworth, blacksmith

3 Richard Cheslyn Esq of Langley Hall.

1 assigns to 2 the remainder of a lease for 20 years of ten yards square of ground on which 2 has built a blacksmith's shop, part of the property which Leonard Fosbrook, who holds it from Christ's College leased to 1, Leonard Fosbrook having since assigned his lease to 3.

Consideration: £5 12s Rent per annum 2d 7th June 1770

PART THREE

FAITH, HOPE AND CHARITY

CHAPTER EIGHT FAITH IN DISEWORTH

From the time of the construction of the Parish Church of St. Michael and All Angels, one can be certain that Christianity has been practised in Diseworth. One assumes that prior to these times when the Romans or Danes were present, other forms of worship took place. But the Parish Church has Saxon construction, so Christian worship goes back a long time.

Through the years of Langley Priory links, through the Reformation, to the present day, the Parish Church has drawn local people to the services held within. However, there are two other branches of the Christian Church, which have long been established in Diseworth, each offering their services and values to the people.

In 1752 Joseph Adkin applied to the General Quarter Sessions of the Peace of Leicester for use of his dwelling house at Diseworth as a meetinghouse for Protestant Dissenters. As the name Adkin appears in both the Baptist and Methodist documents, it is unsure for which group of believers it was intended, but both churches began to thrive, possibly as the result of the visiting preachers of the day who travelled from village to village, first meeting the people in their own homes.

The Baptist Church

The Baptist Church has been established in the village for almost 250 years, and in spite of religious persecution and theological controversy on a national level at its commencement, has offered evangelical witness since that time. The Baptist Ministry was relatively new in the eighteenth century and it is unlikely that meetings were public and the 'dissenting ministers' as they were called held their early meetings in the weavers shop, now known as Lilley's cottage. There was so much opposition that their employers could dismiss workers if it was discovered that they were attending the preaching of the dissenters. However, slowly and surely the enthusiasm for the principles of the Baptist Church grew and was accepted and in 1752 a meetinghouse was erected in Diseworth.

By 1760 the region was divided into five districts, with the principal centres being Barton, Melbourne, Kegworth, Loughborough and Kirby-Woodhouse. The Kegworth district was a large one, comprising Kegworth, Castle Donington, Ilkeston, Smalley, Sutton Bonington, Long Whatton, Belton and Diseworth. There were just two ministers, and in the late eighteenth century, transport would not have been easy and not every village had its own place of worship.

Eventually weekly meetings were held, one at Kegworth and one in Diseworth, and these are faithfully recorded in minute books. Details of prospective members, baptism days, and accounts are carefully noted. Names of prominent Baptists through the two hundred years are Jarrom, Adkin, Mee, Hayes and others. The minute books also mention the Victorian schoolmaster Nathaniel Gayton and describe his affinity to the Baptist Church.

On 10th March1805 '*Nathaniel Gayton and Thomas Draper were proposed as candidates for Baptism and Fellowship in the Baptist Church in Diseworth and a committee was appointed to converse with them*'.

The church had strict rules for its members, and also in 1805 '*a number of Diseworth persons were excluded from the Church*'. The rules must have been too much for one John Harvey as it was noted in September 1805:- '*John Harvey sent a note to the meeting in which he declared that he no longer considered himself a member of this Church. He assigned no reason for this stop*'

Beneath this minute in the book was a phrase '*How absurd and dangerous is such conduct*'.

However other members who had been called to account for their behaviour repented and another minute states '*Brother William laments his conduct and asks forgiveness*'

The religious education of the young people was always foremost in the minds of the Brethren and Sunday School is frequently mentioned, as is the construction of a school room, which after many years was finally built in 1824. This afforded much opportunity for the instruction of the children who were taken on annual outings. Funds seemed plentiful as two cottages were built or acquired next to the church and rented out. But the geographical position of the Church next to Diseworth brook caused concern when the floods came, and often groups were asked to consider the building of a wall against the brook. By 1830 the Church was in serious debt, and a committee was formed which included Brethren Jarrom, Mee, Adkin, and Gayton with the remit:- '*To endeavour to advise members to remove the present debt and to keep free from debt in future*'.

The Baptist books keep detailed records of the Baptisms and Deaths of its members, and there is also Nathaniel Gayton's scrapbook, which records deaths and burials in the Baptist Burial Ground. Often he noted the texts for the service:-

'*John Sheffield departed this life on 2nd December and buried at Baptist Burial Ground. 1st Corinthians verses 56 and 57*'

'*William Brown, son of Robert and Elizabeth departed this life 16th April and interred. Text-Samuel chapter 12, verses 2 and 3*'

Certainly Brother Gayton became indispensable to the Church as the years progressed, and in 1851 at a special meeting the '*friends agreed to request Brother Gayton to preach at Diseworth once a fortnight on Sabbath evenings*' and in 1859, when the Reverend Joseph

Taylor resigned he was requested to conduct the Tuesday evening meeting and to supply ministerial services where no other supply was available. But the schoolmaster was getting on, seventy-three years of age, and in the next two years he was to lose his job as the new village school was nearing completion. The generosity of the church is indicated with the note in the minute book: -

'*May 1863. Agreed to make Nathaniel Gayton a present of £5 for his past services as a supply to the Baptist Church.*'

The following year a balance sheet was prepared in relation to painting the chapel and building a wall to prevent further flooding but the good members still decided to pay Nathaniel another £5.

In 1865 the members of the Baptist church held a special meeting. '*Request Brother Atkin to see Brother Gayton and obtain from him the money to balance the account for the meeting of the chapel, also to appropriate the residue of the money Brother Gayton holds to the purchasing of a Chapel clock.* At the same meeting it was agreed as '*Brother Gayton was now very old and is evidently declining in strength and especially as he wishes to be relieved of some of his duties, that Brother Atkin be requested to obtain the writings relating to our chapel property here and hold them for the church*'.

The Baptist Church did not forget their faithful servant. They resolved that '*Brethren Atkin, Barker, Mee and Russell be requested to wait on Brother Gayton and thank him for all the kindness he has shown toward the cause here and all the efforts he has put forth for many years to promote its prosperity. Also to inform him that we now appoint Brother Atkin as our Treasurer - in conjunction with himself*'.

They further resolved that '*a paper be drawn up by Brethren Jarrom and Yates and read to the friends next Sabbath day that it be then signed by every member at Diseworth who can and will sign it and present it to our dear Brother Gayton as an acknowledgement of our obligation to him and as a small indication of our confidence in him and our affectionate sympathy*'. The pastor, Rev Thomas Yates was the first to sign the letter.

The Baptist Church progressed, and by 1928 numerous alterations had taken place and thanks to many generous donations from members, many of whom were living away from the village, the church continues to be the welcoming place of worship it has been for over two centuries.

The Methodist Church

The Methodist Church in Diseworth is newer than the Baptist Church, the Foundation Stones being laid early in 1887, but the original building was established more than ninety years earlier. The Methodist records show that a cottage, barn and land were purchased at a sale by auction in 1799 for the sum of £73 10s:

'for the purpose of proclaiming and expounding God's Holy Word therein conformable and agreeable to the doctrine (and no other) which is contained in the said John Wesley's Notes upon the New Testament and four volumes of sermons'

The transaction is described as: -
'Bargain and sale of premises at Diseworth upon trust for the purposes within mentioned. Mr. William Hall, surviving trustee under the will of John Williamson, deceased, (shoemaker), to Mr. John Rayns and others, enrolled in the High Court of Chancery 19th March 1800. This indenture was made 14th day October, in the 39th year of the reign of King George 11, and the year of our Lord 1799'

John Rayns was one of the first trustees; he came from Castle Donington and was a basket maker. Three of the trustees lived in Diseworth; John Mugleston, a shopkeeper, John Ragg, a framework knitter and Thomas Stevenson, a cordwainer. The cottage and barn which had been purchased were used very soon afterwards, following a few alterations. A caretaker occupied the cottage, and the barn became the chapel and an application was made for the house and barn to be registered as a meetinghouse. By 1829, a return showed the number of Methodists in Diseworth to be fifty.

As numbers grew, so did the number of trustees, from seven in 1847, to seventeen in 1919, but by that time the present Chapel was in existence. It was opened in November 1887, the same year as the foundation stones were laid, and the President of the Methodist Conference came to preach.

The name Underwood is prominent in the work of the Methodist Church in Diseworth.

Peter Underwood, who it is suggested, was much involved in the construction of the chapel was a devout Methodist, and brought up his three children George, Ann and Mary, to follow his faith. One of his daughters, Mary, moved to Weston-on-Trent on marriage, and one of her roles was to care for a baby who grew up to be Dr Gervase Smith, who became the President of the Methodist Conference.

George Underwood had three sons who all went to Africa and became engaged in missionary work.

Adkin is another name which has been involved with the Church since its inception. John Adkin who served the Castle Donington and other circuits for over fifty years as a preacher lived and died in the same house in which he was born. His son Ernest also became a preacher, and he travelled as a missionary to India for many years before returning to England, to take responsibility for the Mission Halls in Liverpool and Wallasey.

It is from 'Pastor Ernest Adkin's Reminiscences' that the accounts of the older chapel and its members come alive. He knew the children of John Ragg, one of the original trustees of the church back in 1799. Their names were George, Jonathon and Bessie, and Bessie had lived in the Chapel cottage. Pastor Ernest could remember the name Ragg being changed to Wragg, because it 'looked better'. His father had spoken of Peter Underwood with great respect, and it was Peter's daughter Ann, married to Jonathon Wragg, whom he recalled. They were never absent from services, prayer meetings or class meetings, unless they were ill.

'I well remember when the Rev. William Taylor was about to leave the circuit, he came to Diseworth, where he was greatly beloved, to conduct his last service. I remember Ann Wragg finishing her remarks of farewell, with tears running down her face, waving her hand, and saying "Go on, we'll meet you there", and they have met.'

Pastor Ernest fondly recalled his parents, particularly his bed-ridden mother, and the hesitation he felt on whether or not to go to India, but neither parent made any move to stop him. He was away for eleven years, and six weeks after he and his wife returned to England, his mother and his wife's mother died on the same day, but he was grateful his mother had lived to witness his return. His love and respect for his father is portrayed in the following account:

'The old thatched chapel was a dear spot, and was especially so after the revival scenes of 1882, but we often wished for a better building. A scene I shall never forget took place on my father's fiftieth birthday, October 13th, 1880, when he called us together. Holding up a sovereign, he said, "That is for a new chapel at Diseworth". As far as I know that was the first contribution to the present chapel and I am glad to think the first contribution was his'.

The devotion of the members of the church certainly influenced the younger members as so many of them went into the ministry in one form or another. Rev Maurice Russell recalled how much he owed to his uncle, John Adkin, and it was his influence which led his nephew to become a minister.

Maurice Russell also remembered the *'stiff, hard, upright, narrow seats in the Sunday School, where small folk were sometimes fidgety. And Abraham Marshall, quaint, but good, though a bit severe.'*

The Bee family and the Russell family are also well known names from not so long ago. Thomas Bee taught the young people in the Diseworth Methodist Sunday School for forty years and was known for inculcating total abstinence principles. The Bee family donated the altar table and chairs to the church. Also recalled are the Christmas parties and the concerts, and the Sunday School Anniversaries.

Doris Allen, whose husband Tom was a lifelong member of the Diseworth Methodist Church, recalls walking with friends from Castle Donington Methodist Church to help with the singing rehearsals for the Sunday School Anniversaries. They would walk across the 'Windmill' fields, now part of the airport, join in with the many others, and walk back again.

The Methodist community in Diseworth is much smaller at the start of the third millennium, but services are still held regularly and the pastors and people come from nearby villages to continue the devotion to the Methodist Church and its teaching.

The Parish Church of St. Michael and All Angels

"Enter this door as if the floor within were Gold,
And every wall of jewels all of wealth untold,
As if a choir in robes of fire were singing here,
Nor shout nor rush but hush for God is here"

St Micheal and All Angels Church, in the heart of Diseworth.

An estimated 800 years after it was built, the church of St Michael and All Angels retains its position in the very heart of Diseworth, a timeless symbol of tranquillity and continuity.

The parish is situated in the deanery of Akeley East, delightfully translated as *'lying in the lea of the oak'* in the borough of Charn Wood.

There is scant information available on the fabric of the parish church before the 17th century other than that already recorded in the booklet published by the Diseworth History Society. In 1344 it is reported that the rectory was taxed at 8 marks and paid one shilling for peter pence, (annual tax of one penny paid to the papal see by each householder owning land of a specific value).

Parish records are few and far between for the period of the middle ages. Many registers were destroyed but some of those that remain include a number of entries with names relevant to today.

An inventory of weddings, christenings and burials in the parish of Diseworth:

17th February 1577	*Baptism of Richard Jarrom - son of Richard Jarrom*
10th November 1577	*Wedding of Franncys Marshall and Isobel Melbourne*
14th December 1583	*Baptism of Mary Marshall - daughter of John Marshall*
4th November 1583	*Wedding of Rowland Lyllye and Anne Layce*
10th July 1584	*Christening of Thomas Lyllye - son of Roland Lyllye*

At the time of the Reformation the living of each parish was valued at considerably more than the stipend of the parson. Clergy were often non-resident and would install a curate who worked as an assistant, performing all the duties of the parish but receiving only a fraction of its worth. In 1534, there were 6 parsons in the county of Leicester who had stipends of less than £5 a year. One of these had the living of Diseworth and received £4. The clerks put in by absentee clergy were often poorly educated and incapable of carrying out pastoral duties. Many were unable to read and write and as a result left incomplete records of their incumbency. A good example of this is reflected in the report of the Rev Isaac Hoyland in 1707.

Describing how he collected the small tithes in the parish, he wrote that he had inherited no written records from his predecessor, the Reverend Twitty. As a result he was dependent on the word of his parishioners for details of all tithes due and feared that he had *'wronged the vicarage in some particulars, and could not help it'*. Now it was around this time that the undertenants of Diseworth were disputing the increased rents they had to pay to the grand tenant and ultimately to Christ's College. It is by no means certain that they sought to deceive the vicar, but it is not impossible that they would indulge in a little creative accounting and thus mitigate their hardship.

Parish church harvest festival, 1899.

The account of the tithes make fascinating reading but Mr Hoyland confessed that he was uncertain about the previous report sent to the Spiritual Court, being a little forgetful, but '*perhaps with some variation from one another, was in the form here following*'.

The small tithes - taxes of one tenth of all produce and livestock - had to be paid in kind. Wool, lamb, pigs, geese, pigeons, bees (every tenth swarm), apples and all orchard fruits; the eggs of hens, ducks and all other farmyard fowls with the exception of goose eggs. If pigs were not available in tens, they were to be counted in the following litter. Alternatively there was a discount of one halfpenny for those above seven and below ten.

Any sheep belonging to children under age and who were living with their parents, or sheep sold or bought from markets before clipping day were valued at one halfpennny each. Sheep brought in from another town were charged for the length of their stay or fourpence for twenty beasts per month. Any sheep dying after Candlemas were valued at halfpence a hide. The vicar's pastoral rights entitled him to graze his cattle on villagers' pasture with rights of common in '*all commonable places for three cows and a horse or mare*' The Easter Roll for that year was '*threepence for every dwelling house; communion oblations for man and woman twopence halfpenny, every servant and single person 16 years of age, 2d. Servants one farthing further at every shilling wages. Every yardland in the*

Parish church harvest festival, 1910.

parish (25 in all) to pay 3d apiece. The foregoing account of tithing, subscribed by me (Isaac Hoyland) and Robert Mee and Henry Adkin, churchwardens, was delivered into the Ecclesiastical Court in the year 1707. There is due to the vicar 8 shillings per annum for tithe herbage of high wood closes, being a third part of the whole composition, constantly paid by the tenants, and due every Michaelmas.'

The Churchwardens - Officers of the Parish

The churchwarden's post is an honourable office, known to have existed as long ago as the 12th century. Chaucer refers to churchwardens as church reeves. Next to the vicar and the grand tenant of the village, the churchwardens were (indeed still are), two of the most important people in parochial life and are concerned with the maintenance and repair of the church.

Wardens were originally ecclesiastical officers, specified as *'proper guardians and keepers of the parish church'*. Between the 16th and 19th century, they shouldered an additional burden of secular duties, becoming more involved in parish government with responsibility for the relief of the poor and maintenance of the roads. According to historical documents it is the duty of the wardens to: provide bread and wine for Holy Communion, maintain the fabric of the church, obtain a faculty for any major repairs or alterations to the building, take charge of the belfry and ensure the bells are not rung without cause. Further duties were to clean the churchyard, keep boundary fences, hedges and walls in good repair and make sure there was no disorder or irreverence among the congregation. They were responsible for bringing offenders of Church law to book and to this day they have the authority to remove a worshipper's hat during a church service.

Churchwardens were required to keep detailed accounts of all parochial income and expenditure. Few examples of these account books survive today, as many were destroyed or simply lost. Remarkably, a book of Diseworth's Churchwardens' accounts was discovered on a junk stall at a Sunday market in the 1970's and purchased by a gentleman from Leicester. A plain exercise book with cardboard covers, it is mainly in ink with some pages written in pencil and spans a period of 42 years. This document was painstakingly typed by the purchaser onto a computer file and we are fortunate to possess a copy. The transcript provides a detailed and fascinating report, not only of church expenses, but of the setting of church rates, vestry meetings, income from pew rents and the election of churchwardens for the years 1838 to 1880.

Election of Churchwardens

The election of new churchwardens took place each year, usually at the time of the Easter vestry meeting and Diseworth, like many other parishes had a vicar's warden and a peoples' warden.

At a vestry meeting of the inhabitants of Diseworth held in the New School Room pursuant to Notice on Friday April 6th 1866 for the purpose of electing two fit and proper persons to the office of Churchwarden for the ensuing year for the said Parish of Diseworth, Charles Shakespear Esq was elected Churchwarden by the Vicar on his part and Mr Robert Bartram was elected Churchwarden on the part of the Parish.

CF Cooke Vicar
C Shakespear
R Bartram Churchwardens

The Setting of the Church Rate

The church rate was another major source of income for the parish to guarantee funds for the upkeep and expenses of the clergy and officers.

On 10th September 1858, a vestry meeting was held in the new school rooms to make a rate for repairs to the church and *the necessary expenses of performing Divine Service*. An estimate was put in by the churchwardens of one penny and three farthings in the pound. This rate was proposed by George Hinds and seconded by Charles Bowles -

churchwardens. The proposal was agreed without opposition. Three years later, the vestry meeting began as usual in the school room but swiftly adjourned across the road, possibly because it was a warm evening!

At a vestry meeting held pursuant to Notice on Friday June 21st 1861 at the School Room Diseworth and adjourned to the Bulls Head Inn, the accounts of the Churchwardens for the past year were examined and passed unanimously - and at the same time and place a Church Rate was proposed by C Shakespear Esq and seconded by Mr T Hill at the rate of one penny farthing in the pound for the repair and expenses of the Church in the ensuing year was carried unanimously.

Signed.	*CF Cooke*	*Chairman*
	C Shakespear	*Churchwardens*
	George Adkin	
	Robert Adkin	
	Henry Mugleston	
	Thomas Hill	

Pew Rents

In theory, seating in church was available for all, but the practice of renting pews was widespread following the Reformation. Churchwardens were able to derive a considerable income from renting pews, not only to the gentry but also to wealthier members of the congregation. Freehold pews would have doors on them which would have a lock and key, while the lowlier members of the flock would be obliged to sit on benches or stand. It is noticeable that a large number of the pews in our parish church have doors on them and there are itemized entries in the churchwardens' accounts.

Accounts of pew rents taken by the following persons from August 1st 1875 to August 1st 1876.

				£	s	d
20	Mr Orton	2 sittings	@ 1/6d		3	0
11	C Shakespear Esq	10 sittings	@ 10/- each	5	0	0
12	C Shakespear Esq	One pew		1	0	0
16	C Shakespear Esq	2 sittings	@ 2/6d each		5	0
	Rev HC Pryce-Jones	6 sittings	@ 4/- each	1	4	0
1	Mr Barrow	4 sittings	@ 3/9d each		15	0
2	Mr Cross	4 sittings	@ 3/9d each		15	0
3	Mr George Hinds	4 sittings	@ 3/9d each		15	0
4	Mr SW Thirlby	4 sittings	@ 3/9d each		15	0
5	Mr Neal	4 sittings	@ 3/9d each		15	0

6	**Mr Dent**	**1 sitting**	**@ 2/6d each**		2	6
7	**Mr Fletcher**	**4 sittings**	**@ 2/6d each**		10	0
8	**Mr George Adkin**	**2 sittings**	**@ 2/6d each**		5	0
"	**Mr Pountain**	**1 sitting**	**@ 2/6d each**		2	6
"	**Mr Jno Simpkin**	**1 sitting**	**@ 2/6d each**		2	6
9 & 10	**The choir**			£12	6	6

The Expenses of the Churchwardens

The expenses covered every aspect of maintaining the church, from visitation expenses to *a new key for the belfry - one shilling.* A very large part of their outlay was on fuel; ie coal and coke for heating the building and paraffin for the lamps. A huge quantity of candles were needed and in 1870, nine pounds in weight were purchased in one month alone. Other regular expenses were for the cleaning of the church. This involved not just the wages of the cleaner but the diverse cleaning implements and materials. These were variously described as: *brooms, brushes, handbrushes, a turk's head brush and besoms,* not to mention the necessary dustpans.

Altar expenses were naturally a considerable item. A new prayer book for the reading desk cost £1 15s in December 1859 and a communion book was 11s 6d in 1868. The regular purchase of bread and wine for the Sacrament was necessary and in August 1843 there was an entry for *a white table-cover for Communion Table: 11s 6d. Napkin for Communion: 1s 6d.* Payment to the churchwarden's wife, 1s 6d for washing a surplice, for mending a surplice one shilling. In 1858 *a new fine linen surplice - £2 0s 0d.* Whitewashing had to be done every two to three years, no doubt due to the soot accumulation from the boiler which also had to be serviced and repaired. Other miscellaneous outgoings included: *repairing windows; fees to the Town Cryer, (entered in the account book as crying); repair of the Funeral Paul; a mat for the church door -11s, poison for mice 3d.* On May 28th 1841 the sum of 4 shillings was entered for *Journey to Kegworth with Horse and Cart for Confirmation.*

The bell ropes needed to be replaced every five or six years. The cost rose from 18 shillings in 1839 to £1 10s in June 1867. An entry in 1874 read:

July 14th	**Taylor's Bill for repair of Bells**	**£4 10s**
July 14th	**Taylor's men for Beer when repairing Bells**	**3s**

One other major expenditure which appeared regularly in the pages of the accounts was for maintenance of the church clock. Variously described as cleaning, repairing, winding and oiling, the annual cost was between ten and twelve shillings over the 40 year period.

The Bells of Diseworth Church

The history of the six bells of St Michael and All Angels is well documented elsewhere but it is worth repeating here. It is known that there were two bells in the tower in 1626. A third was cast in 1672 and a fourth in 1803. The fifth bell was purchased during the incumbency of the Reverend Herbert Lock. His brother had raised approximately £215 towards the building of a mission church in Africa which was to be dedicated to St Joseph of Arimathea. Tragically, the Rev Lock's brother died before the church could be built. It was arranged that the money be returned to Diseworth, on the condition that it be used, among other things, to purchase a bell. Known as St Joseph's bell, it stood on the floor of the tower until 1921. The sixth bell was a gift from the Reverend JA Palmer in gratitude for the recovery from a serious illness of his young son during the first world war. It is recorded that the first five bells were re-cast by Taylor's bell foundry and the additional one hung in 1921. These six bells are positioned in the tower in two layers of three.

In times past, the bells were rung to mark the passing of a parish resident. There would be a muffled peal followed by a solemn tolling. On and on the bell would toll, 1, 2, 3, one toll for each year of the deceased's life. Workers in the fields would pause and count the strokes and villagers about their everyday business would also stop what they were doing and reflect on this transitory life.

Bell rubbings taken in the latter half of the 20th century.

NAZARENVS REX IVDEORVM 1672

There are countless occasions in recent history when special peals have been rung.

In 1936, as a tribute to his late Majesty King George V muffled peals were rung on the bells at each of the services. A memorial service was conducted by the vicar on the day of the funeral and a muffled peal was again rung in the evening.

On the Coronation Day of King George VI, the church bells were rung at 7 am and at intervals during the day. The dedication of the new church clock in the same year was marked with full peals on the six bells before and after the service. At the Coronation of Queen Elizabeth II, *Holy Communion Services were held at 7, 8, and 9 o'clock followed by merry peals on the church bells.*

On April 17th 1945 at a meeting of the Parochial Church Council, the vicar stated that with the end of the war in Europe in view, he proposed that on VE Day, the bells be rung as soon as possible after the initial announcement and that a thanksgiving service be held in the evening of that day at 8pm. The Thanksgiving Day Collection to be given to the Fund for the Churches of Europe.

In addition to weddings, confirmation services and the call to divine service, the most recent special peal was 1st January 2000 when villagers assembled in church for 'Celebration 2000'.

R·SOWTER & T. HASTINGS & W. JOHN BRIANT HERTFORD & D CORT LEICESTER FECERUNT

The Clock

The church clock is almost certainly unique. The slate dial was installed in 1730 and bears the initials of the churchwardens for that year. The original movement ceased working in the early 1900's and the clock stood silent for thirty years. In 1936 the people of Diseworth launched a fundraising drive to install a new clock mechanism as a celebration of the coronation of King George VI. In a very short time they raised the handsome sum of £108 and the Derby firm of John Smith & Co began the task of installing the new movement.

The dedication of the new clock by the Bishop of Leicester was a joyful occasion although according to accounts of the event, time appeared if not to stand still, to drag.

'The Bishop walked in procession from the vicarage, preceded by the churchwardens. After the

third hymn the Bishop moved to the tower where the dedication took place. He then proceeded to the pulpit where he congratulated the congregation on raising the money in such a short time. He took as the text for his sermon "Lord, teach us how to pray" and spoke for thirty minutes emphasizing the need for devotion'. A brass plaque was placed in the tower to commemorate the occasion.

Shortly before the publication of this book, the clock was refurbished. A fundraising drive entitled '£2,000 for 2,000' was launched and once again the parish and local businesses raised the money in a remarkably short time. Yet another example of Diseworth's sense of community and the reassuring continuity of parochial life!

Part of the refurbishment involved the stripping away of many layers of paint from the slate dial before the hands and numerals were painted with gold leaf. The original Roman numerals were now exposed and it was discovered, with considerable excitement, that there are two elevens. Number nine is carved XI instead of IX. One can imagine the stonemason crawling round the outside of the clock dial, painstakingly chiselling the numerals. From the edge of the face, IX would appear as 9 although viewed from its position on the church tower, it reads XI. The result of this error does of course mean that in Diseworth there are always two opportunities to do things at the eleventh hour!

It is interesting to note an entry in the churchwardens accounts mentioned earlier:

May 6th 1870 Painting and Gilding Clock face £1 0s 0d

In Loving Memory

There are many memorials to the departed in the graveyard and inside the church itself. Although we have been unable to discover its location, there is said to be a slate gravestone of a former gravedigger. The inscription reads:

Graves around for many a year,
Were dug by him who slumbers here.
Till worn with age he dropped his spade,
And in this dust his dust is laid.

To the right of the church tower is the grave of the very first casualty from Diseworth of the First World War:

9435 Private JF Allcroft. Leicestershire Regiment. 31st May 1915. aged 21

Inside the church are some touching monuments to former parishioners. One is to the memory of Trooper George Harris. The story of his untimely death, also at the age of 21 comes from an account by a descendant of his family - Harold Barker:

George Harris volunteered for service with the Imperial Yeomanry and as was customary, supplied his own horse. In bidding him farewell from Diseworth, Ellen, his mother, slapped the horse's flank and said "Well my lad, do your duty". His platoon was galloping through a pass near Dewetsdorp and came under sniper fire from Boer soldiers in the rocks and George was shot and wounded. Another trooper's horse was killed and the soldier, seeing George's horse available, leapt into the saddle and escaped with five other troopers. The Dewetsdorp area was taken in the following few days and the major returned with two other troopers to bury George, unaware that he had lain dying, mainly of thirst, in the hot African sun. Given water, he was able to croak "Tell my mother I've done my duty".

Sacred to the Memory of Trooper George Harris - Aged 21 Years.
Of the 65th Company, Imperial Yeomanry. Killed in Action at Dewetsdorp,
Orange River Colony, December 14th 1901, during the Transvaal War, South Africa.
Erected by Emily Lock in Gratitude to his mother.

A
P + X

One poignant memorial is to Anne Cheslyn of Langley Priory. She drowned in the lake at the Priory and the plaque shows her clutching a piece of pondweed.

O GOD, THY WILL BE DONE

To the memory of Anne, the wife of Richd. Cheslyn of Langley Priory Esq.

She was the second daughter of Thomas Barber of Derby Esq. An excellent heart and manners assured her the esteem of an extensive acquaintance but her delicate form of body and extreme sensibility of mind tended to shorten her life and she died, beloved by all who knew her, and greatly bewailed by her husband and her children on the 10th day of August 1823 in her 54th year.

*"Accept blest shades the tributary star that mourns thy exit from a world like this;
Forgive the wish that would have kept thee here and stay'd thy progress to the seat of bliss.
Tho' thou art free from mortal care, Thy spirit fled to realms above.
Still shalt thou be to mem'ry dear, and ever charm thy husband's love".*

There are several memorial plaques to former clergymen of the parish.

The Reverend Herbert Lock did an enormous amount of good, not only for the church, but for the whole village of Diseworth. He was held in very high regard by adults and children alike and was remembered as "The Children's Friend".

A
P + X
In Jesu

In loving memory of the Reverend Herbert Lock A.K.C. Vicar Of Diseworth from 1894 to 1902, who departed this life aged 39 years on March 17th in the year of Our Lord 1902.

The south aisle of the Church was restored and this tablet erected by the Parishioners and Friends, in token of their deep esteem for his holy and humble Christian Life and incessant labours for his Master's service and the welfare of his people.

"Faithful Unto Death"

Under this monument lie the bodies of Mr Isaac Hoyland, late vicar of Diseworth and Mary his wife, sole daughter of Mr Matthew Trigge, rector of Stretton le Field, by whom he had six sons and two daughters; but two only, Matthew and Mary, do survive him. This truly reverend person and eminent preacher, after he had faithfully served God and his Church in a long course of excellent ministry, and given one of the best examples, both of pastoral and private virtues, resigned his soul to God, April 21, 1712, and of his age the 66th.

His wife, a woman of exemplary prudence, conduct and goodness, died before him Sept 15th 1708. To the memory of her parents their daughter Mary hath erected and devoted this sepulchral monument.

Perhaps one of the most interesting memorials in the church is the one to Caleb Lowdham, vicar of Diseworth for 52 years. It is apparent from the plaque which commemorates his life, that he was in charge of more than one parish, but unlike the clergy referred to earlier in this chapter, he did not neglect his duties or shirk his responsibilities.

In January 1994 the brick floors were removed from the Baptistry and soil was excavated to several inches below where the existing floor finishes. A brick burial chamber was found in this area which contained two lead coffins belonging to Caleb Lowdham and his wife Mary.

Beneath are deposited the Remains of CALEB LOWDHAM MA

He was resident Vicar of this parish	52 years
Rector of Stoney Stanton in this county	42 years
Domestic Chaplain to Theophilus and Francis, Successive Earls of Huntingdon	46 years

After a life uniformly employed in the exemplary discharge of every pastoral, conjugal and parental duty, he resigned his soul into the hands of his Redeemer on the 25th day of March 1779 aged 76 years.

Also near this place lies interred the body of MARY LOWDHAM
The faithful consort and relict of the above named Caleb Lowdham.
She died the 10th day of December 1788 aged 87 years.

In testimony of their filial duty and affection, Francis-Glen and Caleb, their two surviving and only children caused this monument to be erected.

READER PREPARE TO MEET THY GOD IN JUDGEMENT.

Three Charitable Men

There are three men in the history of Diseworth whose generous bequests were to have a significant effect upon the lives of village people. These men were William Langley, William Lane and Caleb Lowdham.

William Langley's will dated 2nd April 1695 bequeathed his college lease in Diseworth and the residue of its income to his executors. He instructed them to sell it and invest the money realized for the purpose of '*educating six poor boys of the town of Diseworth in some school in Diseworth*'

William Lane, in a similar bequest in 1720 *left all his land and hereditaments in Long Whatton and Diseworth and decreed out of the rents and profits thereof to pay £5 annually to each of the liberties of Diseworth and Long Whatton to be distributed in bread at the discretion of his trustees. Sixteen sixpenny loaves and one fourpenny loaf are to be supplied at the church the first Sunday in every month from a baker in Hatherne. These are to be distributed after Divine Service, amongst widows and other poor inhabitants of the parish, the same persons, when once on the list of recipients, being allowed to receive the bread for life.*

He further gave annually, for ever, *the sum of £10 to finance a free school for the children of Long Whatton, on condition that the inhabitants would pay an annual sum of £10 to the school-master.* If villagers in Long Whatton failed to carry out this request, they would forfeit the legacy and the money would be given to Diseworth to fund their own schoolmaster. Twelve years later in 1732, the people of Long Whatton declined to accept this annual gift and the money was duly transferred to Diseworth. It was shortly after this that the new schoolroom and master's house were built in the village. A further £7 was raised by public subscription for the schoolmaster's salary, thus laying a strong foundation for education in Diseworth.

Caleb Lowdham in his will dated 21st October 1817 directed his executors, *at the end of twelve months after my decease, to invest £200 in the purchase of stock in one of the public funds of this kingdom*. This stock was taken out in the names of the vicar of Diseworth and two substantial landowners or parishioners of the village.

He left instructions for these people to use the dividend from the investment to buy bread or meat, or both, to be distributed each year within fourteen days of the 1st January, one half by the vicar, *to such poor inhabitants therein, whether legally settled or not, as he should think proper,* the other half to be distributed by the churchwardens of the same parish to such other poor inhabitants as they should think proper. The benefits were unconditional and were not to be considered as a substitute for existing poor relief entitlement from the parish rates.

When the position of a trustee became vacant, a new official had to be appointed at a specially convened vestry meeting, *four days previous notice given thereof publicly during, or immediately after Divine Service*.

The Reverend Lowdham died on 9th January 1825 and in January of the following year the sum of £200 was invested by his executors. The stock purchased to fund the charity was three per cent Consolidated Bank Annuities in the names of the vicar, The Reverend George Ludford Harvey, and of Richard Cheslyn and Charles Harris who were the two landowners and principal inhabitants stipulated in the Will.

Some of the earliest records existing of the administration of Caleb Lowdham's charity date back to 1913 and make fascinating reading. The cost of beef in that year was 8d a pound and a quartern (4 lb) loaf was 5d. In 1914 beef was the same price but a loaf had gone up to fivepence halfpenny.

In 1916 the income from the charity was not sufficient to provide the usual distribution of bread and meat. The vicar offered to supplement the charity with money from church funds and the offer was accepted. The charity was augmented once again in the following year. Due to the order of the food controller it was not possible to distribute meat but recipients were given 1s 6d and a loaf of bread. From this time onward, the distribution was of money and bread. Although the price of a quartern loaf gradually increased, the cash award remained the same. The following items appeared in the local press:

February 1936 *The annual distribution in connection with the Lane and Lowdham charity took place in the schools. Gifts of bread and a sum of money were handed over to a number of parishioners. Distribution was undertaken by the vicar, a churchwarden (Mr FG Fletcher) and Mr Barnett of the Parish Council.*

1938 *The charity bread list for the Whatton ward was revised and 28 families will receive two 4lb loaves and one small loaf which is to be supplied by Messrs JH Smith & Sons of Kegworth.*

The list of beneficiaries was continually revised during the war years and there was lengthy discussion at the 1943 AGM. The decision was taken that no one in regular employment could be considered poor. After careful scrutiny, ten parishioners were selected for a grant of twelve shillings each and beneficiaries were required to purchase their own food.

The grant was reduced to 6s 9d in 1946 for 20 people. The chairman received a letter from the charities commission concerning the appointment of trustees and suggesting a scheme giving trustees wider discretion:

For the vicar's moiety, Trustees to be named by the vicar as ex officio, one person named by him, one nominated by the Diseworth Ward councillors and appointed by Long Whatton Parish Council. The nomination for the churchwardens' moiety was identical. A resolution was moved and seconded that the vicar and trustees apply for administration of the charity. This would give them wider discretion in the application of the income in the supply of clothing and boots, fuel, medical aid, for sickness and convalescence payments and for educational payments. As no reply was received in this application, they reverted to cash payments in 1947.

In 1966 the vicar received a letter from the Charities Commission regarding the deficiency in the number of trustees. To resolve this difficulty, it was suggested that the Trustees for the Lowdham charity serve for the Lane charity as well. This was agreed unanimously and the AGM of 1967 received a letter from the commissioners approving the amalgamation of the two charities Both charity meetings were conducted simultaneously from 1968. Ten shillings was distributed to 12 people and fowls provided by Mrs Lockett were distributed to 11 persons.

The Lane charity was disbanded in 1972 as no payment had been made from the land which yielded the funds. After investigation, it was decided that the cost of taking legal action against the landowner would cost around £100 or 20 years income from the trust. It was decided with regret to allow the rent charge to lapse making the Trust ineffective.

The Lowdham charity made occasional gifts to residents over the next few years but no specific grants were made as a matter of course. A new law under the Charities Act came into force in 1992 and the charity was required to adhere to new regulations. The income was less than £1,000 p.a. and it became necessary to re-invest the existing investments and use the annual income to meet the needs of the local population.

At the AGM in 1994, the committee had three options for the continuance of the charity:

1 **Transfer the assets to another charity, thus leading to the charity being wound up.**
2 **Alter the trusts of the charity.**
3 **Empower the committee to spend the capital of the charity which would lead to the charity being wound up.**

As the income from the previous 12 months was £5.51, it was decided, after considering the various alternatives and accepting that neither of the first two options was viable, that the capital be spent on helping the poorer people of the parish to meet heating costs and that as a consequence, the charity be wound up. This motion was proposed, seconded and carried unanimously by the trustees and notices were posted around the parish to this effect in accordance with the Charities Act 1993.

CHAPTER NINE EDUCATION IN DISEWORTH

There is little evidence of formal education in Diseworth until the 18th Century. Those that received it were generally those entering the Church or the Law, these being young men thus women did not benefit. Even those who entered the convents depended on the value given to learning by the abbess or prioress. Basic reading and writing would be necessary for chanting prayers and singing hymns, but other aspects of education would be at the whim of their superiors and whether such was important for the well being of the establishment.

In 1440, the Prioress (of Langley), Dame Margery Pole, in accounting to the Bishop, declared she would explain the accounts to him but not to her sisters. The nuns were said to be '*unversed in letters and could not understand the writings*', but this was probably because the writings were in Latin. More than one hundred years later, William Lilly (born in 1602), describing his childhood in Diseworth, complained that farmers did not educate their sons. He was sent to Ashby Grammar School.

The moves nationally to improve the basic education of the populace resulted in Diseworth acquiring two benefactors, William Langley and William Lane.

Two Good Men

William Langley, in his will dated April 1695, left the residue of his college lease in Diseworth, together with the benefits of renewing it, to three people in trust, Henry Brisby, Edward Harris and John Savage. They were then to sell it in order to purchase an '*estate of inheritance for the teaching and instructing in the reading of English, 12 poor boys and girls out of the parish of Ashby-de-la-Zouch, and six poor boys of the town of Diseworth, in some school in Diseworth*'.

William Langley was a devout man. He also decreed that the master should be allowed $1^1/_2$d per week for each boy, and that 6d a year should be allowed to each boy to buy books for learning; at the end of the first year, 2d per boy to purchase a catechism. At the end of the stipulated three years of education, 12d for each boy to purchase Mr Allen's '*Alarm to the Unconverted*', or some such other good book; also 3s a piece to buy each of the said boys a Bible.

The charity was later extended to nine children, boys and girls, but the girls were only taught needlework.

William Lane in his will, dated September 1720, devised all his land and hereditaments in Long Whatton and Diseworth, upon trust, to four men, William Busby, Charnel Wilson, William Cook and William Cox. The rents and profits from the income should go towards bread for the poor of the two villages. He also arranged for an annual sum of ten pounds towards a '*free school for the teaching of the children of Long Whatton to read and write, providing the inhabitants thereof should yearly give unto the schoolmaster (elected by the trustees) the sum of £10'*. The proviso was that if the Long Whatton inhabitants did not give their share, then the money was to go to Diseworth for the same purpose.

Long Whatton's loss became Diseworth's gain, and the parish set about providing a schoolroom and house for the master. In addition to the salary of £10, a further sum of £7 was raised for the schoolmaster by subscription among the inhabitants. The master was duly appointed and required to teach reading *free gratis*, to any poor children in the parish, who applied for admission to the school on the recommendation of the ratepayers. There was a charge however, for learning to write.

Diseworth was fortunate in having Christ's College as lords of the manor, in that they were persuaded to help provide the means of building the school. In a letter of 1744 to the Reverend Doctor Towers, Fellows and Scholars, the forty tenants after bitterly complaining about the rise in rents and their resulting hardship, end their letter with gratitude for '*generosity and kindness towards building our school house*'. This letter may well have been written by Robert Cheslyn, who was then owner of Langley Priory, and to whom the response was requested to be sent.

In the '*Particular and Estimate of the Yearly Value of the estate in the Parish of Diseworth in the County of Leicester belonging to Christ's College*', in 1793, Samuel Wyatt recorded:

House and Croft	*Langley School*	*1 acre*	*yearly value*	*£2 10s*
House and Croft	*Cox's School*	*1 acre*	*" "*	*£2*

The Langley School was clearly continuing, one hundred years after being established, and the Cox's School could well be the William Lane bequest, considering that one of the trustees was named William Cox.

The Cheslyns had a schoolmaster in their family, Nicholas Cheslyn, who was the son of Richard and Elizabeth Cheslyn. Nicholas was the grandson of the Richard Cheslyn who had purchased Langley from the Grays, and the half-nephew of Robert mentioned above.

It is not recorded where Nicholas Cheslyn lived, nor whether he was one of the first teachers in Diseworth. However, when Mr Case wrote his detailed valuation of Diseworth for Christ's College in 1766, he mentions that:

'Nicholas Cheslyn, a schoolmaster aged 70, has written terriers about 40 years since, for the undertenants, to be delivered to the grand lessee, Mr. Barwell'.

The Parish records note that he and his wife were buried in the village.

'Ruth, wife of Nicholas Cheslyn, schoolmaster, buried November 23rd 1768 aged 78 years'

'Nicholas Cheslyn, schoolmaster, buried August 1771 aged 79 years'

A school and master's house was built in Clements Gate, and continued as such until 1862 when the new school was built in Grimes Gate. The first schoolmaster was possibly Nicholas Cheslyn, and the second was Thomas Waldron. A headstone in the Parish Churchyard reads:

'Here lies the body of Thomas Waldron, late School Master of Diseworth who died May 16th 1801 aged 58 years'

Thomas Waldron may well have been a pupil and protégé of Nicholas Cheslyn. He was born in 1743, the eldest son of Thomas and Mary Waldron of Diseworth. He probably became the village schoolmaster around 1762 when Nicholas Cheslyn was 70 years old.

Thomas was well respected in Diseworth, and was called upon to witness many of the marriages in the Parish Church in the 1770's and 1780's.

After Thomas died in 1801, a new schoolmaster arrived in Diseworth who was to have a profound effect on the village as a whole and who was responsible for a great deal of the information on Diseworth from the nineteenth century. His name was Nathaniel Gayton.

A Victorian Schoolmaster

Nathaniel Gayton came from Northamptonshire, and possibly arrived in the village to take up the appointment as schoolmaster. From Census details we know he was born in 1787.

The earliest record found of Nathaniel's arrival in the village is in 1805, when at the age of nineteen, together with Thomas Draper, he was proposed as candidate for Baptism and Fellowship in the Baptist Church in Diseworth.

The evidence available for the account of Nathaniel's life comes mainly from two sources, in particular the wonderfully detailed Minute Books of the Kegworth and Diseworth Baptist Churches. These describe his devotion to the Baptist Church, and there are also, from the schoolmaster himself, scrapbooks and diaries, which he kept from at least 1848 until 1866, shortly before he died. The diaries record village events, marriages, births and deaths, as well as his personal concerns. His academic talents were obviously appreciated; he was Census enumerator for two decades, an onerous task in which the personal details of all the families in the village were recorded.

Nathaniel married Elizabeth, daughter of Joseph Harvey, on 25th October 1813 in the Parish Church. Sadly, less than one year later Elizabeth died and perhaps then Nathaniel threw himself into village and church life in addition to school duties.

Throughout the writings in existence no mention is made of the school or the pupils.

He records himself in the 1851 census as '*Widower, aged 64, Schoolmaster, teacher of reading, writing and arithmetic*'. According to village memories of long ago, only one newspaper was delivered to the village and that to the schoolmaster, so he provided people with news from the 'outside world'.

The school and house included the Parish Rooms, all of which were under the jurisdiction of the Governors of Shardlow Poor Law Union. The premises where the buildings stood were part of three properties owned by the Parish and the Shardlow Union. In 1858 part of these properties were sold to Mr Robert Adkin and at the request of the parishioners, it was resolved that £47 15s be allocated to repairs for the school and vestry room.

His diaries show that while he was very busy throughout 1859 and 1860, sadly, deafness was affecting him and he noted that at a Missionary meeting held at the chapel he could scarcely hear anything said. At about this time, questions were being asked at the Shardlow Union as to what specific repairs had been carried out at the Parochial school room. By then also, plans were being put forward for the new school and school house on Grimes Gate.

In May 1861, Nathaniel notes '*I applied as usual for my salary belonging to the school and was refused payment and have applied a second time and been refused*'. It was not until October of that year that he was informed that his salary as schoolmaster would cease as from January 1862. This was confirmed a couple of weeks later. It may seem harsh to this loyal schoolmaster of so many years in the village, but he was 75years old by then and very deaf. It is possible that the Shardlow Poor Law Union and the Parish permitted Mr Gayton to continue living in the schoolmaster's house. Certainly he made no mention of leaving in his diary.

Nathaniel Gayton wrote his last recorded entry in his diary in September 1866. The Minute Book of the Baptist Church notes his death at a May meeting in 1867 and less than a year later on 13th April 1868, the old school house and premises were sold to Robert Adkin.

A School for the Village

The new school on Grimes Gate heralded the 'Education for All' call from the governments of the day.

The Committee of Management consisted of: -

Charles Shakespear - also Member of Building Committee
C.F. Cooke " " " "
Edward Barnett
Marcus Huish
R. Dalby
Joseph Clarke
George Adkin - also Church Warden

This Committee made a detailed statement for the information of the *'Right Honourable the Lords of the Committee of Council on Education'*.

It included the following points for their notice.

1 That the new School Buildings and Teacher's House, in aid of which Your Lordships were pleased to grant £190, have been carefully examined by us, and are completed in a perfectly satisfactory and workman-like manner.

2 That all subscriptions and donations have been received, expended and accounted for as set forth in the annexed balance sheet of receipts and expenditure.

3 That the entire premises have been conveyed to trustees by the deed approved by your Council; that the said Deed has been unrolled in Chancery…and that the said Deed, having been returned to us, is now lodged in the Diseworth Parish Chest.

4 That we are ready to submit to any audit of our accounts for building which your Lordships may direct; to make such periodic reports respecting the state of this school as your Lordships may call for; and to admit Her Majesty's Inspectors of Schools according to the annexed Regulation.

5 That the School will be opened on the 12th day of May 1862, under a Master and Mistress.

6 That we consider it practicable, and will endeavour by our exertions, to maintain the school in efficiency.

Details of the plans and accounts of the new school in Diseworth in 1862.

Balance Sheet of the Building Account of the Diseworth Parish School. As certified in the second clause of the annexed Certificate.

C. F. Cooke, Treasurer in Account with the Diseworth Parish School.

Building of School (14) 1862

Dr.	£	S	D	Cr.	£	S	D
Local							
By voluntary Contributions	260	2	3	Paid for Site	–	–	–
" Collections in Church or Chapel	–	–	–				
" Value of Site (if given)	80	–	–	By Value of Site (if given)	80	–	–
" Sale of old Materials	83	5	10	Buildings	348	15	10
" gratuitous Cartage	52	4	–	Value of gratuitous Cartage	52	4	–
" other means	–	–	–				
Not Local				Legal Expenses	8	8	–
By Contributions or Collections	20	–	–	Sundries	6	4	3
" Grant from — ...... Society	–	–	–				
...... Board	–	–	–				
" other means	–	–	–				
Total amount already received	495	12	1	Total amount already paid	495	12	1
Amount of Grant to be received from Committee of Council	190	–	–	Payments to be made from Grant of Comm: of Council on Education, when received: — For Buildings	190	–	–
Total	685	12	1	Total	685	12	1

Local			
Christ's Coll: Camb:	100.0.0	Brought forward	227.15.0
Do. The Site	– – –	Mr. J. Hayes	1.0.0
C. Shakespear Esq	50.0.0	Mr. G. Hinds	1.0.0
Do. Lease of Site	– – –	Mr. G. Hudson	.10.0
J. Copestake, Esq	50.0.0	M. Huish, Esq.	8.8.0
Rev: R. Dalby	10.0.0	Mr. Jos. Jarrow	.10.0
Mr. G. Adkin	1.0.0	Mr. W. Jarrow	1.0.0
Mr. Jos. Adkin	.10.0	Mr. R. Ince	5.0.0
Mr. R. Adkin	1.0.0	Mr. G. Moore	.2.0
Mr. W. Adkin	2.0.0	Mr. H. Muggleton	1.10.0
Mr. Bartram	.10.0	Mr. Oldershaw	2.0.0
B. Brock, Esq.	2.2.0	Mr. Simpkin	.10.0
Mr. Burkett	.5.0	J. Story, Esq:	5.0.0
Mr. Carter	.5.0	J. Towle Junr. Esq.	2.0.0
Rev: C. F. Cooke	3.3.0	Mr. W. Upton	.5.0
Mr. J. Cross	2.0.0	Bank Interest	3.12.3
Rev: P. Fosbrook	2.0.0		260.2.3
Mr. Gee	1.0.0	**Not Local.**	
Mr. A. Harris	1.0.0	Bp. of Peterborough	10.0.0
Mr. G. Hayes	1.0.0	J. Bowles, Esq:	5.0.0
Carried forward	227.15.0	Rev: H. James	5.0.0
			20.0.0

Building	
Messrs. Broadbents Contract	415.0.0
Value of old Materials given to Contractors	83.5.10
Surveyor's Charge for Quantities for Builders Tenders	10.10.0
~~Trustees~~ Architect	30.0.0
	538.15.10

Village school and schoolmasters house, Grimes Gate.

The cost of building the school was set out.

Building - Messrs Broadbent's Contract	£415		
Value of old materials given to Contractors	£83	0s	10d
Surveyor's Charge for Quantities for Builders	£10	10s	
Architect	£30	0s	0d
TOTAL	£538	15s	10d

A considerable number of people contributed voluntarily towards the school, many of whom were villagers. Christ's College again supporting a school, and donating £100 and the site. Mr Shakespear and Mr Copestake also gave £50 each.

The first Head Teacher is recorded as Mr Turner In the thirty two years between the opening of the school and the arrival of Mr Samuel Taylor as Headmaster in 1894, the school had seven head teachers.

Mr. Samuel Taylor, Head Teacher for 25 years at Diseworth
Detailed logbooks were kept and the ones that have survived date from 1899 to 1960.

Mr Taylor ensures his credentials and success are listed at the front of the 1899 Log Book.

'January 2nd. Samuel Taylor (Certificated Master) and Fanny Clara Taylor took charge of this School, December 31st 1894, having held a similar position for nearly eleven years at Dunham-on-Trent, Notts. Average attendance at Dunham School being 250.

1894 Average of Diseworth School 58. 1898 Average Attendance 76.'

The vicar, Herbert Lock, took a great interest in the school as did Mr and Mrs Shakespear from Langley Priory. Mr Taylor appears to have been a strict master, his first report in the logbook of 1899, after noting that the vicar had opened the school following the vacation was to record the punishment of six boys for bad conduct towards *'Maggy Ferguson on their way home from school'*. Unfortunately the *'bad conduct'* is not described.

Mr and Mrs Samuel Taylor (also pictured with the school on page 116).

Days off were taken at special occasions, such as the marriage of Miss Shakespear. Poor attendance is noted when Fairs and Wakes took place or when there was a Sunday School Outing. Other irregular attendances were seemingly acceptable such as when the harvest or potato or fruit picking was in season. During some harvests the managers and the head teacher closed the school early or made the holidays later in order that the boys could help out. Shooting parties at Langley meant many boys absented themselves from school.

Illness is also reported and when scarlet fever hit the village in 1903 the Medical Officer sanctioned the closing of the school, after which, understandably, some parents hesitated to send their children back. The epidemic lasted from February through until May of that year. Influenza also caused much absence, on one day the Head reported that the registers were not worth marking! Such comments ensured that the School Attendance Officer visited the school regularly, but in some cases did not have much effect. Illnesses certainly were a major cause of non-attendance. Whooping Cough, Mumps, Measles and Diphtheria were mentioned in the early years of 20th Century, the latter two often causing the school to be closed for some weeks at a time. Influenza again caused much absence, and in the whole of November 1918 and a couple of weeks either side the Medical Officer closed the school. When it was reopened many children were deemed still too weak to attend.

However in spite of numerous comments about poor attendance, various illnesses and other reasons for absence, the Diocesan Reports were always of a very high standard, with the new vicar, Rev Huntley Heath testing the pupils and visiting the school.

Surprisingly, there is little mention of the First World War. Apart from the Red Cross taking over the premises for some days, the only other reference was when the children were given an afternoon off to collect blackberries for the Army and Navy on one occasion and for the Government on another. Empire Day was always marked with marching in the playground and songs and the National Anthem.

Miss Elizabeth Adkin, who was a pupil during the First World War, recalls the school being blacked out, and when all the children were issued with small circular badges. Before leaving school in the afternoon, the badges were warmed in front of the fire till they glowed, they were then pinned on the child's clothes, and body heat kept them glowing on the journey home.

Mr and Mrs Taylor had ten children, one of whom, Miss Carmen Lily Taylor, also helped in the school as assistant mistress. The Headmaster was rightly proud of his family and noted their successes in the logbook.

1900

Feb 1st. C L Taylor of Castle Donington National School entered upon her duties at Diseworth Parish School as Assistant.

March 27th. CL Taylor of Castle Donington National School has obtained a 2nd Class in the Queens Scholarship list. Holiday given in the afternoon.

April 2nd. H Taylor Standard VII has left the School and entered GJ Shield's Esq Office.

1902

August 14th. At a meeting of the managers, HE Taylor was appointed assistant Mistress...In the place of Miss CL Taylor who has obtained an appointment as Head Assistant in the Infants Department of the Ashby-de-la-Zouch National Schools.

Mr Samuel Taylor certainly made his mark on the education of the children of Diseworth. His regular accounts of the curriculum, health and attendance of the pupils in his care show the extent to which he took his role. The vicar of his previous school sometimes visited him, and in 1905 James Francis, Vicar of Dunham-on-Trent wrote in the logbook: -

'Visited the schools this morning and was much pleased with the artistic appearance of the rooms, and the brightness and orderliness of the dear children. Mr and Mrs Taylor fully maintain the reputation they acquired when in charge of the school in Dunham-on-Trent.'

His greatest concern, which is noted on almost every page of the logbooks, was the irregular attendance of some pupils. In 1915 he wrote that it was impossible to make satisfactory progress under the circumstances when pupils take time off to go potato picking. When the weekly attendance is over 90% he notes with delight that good progress will have been made. Children are reported to the attendance officer regularly, and on one occasion he notes that the attendance officer had not been to the school recently. Samuel Taylor covered over three hundred pages of school business in the logbook, and when he left, he of course took with him, as they were his family, all the teaching staff of Diseworth School.

In addition to his school duties, Mr Taylor was organist at the Parish Church. He was renowned for arriving at the church, and prior to taking his place at the organ, would scrutinise the children. He would then solemnly call forward the child with the cleanest pinafore, proceed to polish his glasses with the edge of the pinafore, and then send the child back to her place.

On September 30th 1919 Samuel Taylor wrote in the Log:

'I give up charge of this school having been Head Master since December 1894. Twenty five years.'

The school appointed temporarily, a Miss Jackson with one of the older children helping with the infants. There followed a most unsatisfactory few weeks, with no permanent appointment. Almost fortunately there was an outbreak of whooping cough and the medical officer ordered that the school be closed for four weeks. On 8th December Mrs Larkin commenced as Head Teacher still with older girls helping with the infants.

A Selection of Head Teachers and the Helpful Miss Grimley

Unqualified supplementary teachers were appointed but did not stay, and Mrs Larkin coped with various help. She encouraged the older girls to attend cookery and housewifery at Castle Donington, and obtained favourable examination results.

However by the end of 1921 the Head Teacher reported to her managers that she was running the school single-handed and urged them to send to the Education Authority for immediate help. Another temporary teacher was appointed by the end of January, who did not stay long and Vera Grimley replaced her.

The school then progressed well, until Ada Larkin retired at the end of September 1923.

A selection of school photographs. Above: 1895, below: 1914.

Above: 1932, below: 1955.

The next Head was Mary Hunt, but within two months she was absent from illness, and a supply teacher took over the school. Mary Hunt returned in January 1924 but resigned soon afterwards and Jessie Pearson became the new Head. For many years the school had the same Attendance Officer, Mr Gray, who visited regularly. The infant teacher Vera Grimley stayed a number of years and steadily worked for her certificates and examinations. This ensured continuity, as the head teachers changed again. Jessie Pearson resigned in August 1927 and was followed by Edith Charles who stayed three years and made a good impression on the School Inspectorate. The next Head Teacher recorded many details about the visits of the school nurse and the school attendances. Descriptions of sores and illnesses are mentioned, as are children who did not come to school in an acceptable state of cleanliness, especially their boots!

In 1932 she noted *'men finished putting in electric light'*. On specific days, such as Ash Wednesday and Ascension Day the children had a day's holiday after attending Church. Certainly the Religious Instruction was of an acceptable standard, the Diocesan Inspector wrote positive notes about his questioning of the children both infants and older ones. The pupils were often ill with colds and influenza, which was not surprising considering that *'On cold days it is impossible to get the temperature of the big room higher than 50 degrees'*. This cold might have been the reason the visiting dentist *'fainted during the lunch hour and in falling slightly injured his face and cut the end of one finger'*. The dependable Miss Grimley, the trainee teacher gave first aid.

School Outings were important, the managers giving a day's holiday for the Skegness Outing, and many children would attend the Baptist Church annual outing.

By 1932 there was another change of Head Teacher, and a report noted that the previous one did good work during her time and was ably seconded by her assistant, (Miss Grimley) but concern was expressed as to what the children *'lose by not going forward to a Senior School'*. By the end of the year the managers consented to the reorganisation of the school. It was agreed that the senior scholars be transferred to Castle Donington Senior Council School at the end of the autumn term.

As a result of the reorganisation thirteen children were transferred to the Castle Donington School and Miss Grimley, who had faithfully given her services to the school for over ten years as she studied for her examinations was given notice. However Miss Grimley did not go far, and in 1934 when the Head teacher was ill, she was *'borrowed from Castle Donington'* to help out.

1933 was a sad year, which started with 28 children on roll but through illnesses, whooping coughs, influenza and colds the numbers dwindled seriously and on a number of occasions the children were sent home. Sadly a child died, and the numbers attending dropped to as low as seven. Special entries were made on the registers to note the seriousness of the illnesses. As a result of the reorganisation the infants and older children were taught altogether and this was considered a disadvantage by the Diocesan Inspector, and by April 1934 the Head Teacher enquired whether a suitable girl might help with the younger children. A monitress, Ivy Laban was duly appointed. This young lady took her work seriously and each Wednesday afternoon attended the Pupil Teachers Centre in Leicester.

However in the Spring term of 1935 there was a problem involving the vicar, the Head Teacher and the monitress, which resulted in the vicar calling at the school every day for while, the vicar's wife turning up in the playground, and not on school business according to the Head. When school reopened at the end of April, the monitress had been transferred to Kegworth and Miss Dorothy Adnett took her place.

Fuel Problems

In January 1936, the coal supply had not arrived and the Head was using her own coal to heat the school. Despite postcards sent to the office no coal was received, the assistant teacher was off ill, and the Head commented that in 1929 and in 1930 the records showed difficulty in obtaining coal and the poor quality of the coal when it did arrive. When the school closed for the polling day on 23rd January coal was provided for that event and there was sufficient for three days fires in one room only. After much consternation the coal finally arrived on 3rd February. However when the fires were finally lit, one went out and the other did not heat up. The temperature recorded that day was 35 degrees F. The problem continued with the coal in the schoolroom being used up and the caretaker taking the key to the coalhouse home with her. Some altercation took place when the caretaker came back to school and it took Mr Fletcher, one of the managers to come in and sort it out. The Head reported that a new lock was put on the coal house door with a key for the Head and one for the caretaker!

A New Name and Old Problems

In 1936 the Education Office informed the Head that in consequence of the boundary changes the school was to be called 'Long Whatton and Diseworth Church of England School'.

The last entry for the current Head was 30th October and on 16th November Alice Tunnicliffe took temporary charge of the school. When the school closed for the Christmas holidays Miss Adnett left to get married, and Mrs Wardle was brought back on supply pending other arrangements. On 25th January 1937 Miss Shaw, the Head returned to take charge of the school. But the detailed notes in the logbook dwindled and on July 13th Miss Simpson commenced duties as temporary Head Teacher. Miss Shaw returned on 7th October.

January 1938 the school reopened with the information that Miss Shaw the Head Teacher had left the village and that Mrs Wardle the assistant teacher had also left. Miss Simpson came back to take over. This was another temporary appointment and in May 1938 Miss B Anderson commenced as Head Teacher.

The HMI reports continued, each time mention was made of the unsuitability of the backless benches for the infants but nothing appeared to be done.

School in Wartime

In September with the outbreak of war, instructions came by the wireless that all schools were to remain closed for one week. Shortly afterwards the evacuees arrived and were admitted to the school. The weather at the beginning of 1940 was severe and on one day only two children turned up for school. Throughout the week the numbers at school did not rise above eight. The Head wrote that with such frosty weather it was impossible to raise the temperature of the larger schoolroom above 38F. As the numbers improved the children began to go down with mumps!

In the middle of May further instructions via the wireless informed schools that they need not reopen, only to be followed by instructions that they were to reopen. This resulted in some children arriving and not others so the Head posted a notice saying the school would definitely be open.

The weather improved with the advent of summer and in June the school closed for a fortnight to enable the children to help with the hay harvest.

In July the boys began sticking strips of gummed paper to the windows to prevent splintering and plywood was also fixed to the windows for safety during an air raid. Wartime Britain certainly brought a change to the school time table. When the siren sounded, the children from Diseworth were sent home whilst those living further away were kept in school. When the all clear was heard the children returned. With the night raids becoming frequent the children were allowed to arrive later in the morning because of broken nights. On 30th August the school was damaged during an air raid. Windows were shattered and tiles fell off the roof. The school was closed and the HMI called to inspect the damage. Repairs were completed by the end of September in time for the further arrival of a large number of evacuees in the village. With the school numbers rising another teacher was expected to help, and until then the vicar arrived to assist with teaching. However by the middle of November the measles outbreak which had been mild throughout the year, suddenly erupted and local children and evacuees alike went down with the illness. For one week, only four Diseworth children were in attendance at school. By March of 1941 'alerts' were sounded frequently, and children who were not sent home went to the 'strong' room, always taking their work with them! In September of that year the school closed for a fortnight to help with the potato picking. Some of the evacuees did not stay long their parents claiming they were as safe in London, but new additions to school included children whose fathers were stationed with the RAF at the airport. By early 1942 these too had left. The proximity of the aerodrome caused the Head to ask for an air raid shelter for the children, as apparently some residents in the village were to be provided with them. However this request was turned down.

The Head Teacher resigned her position on 1st July 1942, giving the required three months notice. But as another Head was not appointed she returned in September and a Mrs Parsons from Breedon was appointed assistant mistress. Coal was again a problem this time the difficulty was transport, and the school was informed that if any lorries returned empty to the Coalville area they would be used to take coal and coke to the school. By the end of September a new Head was taking over the school, Miss Evelyn Ross. In November a new assistant, Mrs Nichols was appointed. But again the Head did not stay long and in November 1943 one of the most well known Head Teachers of Diseworth took office, Miss Francis Rigby.

Miss Rigby Takes Over

1.11.43 *'I, Francis Majorie Rigby, took over duties as Headmistress of this school today'*

So began a remarkable stage in the history of Diseworth School. Miss Rigby, like Mr Taylor many years before, brought stability to the school, and like Mr Taylor, stayed for twenty-five years. Many adults in Diseworth still recall her as *'firm but fair'*, and it has been suggested that pupils and parents went in awe of her.

Miss Rigby kept detailed accounts of daily life in the school. The assistant teacher had difficulty with transport and distance and again the school was short staffed, but the vicar or the vicar's wife always seemed prepared to come in and help out.

In January 1944 Mrs Perry was appointed as assistant. When the Head was unwell, Mrs Perry took over as Miss Rigby noted, *'useless to ask the Office for help'*.

In March 1944 'emergency rations' of food arrived in the event of school dinners not turning up. These rations consisted of tinned meat, rye-vita, margarine and jam.

Miss Rigby confined her comments generally to the well being or otherwise of the children in her care, and wrote much about the Christmas Party, when *'CB Shakespear Esq donated the tree and money towards a Christmas present for each child'*.

The Headmistress made no mention whatever concerning wartime arrangements or concerns, except to write that on 8th and 9th May 1945, the school closed for VE days.

Miss Rigby continued her good work through peacetime Britain, but by the early 1960's she became increasingly unwell, and retired. A presentation was made to her from the pupils and parents and she resided in Long Whatton until her death in 1993. She had been influential in the village throughout that time, helping with various organisations.

With her departure, the logbooks finished, as did the occupation of the schoolhouse by the Head Teacher. But Diseworth School carried on, with continuing success, and in 1973 the new school was constructed behind the old one which was demolished.

Head Teachers have come and departed, a thriving *'Friends of Diseworth School'* exists, and the school, and the education of our children, continues to be a central part of the village.

CHAPTER TEN POVERTY AND PROGRESS

Throughout its history Diseworth has been an agricultural community. The predominant occupation was farming of one sort or another. The land given to Langley Priory would have been farmed and the Prioress, in 1300, referred to *'arable lying in the open fields which provided much corn for the house'* and *'thirty acres of pasture…for her sheep'*. Such land required people to work whether as farm hands or shepherds. Wood was essential for building and fuel and the skills for ensuring a continuous supply would have been passed down through families.

It was the income from the farms that was used to educate the young men of Christ's College. The letter written for the tenant farmers in 1744 shows forty farmers in the village. However, possibly following the Enclosure Act and poverty through farming, a new trade was to sweep through the Midlands, involving, as did the farms, the whole family, but like the farms, did not result in great wealth for the workers.

Framework Knitting

Although the knitting industry was popular in the early part of the seventeenth century, and the Company of Framework Knitters was formed in London in the middle of the sixteen hundreds, it was somewhat later that people became interested in the business in the East Midlands. This was probably because the land still offered the only work with which people were acquainted from an early age. But when the stocking frames, which had been made for silk garments for the wealthy, were adapted for the worsted yarn, which was spun in the Midlands, mills began to spring up in Nottingham and Derby. Trade moved from London and by 1782 nearly 90% of the twenty thousand stocking frames in use in Great Britain were located in the East Midlands.

This was truly a cottage industry.

At the beginning of the nineteenth century homes began to be adapted to take the stocking frame which was usually placed under a window to obtain the best light. The family would work as a unit, with the man generally operating the frame, the wife seaming the hose and the children winding the yarn on to the bobbins. Owing to the expense of the stocking frames these were rented, so the family had to work hard to cover the initial costs. Carriers became agents for both manufacturer and knitter.

These 'middlemen' or bagmen, whilst performing a useful function, were often suspected of keeping rather more of the percentage for service, by charging the manufacturer for completed hose and not paying out to the knitters their due wages.

At first, as with most new inventions, there was a high demand for knitted hose. The American colonies were an important market until the conflict between Britain and America in the middle of the 18th century and the early part of the 19th century. War against France created a short term demand for clothing for the armed services. But it was not the knitters, working far longer hours than they had at farming, who made the money, but the factory owners and the bagmen, and like their ancestors the farmers, the workers sent a desperate petition for help.

The Leicestershire Framework-Knitters Petition

Pardon our visit in this place,
And wait while we explain our case,
And then we think you'll pity take,
Nor us in our distress forsake.

Could we obtain our food by work
We'd labour like the hardy Turk;
But all our hopes from thence are fled,
And now we pine for want of bread.

Our children though to us most dear,
Must die for want, we greatly fear,
Unless some humane gen'rous heart,
Some food for them to us impart.

Could you our habitations see,
The seat of abject misery,
We think you would afford your aid,
Till we return unto our trade.

On heaven and you we now depend,
And trust in you we've found a friend;
And what you give God will repay,
Both here and in the judgement day.

It was to no avail and finally, desperation led the workers to the destruction of the knitting machines and the organisation of the Luddite movement. Whilst there is no evidence that Diseworth workers were involved in the destruction of machines, Nathaniel Gayton, in his diaries, noted in August 1849:

'The Framework Knitters have commenced work again after a strike for more wages which has continued sixteen weeks and have obtained a small advance'.

The numbers who applied for parish relief in the middle of the nineteenth century shows that framework knitters were extremely poor.

The Poor Law Act

In 1834 the Poor Law Amendment Act grouped together parishes in Unions for the purpose of poor relief. Diseworth was included in the Shardlow group. The first meeting of the Shardlow Board of Governors was held in April 1837. This continued until 1930 when the functions of the Guardians was taken over by the Public Assistance Committee of the County Council. This continued until 1948 when Poor Law was abolished by the National Assistance Act.

Poverty in Diseworth

The Diseworth Records of the Minute Books of the Shardlow Poor Law Union offer an insight into the needy state of many people. A Diseworth man represented the interests of the village at the meetings. The average offer of poor relief consisted of 4lbs of bread and 1 shilling and sixpence (7½p) per week. If the applicants were unable to look after themselves they were admitted to the Diseworth workhouse (situated at Town End).

At the end of each quarter Diseworth Parish had to pay towards the Establishment, and the maintenance of the paupers. In some cases a kindly Medical Officer would order extra comforts, but if the person died these had to be returned or paid for. Some cases were obvious hardship, some may have pushed for relief and some had been deserted by their families. The records show that the majority of those applying for relief were framework knitters

'August 1838 Maria. 18 years old applies for relief. Maria lives with her father who is 61 years old, and has a brother of 20 years and a sister of 12 years. All three children are very ill and confined to bed. Another sister Hannah made the appeal. The Medical Officer ordered wine for the two girls at a cost of 2 shillings each and extra bread. Three weeks later they were all well and were presented with the bills for the wine. The young man asked for new shoes but was refused'.

'May 1839 Anne. 56 years old, earns 4 shillings a week seaming. Son at home, earns 4 shillings a week framework knitting. Daughter works lace, two sons in Nottingham, framework knitters. Relief discontinued.'

Occupations

However progress was being made, possibly as a result of the education of the young people. The Census returns shown in the 19th century directories of the day indicate a variety of occupations in Diseworth.

White's Directory of Leicestershire 1846 Census:

Annibal	**George**	**shoemaker**
Adkin	**John**	**blacksmith**
Bailey	**Thos. Jackson**	**grazier, maltser & vict. Bull's Head**
Begbie	**Rev. Francis R.**	**vicar**
Brown	**Robert**	**shoemaker**
Gayton	**Nathaniel**	**schoolmaster**
Jarrom	**John**	**brick and tile maker**
Mee	**Thomas**	**butcher and beerhouse keeper**
Muggleston	**Robert**	**wheelwright**
Upton	**Joseph**	**wheelwright**
Wheatley	**John**	**blacksmith**

Also included are 13 farmers.

Five years later another directory identifies a more detailed list of occupations.

Hagar & Co Commercial Directory 1849
Gentry:

Adkin	**Mr John**
Nash	**Rev Frederick Gifford BA**

In the 'Trades' list are included milliner and dressmaker, tailor, ironmonger and shopkeeper, baker, butcher, brickmaker, coal dealer, the victuallers of the 'Plough' and the 'Bull's Head', twenty-five farmers, and the Post Office. It is possible this directory took greater detail than White's, certainly it numbers the children at the school as twenty-seven. Letters arrived at 9am and departed at 6.45pm.

By 1883, Wright's Directory listed three dressmakers, four cottagers and cowkeepers, three shopkeepers, two carriers and nineteen farmers. In addition the vicar, Rev Henry Charles Pryce Jones MA is mentioned, together with the master and mistress running the National School, the occupants of the two Public Houses, and the blacksmith, wheelwright, tailor and bootmaker.

Apprenticeships

As young people became more educated, opportunities arose for training at the place of work. These young people, as young as fourteen, lived away from home for the period of apprenticeship (if the workplace was not in the village), and signed, or maybe their parents also signed, an agreement to stay for the required length of time. This was an Indenture. On the 12th January 1874, a young boy from Diseworth, George Edward Bryan, agreed to become an apprentice to Mr Everard Harris Adkin of Kegworth, who had himself come from Diseworth. For the next five years young George was to learn the *'Art of the County Joiner and Wheelwright'*. The details of the apprenticeship required the lad to do *'no damage to his said master nor see to be done of others but to his power shall give warning to his said master. He shall not waste the goods of his said master nor send them unlawfully to any.'*

Furthermore, George had to agree *'not to commit fornication nor contract matrimony within the said term'*. He was not to play dice or cards, or frequent taverns or playhouses nor absent himself from his master's service. In return the 'said master' agreed to teach the apprentice in the art of a joiner and wheelwright, and supply sufficient meat, drink and lodging during the term of the apprenticeship. The young boy conformed and lived in the attic room of his master and helped to modernise the house. When the wheelwright's shop was closed down in 1910, the new owner converted the building into a Motor Garage. It might be presumed that George stayed on, because when the owner moved on to Nottingham in 1919, it was George's son who took over the business.

20th Century Work

With the advancement of motorised transport, people travelled from Diseworth to neighbouring towns for work. The survey by Mr Orton and Rev Lock in 1900 shows how much the village had changed by the turn of the century. With the construction of the airport, and the rise of the nearby towns, the main village occupation returned to farming, but with the majority of young people travelling in the interests of continued education and varied employment. The building of the small housing estates in the village, with most of the workforce commuting, thus taking advantage of the work offered outside of Diseworth, while at the same time enjoying the benefits of a rural community in which to live.

FIRST EDITION 1884

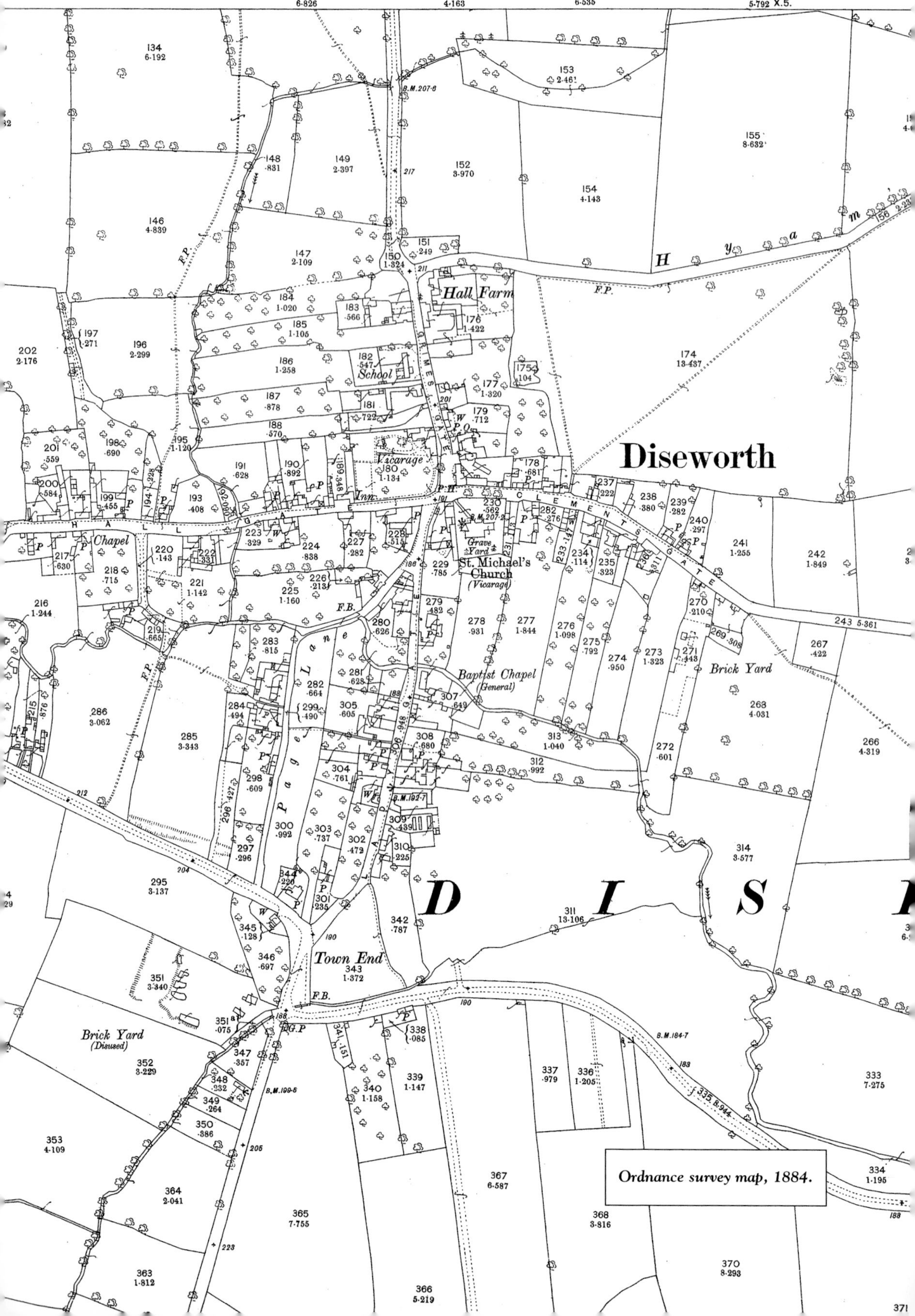

Ordnance survey map, 1884.

PART FOUR
20TH CENTURY DISEWORTH

CHAPTER ELEVEN THE PARSON AND THE POET

The Reverend Herbert Lock became vicar of Diseworth in 1894. Just 31 years old, he brought with him not only a deep love of the church and his fellow men, but an innovative approach to village life. A man of letters, Herbert had written a book called '*The Sad Story of James Kethring*', a cautionary tale about temptation and the sad outcome for one young man. One of the first people the vicar became friends with was Henry Orton, affectionately remembered as the blind village poet and musician. The two men soon became kindred spirits and together they set themselves the task of making the village a happier and more interesting place to live.

Within months of his arrival, the new vicar set up *The Diseworth Men's Recreation Club*, and the venue of the meeting room was *House No 315, Diseworth c/o Christ's College*. Meetings commenced on September 22nd 1894 and it was decided to take two daily papers, the Leicester Daily Express and the Nottingham Evening News. '*A meeting was held at the school on October 5th to decide on whether smoking should be allowed in the meeting rooms. On the 12th October it was proposed that there should be smoking in the upstairs room and that the lower room be reserved for non-smoking.*'

Rules of Diseworth Men's Recreation Club - 1st December 1894

1. **Club shall be open from 9am - 9pm daily. Fires alight 6pm - 9pm.**
2. **Club to be governed by an annually elected committee.**
3. **Weekly subscription of 1d to be paid monthly in advance. Any members 4 weeks in arrears to be brought before the committee.**
4. **All cases of bad language, gambling or disorderly conduct to be punished at once by the committee as it seemeth them good.**
5. **Names of candidates (probationers) to be brought before the committee who will have powers to sanction or forbid their entrance as members of the club.**
6. **Age limit is to be 15 but exceptions as to age of members may be taken at the discretion of the committee.**

Herbert Lock. Diseworth 1st December 1894.

The committee members included J Adkin, C Adkin, H Orton, H Moore, Rev Lock, T Saddington, W Bexon, Mr Crow, J Simpkin, C Saddington, G Hinds, A Newton, T Danvers and S Gascoigne. The following members were admitted to the Recreation Club on the 7th December: Samuel Lester, John Halford, William Archer, Walter Gunn. By the end of December two more members had been admitted, Harold Sylvester and Sam Poxon. Within the space of one month the club had a healthy membership of twenty men. On the 3rd January 1895 it was proposed and accepted that Mr CB Shakespear of Langley Priory be president of the committee.

There are several items recorded in the minute book. The members held a concert in the school for the Band of Hope and it was proposed from time to time to hold a debating evening. The first debate was held on the 7th February 1895 and the subject was 'Courtesy'. The chief speakers were J Orton, C Adkin and the Rev Lock.

The following month it is recorded that the Rev Lock loaned the sum of £1 to the club. Members proposed repayment by way of entertainment. The health issues of smoking were apparent even 100 years ago for on October 30th 1895 it was decided that smoking should no longer be allowed on the club premises. Another example of generosity is recorded in the following minute. *It was proposed at the meeting on 2nd December that as the vicar had kindly promised to give the oil and fuel and the only other expenses being the care-taker, half the balance each month shall be given to the funds of the day school.*

Sadly there are no further records of the Men's Club and it is not known on which date it ceased to operate.

It has been mentioned before that the Rev Lock's brother had raised a considerable sum of money to help build a mission church in Africa to be dedicated to St Joseph of Arimathea. Due to the brother's untimely death it was arranged for the money to be transferred to Diseworth and spent on the installation of a bell, two windows and three oak seats *'for the children'*.

Like his brother, Herbert Lock died very young. He departed this life on March 17th 1902 at the tragically early age of 39. His death left a large gap and an indelible imprint on the lives of his parishioners. His eight years as vicar of Diseworth is perhaps best summed up with an entry in the school log book on the day that he died. *'The deeply beloved vicar of this parish, The Reverend Herbert Lock died today. The children's friend!'*

The Poet - Henry Orton

Henry Orton was one of Diseworth's most notable residents at the turn of the century. He is affectionately remembered as *the blind poet and musician* and as has been noted before, was a great friend of the well loved Herbert Lock

He was born in 1833 in the neighbouring village of Kings Newton. Henry and his wife Emma raised a family of six children and his youngest son, Bertram was born in 1882. Bertram enlisted in the army at the turn of the century and in 1904 was posted to India. Henry was very unhappy that his son had enlisted and even more so about the posting. He was by this time 71 years old and understandably anxious for his beloved son's safety.

He wrote this poem on November 22nd 1904, shortly after Bertram's departure:

> That last fond blest remembered kiss will never be forgot by me.
> My darling Bert had gone away to sail across the deep blue sea.
> He's gone to India's coral strand to guard that portion of the land
> That doth belong to the British Crown, that famous empire of renown
> Who's sceptre sways in splendour there and hath their souls beneath her care
> To govern them in righteousness their Lord and Saviour fond to bless.
>
> I'll love my Bertram. God doth know why he did for a soldier go.
> I do not know or cannot tell but sad misfortune us befell
> When he enlisted in the field to die or make the fame and yield
> To England power and honour to a work which Britain means to do
> To civilise the heathen world the gospel flag to be unfurled
> In distant shore till time shall wane and be no more.
> XXXX Amen.

Henry wrote many verses, many of which were sung as hymns in the parish church. One in particular was sold in aid of the church restoration fund and the verses encompass not only the purpose of the project but all the people working so hard to accomplish the task:

'St Michael and All Angels, Diseworth, Leicestershire'

> See the Church in all her grandeur stand,
> The pride and glory of our land,
> May Church and State go hand in hand
> To keep the enemy from our land.
>
> She has for many centuries stood,
> Thousands her sacred aisles have trod,
> Where they were wont to worship God,
> They're laid around beneath her sod.
>
> The priests in Holy Vestments there,
> Out of God's Word the Truth declare,
> And pray that they might be forgiven,
> And go to rest with Christ in Heaven.
>
> Oh God who art the King of all,
> Help us to obey the Gospel's call!
> Christ died to save us from the fall,
> He invites us both great and small.
>
> He is our Advocate with God,
> To save man from the avenging rod,
> And Jesus wishes all to come,
> To dwell in His eternal Home.
>
> The Bells their silvery notes declare,
> It is the hour of solemn prayer,
> The choir their sacred anthem sing
> Loud praises to their Heavenly King.
>
> The organ with its sweetest charm
> It helps to harmonise the Psalm,
> But now it's had an overhaul,
> So we appeal unto you all.
>
> Our dear old Church, out of repair,
> It needs our aid and earnest care,
> For to repair and make it good
> A temple meet to worship God.

Our worthy Vicar does not shirk,
For he has set his head to work,
By all the plans he can devise
To raise the funds and help likewise.

The Mistress of the Village School,
Is no exception to the rule,
For she is doing all she can,
The children sharing in her plan.

We know the Lady at the Hall,
She has responded to the call,
We know she has the cause at heart,
And is ever glad to take a part.

The Ladies in the Village too,
They have their share of work to do,
By making fancy goods for sale,
We hope their effort will not fail.

They are all doing what they can
To help in this most holy plan,
Their means, though small, since
freely given,
Will be recorded up in heaven.

Henry was a jolly man and as well as being a prolific poet, he also composed music to play on his piccolo. He also told of how, when walking from Diseworth to Castle Donington he was held up by a highwayman. There are no further details of this story but it makes for another romantic tale.

'Ye Parish of Diseworth'

In 1900, Henry and Herbert carried out a survey of the village to mark the beginning of the twentieth century. It contains a fascinating observation on the village in general and the church in particular during the 1800's: *'Ye Parish of Diseworth in the County of Leicester, drawn up by Henry Orton, Diseworth Village Poet and Herbert Lock, Vicar of Diseworth, August 20th in the Year of Our Lord 1900'.*

They recorded that the vicarage orchard had extended from the south side of the vicarage to the Old Plough and that two cottages had once stood on this ground. It was obvious that many properties had been allowed to fall into disrepair in the previous century, a fact which the two friends regretted and deplored. *'These few remarks will show the dilapidated state of the village of Diseworth within the space of fifty years which came under the observation of one of the authors (Henry Orton). There have been 83 houses either pulled down or condemned as dwelling houses under several holdings'.* They went on to list the trades which the village had lost in that time including framework knitters, lacemakers, butchers, bakers and brewers. It appears that six public houses and four malt-houses had also disappeared. The siting of these hostelries has defied investigation and it seems that these may have been 'beer-offs' where cottagers brewed their own ale for sale to the public but were not strictly licensed premises worthy of the name public houses.

The report went on to describe the various alterations to the church fabric in the previous 60 years. '*The choir and the schoolchildren used to sit on benches in the chancel*'. In 1840 the old high backed oak pews had been taken down and replaced by lower backed seats. Records show that after morning service, the churchwarden would call out the names of eligible parishioners and the clerk - *from his clerk's pew* - would distribute the William Lane's charity bread. It was around this time, when the Rev Begbie was vicar that the font, *a massive circular Saxon font* was moved to its present position by the south door. The altar was moved in 1885 from its previous position in the centre of the sanctuary to the east wall and in 1896 the churchyard was enlarged at the cost of £20 with land donated by Charles Shakespear Esq of Langley Priory. In the same year a lightning conductor was run down the side of the spire when the tower was re-pointed in Portland cement. The survey concluded with the information that there was formerly a footpath through the churchyard, leading from the north side to the Long Whatton road and added that there were two paths leading into Clements Gate'.

'There was once a gallery where the belfry now exists, where a mixed choir sat. During the singing the congregation turned round to face the choir. A barrel organ was installed in 1824. Before this the choir was assisted by reed instruments: clarinet, bassoon and violincello. The barrel organ could only play the fixed tunes which were on the two barrels'.

It seems that three people were required to play the organ. One to turn the handle, one to blow the bellows and one to press 'certain knobs' (which were lettered), to produce individual sounds. However as the organ contained bass pipes, one man could play music when the bellows supplying wind to the pipes were worked. An amusing story is recorded about the organ.

'The Organist and the Bellows Boy'

One Sunday after the singing of the psalm, the young lad working the bellows for the large bass pipes remarked to the organist, "We've played that well"! The organist replied "We? You had nowt to do wi' it. It was me that played the tune well, not you". The lad thought, "If I had nowt to do wi' it, I wunna blow". On resuming the next psalm, the organist perceived that the bass pipes would not blow. He asked the lad "Why don't you blow"? "I've nowt to do wi' it" said the lad.

"Oh go on", said the distracted musician, "It shall be we in future".

CHAPTER TWELVE THE GOOD OLD DAYS

Down Memory Lane

Distance lends enchantment, but the latter part of Queen Victoria's reign is remembered as a halcyon period. Despite the hardship suffered by many in the village during this time, it remained a period regarded by many as the 'Good Old Days'. People of all occupations, agricultural and industrial, were required to work extremely long hours in return for pitifully low wages. Food was often poor, both in quality and quantity and the only documented diversions from the humdrum were the devotions of the Sabbath.

The village schoolmaster received the only newspaper delivered to the village and he would pass on news of national importance. Diseworth was also fortunate to have the services of two town criers who would inform villagers of events both parochial and national. (Today we have the *Diseworth Dialogue*).

Transport at this time was by horse and cart or donkey and trap and donkeys would often be used to carry churns *pannier fashion* for the twice daily milking. Farm workers were obliged to walk to their work, often several miles distant and then work a twelve hour day for an average wage of twelve shillings (60p). Every aspect of farm work was covered and it was an exhausting occupation with little leisure time. There were no combine harvesters, mowing was done with a scythe and men would spend the winter months threshing the corn with flails.

One way that people could supplement their diet was by gleaning (combing the fields for ears of wheat left by the mowers). These gleanings were taken home, the grains removed and ground to make a coarse flour for bread. It is said that the finished product was often disappointing with the dough being discoloured and unsavoury in flavour. Another use for the gleanings was to make 'thrummaty' or frumenty. The grains of wheat were boiled in milk and flavoured with sugar and cinnamon to make a form of porridge. For a few weeks of each year, this dish would provide a nourishing and satisfying addition to the staple diet.

Crime was dealt with in an arbitrary way. There were no stocks in Diseworth but there was a village pound in Church Street (Clements Gate). Wrongdoers were locked up here for the night before being taken to Loughborough to be dealt with by the appropriate authorities.

Christ's College in Cambridge is remembered as being a benevolent landlord with houses let at around 1s 4d (7p) to 2s (10p) a week. One villager is reported to have been

View of Hall Gate.

View of Clements Gate.

compelled to leave her privately rented cottage. She sent word to the college agent who was able to provide her with a college-held property within one week.

The village pound.

Although wages were low money went a lot further. The price of *'The Weekly Shopping Basket'* of groceries was 4s 6d (23p). A 'hefty' joint for roasting could be bought for 25p and eggs were 18 for one shilling (5p). Most households would keep chickens for eggs and meat. Many would also have a house cow to provide butter and milk, both for consumption and for sale. Some villagers would rear turkeys for the Christmas trade, fattening them up for the festive season. Only in very recent years has this practice sadly ceased. E.U. regulations stipulated strict controls on the environment in which the fowls were reared and subsequently prepared for table. There are many of us in Diseworth who have fond memories of collecting the turkey on Christmas Eve, bearing the splendid specimen home with exhilaration and anticipation only to be confronted with the dilemma of how to fit the turkey into the oven, let alone 'all the trimmings'. Good Old Days indeed!

The Evening School

One of the innovations of the Education Board at the end of the 19th century was the introduction of an Evening School. The aim was to help further the education of those young people who had left school between the ages of 12 and 14. The Diseworth Evening School opened its doors on the 11th September 1893 to 7 girls and 16 boys. Albert Crew who was Head Teacher of the Day School and *'a trained certificated master'* took charge and the curriculum included Civic Duties, Vocal Music and Letter Writing. Classes met twice a week from 7.15pm until 9pm which must have seemed very late for those who had to rise early the next day.

Each pupil was provided with an exercise book for the purpose of taking notes on the various subjects. Due to the tender years of the scholars and lack of knowledge in the subject, Civic Duties consisted only of elementary facts previously agreed with the school inspectors. One of these was to be shown the postcard and envelope issued by the Post Office to commemorate the Jubilee Penny Postage. It soon became apparent that many of the pupils had difficulty with spelling so the letter writing lessons became exercises in word building. Attendance was a problem due to weather conditions, illness and distance, (some pupils travelled from Long Whatton and Kegworth). The classes continued to succeed with the introduction of History (much is made of the interest in history lessons, particularly that a *'lantern is used for them'*) and also Arithmetic when the importance of making out a bill was emphasised. Students were also shown how to open a bank account. The Evening School prospered as the number of pupils rose. The curriculum expanded and standards improved which led to the class being divided into two sections according to ability. In 1897 the school received a visit from the Secretary to the Technical Education Committee from Leicestershire County Council and the students were informed that having attended three consecutive sessions, with nine out of ten hours possible for each session, they were eligible for the Authority's Special Certificate.

By 1898 there were 21 students receiving classes in Composition, Arithmetic, Geography, Needlework and Drawing. Good examination results were recorded and duly rewarded. On March 15th the vicar (the esteemed Herbert Lock), *returned the fees to those pupils who achieved marks of 80% & 90% to the amount of £3 2s 6d.* Detailed records were kept on the progress of each subject including needlework where, over a period of five months the students were required to: *cut out a flannel petticoat; mend with calico patch and print patch; darn thin places in flannel and socks; learn buttonhole making, feather stitch and tuckmaking and knit stockings.*

1899 saw the introduction of a new subject called *'Ambulance'*. This involved the study of the human body, a comprehensive course in first aid including bandaging, the function of the heart and respiration, also how to deal with burns and poisoning, apoplexy, insensibility and epilepsy. This subject involved periodic examinations to assess competence and capability.

Attendance at the Evening School continued with an average of 24 students reflecting both the good standard of teaching and the results. There were times when the school did not open if the room was required for another function. When 'hirings' took place, the numbers often dropped considerably as the students found employment elsewhere. Other reasons for low attendance were social events such as 'Plough Boy Night' and Castle Donington wakes week. The classes continued to benefit the young people of Diseworth and surrounding villages until 1906 when a final sentence in the log book reads: *'Session 1906 - 1907 No Evening School owing to Long Whatton being made a centre. Much regretted by Managers and Parents'.*
Correspondent S H Taylor :- Responsible Teacher.

Village outings (late 19th century)

CHAPTER THIRTEEN STORIES FROM THE SCRAPBOOKS

During the period 1936 to 1966 many news stories were preserved for posterity in scrapbooks.

Parish Council

The reports on parish council meetings make fascinating reading and some raise issues that have a marked similarity to those of present day Diseworth.

'The plight of young married couples was raised due to the lack of housing in Diseworth'.

Election Excitement in Diseworth Following the death of Mr HW Jarrom, Diseworth's only representative on the Castle Donington Rural District Council, an election was held to fill the vacancy. Two candidates stood for election: Mr Sidney Barnett and Mr William Jarrom, son of the late HW Jarrom. Polling took place at Diseworth and when the result was declared it was discovered that each candidate had received 78 votes and there was some excitement. It was agreed to decide the issue by casting lots and the names of both candidates were put into a hat. The first to be drawn would be declared the winner and this was Mr Barnett. This was the first local government election in Diseworth for 40 years and polling was exceptionally heavy. Of the 189 electors at Diseworth, 156 went to the poll.

A resolution was passed at a later meeting that the electing of parish councillors by show of hands was undemocratic and undesirable. It was urged that the election rules be altered to a method of secret ballot instead of a show of hands.

Let there be light A meeting was held in December 1936 to consider extending street lighting to Diseworth. After general discussion a proposal was put to the meeting and carried unanimously that lighting be installed. A representative of Leicestershire and Warwickshire Power Company was present and submitted proposals for twelve lamps, work to commence early in 1937. The new agreement was for lighting to be provided by Leics & Warks Electric Power Co for 7 years. Under this new agreement the cost to be covered by 3d rate, showing no increase on the charge when lighting was originally introduced to Diseworth. 12 powerful lamps were installed. *'Diseworth is considered to be the best lighted village of its size in the neighbourhood'*. A meeting in 1946 urged the need for economy in street lighting and consumption should only be 50% that of pre-war.

The Floodgate in Ladygate At one annual parish meeting, attention was drawn to the condition of the floodgates in Town End and Ladygate and a request was made to give the matter some attention. At a following meeting of the Parish Council, the chairman stated that periodically the village became flooded and the floodgate, which was an inlet in a wall, was for the purpose of allowing water to flow into an adjoining field. Unless the floodgate could be opened during floods, neighbouring houses became surrounded with water and considerable damage was done. The clerk was instructed to ascertain the cost of repairs. Further investigations revealed the necessity for drainage underneath the path near the floodgate to alleviate the flooding problem in Ladygate.

Drains and Mains In 1938 pipes were laid just outside the village to carry running water and the hope was expressed that the necessary connection would soon be made. The operation inevitably caused disruption, as in 1939 it was reported that complaints had been made of the bad state of the roads in the Diseworth ward since the laying of the water mains. The clerk was asked to communicate with the RDC on the matter. It appears that the outbreak of war interrupted the installation as a news item concerning the Diseworth Fire Brigade reported that water from the mains was scarce in wartime.

In 1955 it was proposed by Castle Donington Rural District Council to borrow £32,460 for a new sewerage disposal scheme for Diseworth and Long Whatton and the county sanitary inspector said the proposal had his whole-hearted support. This was followed only a few weeks later with a report of protests about the operation. One Councillor pointed out that the scheme was likely to take 12 years, not 12 weeks as trenches were being improperly filled and '*causing traffic dislocation and considerable inconvenience*'. Another councillor said that as soon as trenches were filled in they were re-opened and he urged a move to find out who was responsible for such distressing conditions which he described as deplorable. It is apparent that the matter was resolved to everyone's satisfaction and no further reports are recorded on the matter.

The Bus Service and the Bus Stop! One item of interest from 50 years ago is particularly relevant to Diseworth today. A request for a bus service between Diseworth and Loughborough was declined on the grounds that the village was adequately served by two other operators. It was also mentioned on another occasion that the bus route from Diseworth to Melbourne was one of the prettiest in England. After many requests from the public, moves finally went ahead to place a bus shelter in the village. Unfortunately it appears that the finished product did not meet with approval. A press release from the parish council stated *'The new bus shelter erected in Diseworth has brought protests of unsightly and ugly and not at all in keeping with its surroundings!'*

In 1955 - *'White lines with 'SLOW' are to be painted as a matter of urgency on The Bowley and Ladygate approaches to Diseworth Town and The Green.'*

And Finally *'Evidence that parishioners of Whatton and Diseworth ward were satisfied with the conduct of parochial matters was borne out by their non-attendance at the annual parish meeting'!*

The Letting of the Lanes

At annual parish meetings, the ancient custom of letting of the lanes would occur. The lanes: Long Holden, Hyams Lane, Langley Mere, Salter Road, Emery Way and Kegworth Lane were let on an annual basis by the Parish Council of Long Whatton and Diseworth. Local farmers would bid for the rights to roadside grazing or '*the letting of the herbage on the by-lanes*'. There were two methods of bidding, by candle and pin or the timing of sand falling through glass.

Candle & Pin Each lane would be publicly named before the chairman proceeded to light the candle. He would place an ordinary hat pin on the candle just below the flame. Bidding would then begin and the person making his bid as the pin fell from the candle was successful. The process was repeated until all of the lanes were let.

Hourglass As in the candle and pin method, the name of the lane would be announced and bidding would begin as the sand started to fall through the glass. When the sand began to run low, bidding became fast and furious and the lucky man to shout his price as the last grain of sand fell through would secure the 'let' for the season.

This ancient custom used to be a lucrative form of income for the council, realising the sum of £30 in the mid-1930's but only netting 5/- (25p) in April 1939. It is not known when the practice ended.

Diseworth Village Hall

April 1945 Negotiations are to be opened immediately with the view of purchasing part of Diseworth vicarage ground as a site for a village hall. Mr C Dakin advocated an appeal for funds throughout the village.

'*We shall get financial help from the Government, but they will expect us to find our own site*', remarked Mr Barnett, Chairman of Diseworth-Long Whatton Parish Council. It was agreed to make an appeal on behalf of funds, and the committee were asked to do everything possible to further the interests of the scheme.

August 1945 A successful fete, in aid of Village Hall funds was held August Monday in a field opposite the school. The proceeds amounted to £50.

April 1947 The vicar, the Rev PB Hacker, was re-appointed chairman and Mr C Dakin vice-chairman at the second annual meeting of the Village Hall Committee. Arrangements are in hand for a 'bring and buy' sale at Whitsuntide and garden fete and flower show later in the summer. Since the opening of the Village Hall Fund more than £600 has been raised.

Diseworth Fete on site of future village hall, 1946

'*Mr CB Shakespear of Langley Priory, opening the first flower and vegetable show on the Village Hall field, congratulated the exhibitors on their good display of entries, numbering 228. A prize for most points in the show was won by F Mitchell, and Mr C Dakin was the winner of the prize for most points in the village classes*'.

Rev Hacker stated that upwards of £600 had been raised and asked those present to spend freely to help avoid taking up a large loan when the time came for building the village hall. Throughout these years many villagers raised the funds for the Village Hall, through raffles and house to house collections. Our Village Hall stands as a result of their consistent efforts.

1948 Heavy rain on Saturday afternoon spoilt the efforts of the Show Committee at the third annual flower show and fete. In his review of the past efforts of the committee, the Rev Hacker revealed that the arrangements for the temporary Village Hall were complete and all that was now required before building commenced was '*a stroke of the pen by some official of the Ministry of Education*'.

Draft rules for hirers of the temporary village hall were completed. Building operations commenced and it was expected that the hall would be ready for use in about three months.

February 10th 1949 Loughborough Monitor headline.

'Diseworth to have temporary Village Hall - will accommodate 200 people.'

The ambitions of Diseworth Village Hall committee have been partially realised and work is in progress for the erection of a temporary village hall. A central site has been secured. The temporary hall, which is provided by the Council of Social Services (Rural Community Council) at a nominal rental, is capable of accommodating 200 people. The hall is to be used for physical and mental training, recreation and social and intellectual development through the medium of reading, recreation rooms, library, lectures, classes and entertainments without distinction of sex or of political, religious or other opinions. A committee has been formed representative of each public body in the village, including the Parish Church, deacons of the Baptist Church, trustees of the Methodist Church, Parish Council, Cricket Club, British Legion and Women's Institute.

July 28th 1949 An eventful day in the life of the village of Diseworth was the opening of the temporary village hall by Lady Martin. The hall is fitted with electric lighting and is connected with public water, is centrally heated and has modern kitchen facilities. The permanent stage rising about three feet above floor level is effectively curtained, the material being an army parachute, and is the work of Mrs JH White and Mrs AH Cherry. The hall has a wooden block floor. Since the scheme was inaugurated four and a half years ago, the committee has raised sufficient to purchase the site of several acres (at the present time there is a balance of about £600) in addition to equipment. The temporary hall is scheduled to meet the village requirements for five years during which time efforts will continue to augment funds for the erection of a permanent village hall. To meet the cost a further £2,000 is required.

Sir Robert Martin said the Rural Community Council did not make a practice of dropping 'village halls' in every place. The people of Diseworth had shown great initiative and they received the support of the Rural Community Council.

Since that eventful day Diseworth Village Hall has hosted very many events, from afternoon whist drives to the Quorn Hunt Saturday Wire Fence Fund Ball. The Flower and Vegetable Show has taken place most years, and a thriving toddler and playgroup meet regularly. It has been consistently maintained and improved and is open to all village organisations.

In 1998 a committee entitled Swings, showing tremendous enthusiasm, raised a considerable amount of money, and a children's play area was created in the Village Hall grounds, complete with modern, colourful equipment.

Sports

The Cricket Club Diseworth has boasted a cricket team in one form or another for nearly 200 years. In 1838 they attained the dubious honour of a world record according to the book 'Curiosities of Cricket' by Jonathon Rice. '*Derbyshire in 1838, the village of Kegworth were dismissed for a mere 1, courtesy of the vicar's groom, and then got rid of their opponents, Diseworth, for 0*'.

Almost exactly one hundred years later, came the banner headline in the Loughborough Monitor. '*Diseworth Makes Cricket History. Alf Poxon is a proud man*'*!* The report went on to give an account of Alf's first year as captain of Diseworth Cricket Club culminating in the team winning the Shields Challenge Cup and the Castle Donington Hospital Cup. '*Never before in its history has Diseworth won a cup but the season has seen the club at its best: played 15, lost 2, drawn 2. The others were won with scores mostly over 100*'. In the final round, Diseworth met Cox's lead works of Derby. Diseworth and Cox's were known as 'Tie Champions' as in the previous year they had met three times in the first round before Diseworth finally won through. Said Alf "*I am very proud that in my first year as captain of the club, we have won the cup for the first time on record. Over 1000 runs have been scored so far. The team members have backed me in every way and this is the reason for the success*". To celebrate their triumph it was proposed that a victory supper be held at the end of the season to which Cox's lead works would be invited. A poignant press release in 1939 read '*At a meeting of the cricket club it was decided for the present to defer arrangements for next season owing to many of the members falling within the age groups of the Armed Forces Act*'

The next press release was in 1945 when it was announced that the cricket pavilion, damaged in the bomb blast was shortly to be restored. At a well attended meeting it was unanimously decided to take down the notice '*War Stopped Play, 1939*'.

There was a call for membership to include players from outside the parish and for a concerted fundraising effort. New fencing was required in addition to the necessary restoration of the pavilion following the bomb damage.

1950 saw the addition of a boys' team which fielded a junior and senior eleven. The team enjoyed considerable success which was recognised in the local press when a Diseworth boy's prowess proved too much for the opposing Castle Donington side. '*Not many local schoolboy cricketers have equalled the performance of a Diseworth youngster last Saturday! Playing for his school, 15-year-old Andrew Crowe hit a sparkling 82 - a local record. Andrew is not only handy with the bat; he's a most successful fast-medium bowler*'.

The team often travelled to fixtures on foot or by bicycle and were prepared to take on

The cricket pavilion at Cheslyn's Field.

any group, whatever their ability. One very unusual match was played between the junior and senior boys of Diseworth school. In order to give the juniors an advantage, the seniors elected to bowl and bat left-handed. They were successful in dismissing the juniors despite a fair number of 'wides' but rapidly came unstuck when they came into bat. Despite their handicap they fought valiantly and were only two runs short of the juniors as the final wicket fell. Sportsmanship indeed!

By 1951, club funds were considerably healthier and at the annual meeting, the financial report revealed a balance of £23 and membership had risen to nearly 30. Permission was given for a fixture with New Lount Colliery to be played at Langley Priory on the occasion of the village fete.

The Cricket Club continues to thrive and in 1997 the team became Midland Bank Notts Village League Division Six Champions. This deserved success followed a run of bad luck. As reported in the Diseworth Dialogue '*An inauspicious start to the season was put down to inadequate pre-season training - bending the right elbow over the bar is not enough*'!

The old cricket pavilion was sold several years ago and is now used as a domestic garage. Two people approached separate members of the committee with a view to purchase with the result that it was sold twice. It was decided in a gentlemanly manner that the first to offer the cash would secure ownership. After all, anything else would not have been cricket!

The village football team, 1959.

Football in Diseworth There were two football teams in Diseworth, a pre-war team which was disbanded at the outbreak of war, and a post-war team which was formed in the 1950's. The new team had the additional luxury of changing facilities when an old commentator's box was brought from Castle Donington race track, painted and converted into a dressing room. This was then placed on the football field belonging to Sid Adkin. The field boasted the ancient ridge and furrows and although it had been filled in, the pitch was still on a slope, much to the detriment of the game. The team was made up of players mostly from Diseworth or surrounding villages and was a member of the Loughborough Football League. This team used to play a charity match on Boxing Day afternoon which was purely for fun. The inexperienced opposing team players would often turn out in casual clothes and ordinary shoes. As many were unfit, extensive injuries were often incurred through players falling on the uneven and frozen ground. These injuries, ranging from severe bruising to torn muscles often resulted in considerable time off work to recover. One match in the winter of 1963 was completed in appalling conditions during a blizzard. This was the onset of one of the most severe winters in recent memory.

The team ceased to exist in the 1970's due to lack of interest but was revived as a Sunday side - Diseworth Wanderers - in 1980. The team played at a pitch in Hemington and continued for 10 years, before sadly hanging up their boots in 1990.

Village football teams in the 1980s.

The Fun Run The Boxing Day Fun Run continues to draw energetic competitors each year as they complete two circuits of the village. The race attracts entrants from outside the village and is well supported by those whose marathon session with the turkey and plum pudding precludes such strenuous activity. The event invariably raises around £250 for school funds. The kitchen of the Plough is opened at 9.30 to the organisers and post race celebrations are held in the pub amid congratulations and commiserations.

Socials

Diseworth has always been a sociable village. Whether fund raising or 'fun' raising, many parties have been enjoyed to the advantage of a broad spectrum of local causes. Fetes, pork pie suppers, whist drives in aid of the Blind Association and Cancer Research, collections for the Red Cross, dances, raffles and road races. One of the biggest ongoing fund raising drives is for the upkeep and maintenance of the parish church. This symbol of the heart of our community hungrily consumes cash and is a constant source of concern for those responsible for its continuance. In the 1950's an appeal for £1000 was launched to restore the parish church but it appears that the fund raisers were hampered by the constraints of the church hierarchy. At the launch of the appeal, the vicar spoke of the danger of getting *'light hearted donations for religious purposes'*. It seems that at a recent Lambeth Conference, 320 bishops had unanimously urged church people not to raise money by raffles, prize draws or any other form of gambling. The vicar of the time stated publicly that the appeal would be made and conducted along those lines. Even so, the target was met in a commendable time.

Village fetes boasted an enormous variety of activities with fancy dress parades; displays of judo, archery and national dancing; competitions in bowls, golf, skittles plus the deafening activity of balloon bursting. Bowling for a pig was another popular fund raiser. People attending fetes were often entertained with songs by the church choir and items by the Diseworth skiffle group. Gymkhanas were also held on Cheslyn's field in the 1950's. Sunday school outings, treats and parties were another feature of the social scene.

Coronation Celebrations Many people living in Diseworth today remember celebrating two coronations, that of King George VI in 1937 and of Queen Elizabeth II in 1953. Following the death of his Majesty King George V in 1936 and the subsequent abdication of Edward VIII, plans were put into place to discuss the coronation celebrations. It was decided that there should be no levy on the rates and it was confidently expected that the necessary funds would be found through public subscription by means of a house-to-house collection. The sum of £50 was raised and it was proposed that celebrations would be on similar lines to the jubilee celebrations. A suitable souvenir would be provided for each child under the age of 15. An additional three prizes were proposed for the best decorated houses. The celebrations commenced with a fancy dress social on Coronation Eve.

'*Coronation Day found everyone early astir decorating their houses ready for judging by Miss Shakespear of Langley Priory*'. The church bells were rung at 7 am and at intervals during the day. The Rev Wood conducted a united service at 11 am near the war memorial and this was followed by lunch in the schools for all the inhabitants of the village. A fancy dress parade was held in the afternoon judged by Miss Shakespear and Mr CB Shakespear after which the younger children were conveyed round the village by decorated lorries. A few items of childrens' sports were held before all returned to the schools for tea. Villagers spent the remainder of the evening merrymaking and dancing until the early hours. During an interval each child was presented with a souvenir mug, a bag of sweets, an orange and an apple.

The Coronation of Queen Elizabeth II excited similar enthusiasm and it was proposed at a meeting in the Village Hall that the sum of £200 be raised by voluntary donation. The suggestion that one shilling be collected from each adult aged 18-60 was rejected. The chairman pointed out that at the previous Coronation celebration, Diseworth had raised more per head than any other village in the district and a house-to-house collection was proposed once again. The judging of decorated houses took place on Coronation Eve and on Coronation Day, Holy Communion services were held at 7, 8 and 9 0'clock '*followed by merry peals on the church bells*'. After the fancy dress competition the children climbed onto decorated lorries and were '*paraded around the village accompanied by decorated bicycles and perambulators*'. The procession ended at the village hall where a sumptuous meat tea with salads, cakes, cheese and biscuits awaited and each child was presented with a Coronation teaspoon. The meal was provided for all inhabitants of the village. The aged and infirm who were unable to attend were not forgotten and a parcel of food was sent out to each. From 8 pm until the early hours of the morning, the village hall was crowded for a social with '*games, singing and merrymaking*'. It is estimated that a total of 450 people were catered for on the day. To commemorate the Coronation, 47 trees and shrubs were planted at the village hall.

Sundries

The Diseworth Amateur Dramatic Society came into being in 1948 and presented many plays for the entertainment of the village and boasted an enthusiastic membership under the competent direction of the school's Headmistress, Miss Rigby. Plays by Noel Coward were popular and the performances drew supportive audiences.

The church had their own drama group with plays being performed by members of the Sunday school. These included *The Currant Bun; Mr Sly-One and his Cats, Black*

The village drama group. Back row from left; Nancy Moore, Ray Allen, John Whitehouse, Rose Edwards, Fred Fletcher, Nancy Poynton. Front row from left; Margaret Mills, Lionel Windy, Nellie Russel, Eileen Fletcher.

Coupons, *Mothers' Meeting*, *Mr Stick-it-up* and *the House of Mary*. On one occasion, German prisoners of war were members of the audience of a nativity play put on by the church drama group.

The vicar during this time, the Reverend PB Hacker wrote a Nativity play called *The Dayspring from on High* which was performed by the pupils of the Sunday school with the vicar taking the role of Simeon.

The Retired Residents Entertainments Committee was formed in 1965. The object of its constitution was to *raise funds for the purpose of entertaining the Retired Residents of Diseworth by organising outings, social evenings etc.* Membership was open to any person over the age of 65 and if only one partner of a married couple was 65, both were eligible to attend functions. Single people living alone were eligible at the age of 60. The association took responsibility in 1969 for organizing the Village Flower Show and Fete, and continued to make it an annual success for the next twenty years with the added attraction of entertainers such as a Punch and Judy Show. The members also enjoyed a variety of activities ranging from theatre and concert outings to whist drives and dances. Day trips to the coast and country venues were well supported and fund raisers in the form of coffee mornings and rummage sales were a good source of revenue. The annual Christmas dinner parties were a welcome diversion each December. The committee owned a set of skittles and matches were a regular social event. The skittles were also available for hire to outside organisations in return for a small fee and deposit in case of damage. Diseworth organisations were able to borrow at a cheaper rate than those outside the village, but there was no charge for church events.

Four Legged Friends One cheerful item from the newspaper scrapbook reported the impending arrival of a group of seaside donkeys. *Five Diseworth youngsters and their friends are anticipating a happy time with the arrival of five donkeys from Cleethorpes which have been found winter quarters in the village until Easter.* The animals arrived at the end of the summer in 1952, to the great excitement of the little girls.

The four-legged visitors arrived by train and travelled to Diseworth in a cattle truck where an excited reception party awaited them. The children were ecstatic to discover the donkeys each had a bridle and saddle and could be ridden. That winter appears to have been idyllic as the children followed the Quorn hunt, riding up Mill Hill with the wind in their hair and cantering over land where the airport is now situated. All too soon the winter months passed and it was time for the donkeys to return to their beach, leaving behind fond memories for those who had cared for them, and not a few tears.

The village continues to enjoy a host of activities with many social groups. Brownies, Guides, Pre-school Playgroup and the Youth Club are flourishing organisations under the guidance of dedicated volunteers. The Women's Institute underwent a metamorphosis several years ago and has become a well supported Women's Group and a women's discussion group meets once a month for lively and in depth debate. In addition, an active and vocal pressure group has developed in recent years. Its function is to protect the boundaries of the village from further industrial and commercial encroachment and from the services demanded by the trunk roads and motorways nearby. Diseworth remains, to this day, a sociable place to live.

CHAPTER FOURTEEN DISEWORTH IN WARTIME

The outbreak of the second world war made it necessary for Diseworth, as in all communities nationwide, to re-organise the pattern of daily life. A considerable amount of grassland in the village went under the plough for the sowing of extra crops, with a team of three horses pulling the plough. All food production was controlled by the Ministry of Food and farmers were instructed what crops to grow and where to send the harvest. Cereal crops were sent direct to the mills by train and the farmer was left with 'seconds' and 'sweepings' for his own use. Eggs had to be wiped clean before being packed and sent to Loughborough. It was the practice for farmers to receive payment in the form of coupons which would then be used to purchase chicken feed and dairy cake for the cattle. There was also a small food allowance for the sheep dogs.

Women's Institute

The Women's Institute was formed in Diseworth in 1939 and shortly after, the Ministry of Information gave a film show in the schoolroom for the entire village. Presented through the WI, it featured films on handicraft as well as the working of the Country and Empire in wartime. During the second world war a call went out for jam making. There was a talk at Loughborough Town Hall explaining the working of the fruit preservation scheme and many ladies from Diseworth attended. With the shortage of sugar and fuel, it was necessary to receive instruction on the most economical method of preserving fruit.

A Jam Centre Committee was set up and all members were requested to notify the secretary of the amount of spare fruit available. Work was carried out in Mrs Jarrom's kitchen and as there was a plentiful supply of fruit in the village, jam making became big business. Each lady took along her own preserving pan and jam jars. Labels and the parchment for jam pot covers were supplied.

The resources of the ladies were severely stretched one evening when a knock at the door revealed a villager with a huge laundry basket full of golden plums. He went on to say that there were more in his bath at home. The jam had to be made quickly while the fruit was still fresh but extra sugar and coal (for the range) were needed. There was only one man to approach, Sidney Barnett. Sid was the village A.R.P. warden and possessed the only telephone in the village. Thankfully he was able to secure the necessary supplies and the jam was made within the next two days. Yet another example of triumph over adversity!

There was an added perk when the jam making was completed. The ladies would take a quart jug to Mrs Jarrom's kitchen. The preserving pans were rinsed with boiling water and scraped clean with a wooden spoon. The sweetened water was poured into the jugs, taken home and either used as a basis for home jam making or for consumption as a fruit drink.

During the winter months in wartime, it became impossible to obtain speakers and demonstrators. It was decided to use the time at the monthly meetings knitting socks for the army and navy, and bed socks and operation stockings for the hospitals. Supplies of wool and patterns for knitting comforts for the troops were supplied by Miss Shakespear and Mrs Hacker, the vicar's wife.

Air Raid Precautions

Shortly before the outbreak of World War II the parish council met to discuss air raid protection. A telegram had been received from the Home Secretary urging all authorities to make arrangements for recruiting volunteers and participation in a course of instruction. It was decided that the council would co-operate with the Rural District Council's air raid protection scheme and liaise with surrounding villages. Steps were taken to secure a lecturer but, as was necessary in the first world war, each village would be required to train its own instructors.

The question of special emergency vehicles was raised and it was decided that one would be marked as an ambulance. There would be two motorcycles for use if other communication was not available and volunteers would be at the council's disposal. Councillor JG Shields observed that as they had some very fine hunters at Belton, these might be used. The possibility of A.R.P. wardens leaping into the saddle and galloping through the village in times of emergency caused some amusement.

Then, as now, apathy reigned and it was often the faithful few who attended meetings. Another local councillor, Mr TV Deane deplored the lack of interest in precautions and stated publicly that if people showed no interest, *'it was their own fault if they got done in'* if and when there was a war.

An inspection of cellars which the council considered suitable for air raid shelters revealed 16 in the Diseworth ward but it was noted that there was an inadequate number of hydrant points on the water mains in the village. A.R.P. Wardens were kept busy on two consecutive evenings in the schools as they fitted the inhabitants for gas masks and they presented badges to those who had passed recent examinations in air raid prevention work. A further meeting was held in the schoolroom for the purpose of appointing firewatchers and there was no shortage of volunteers willing to serve.

Material was purchased to black out the schools. Following the cancellation of an evening service and social arranged for Michaelmas Day because of lighting restrictions, arrangements were made to black out the church as well so that evening services could continue during the winter months. A mock airfield was established on Long Holden (at the top of Clements Gate), to decoy enemy bombers away from the military airfield situated where East Midlands Airport stands today. In addition to these precautions, a captain and five other men were appointed to form a fire brigade for Diseworth.

The Diseworth Fire Brigade

The members of the Diseworth Fire Brigade were drilled and ready for action at the first sound of an air raid alert. The leader of the brigade was Len Purday and he had charge of the pumps which were kept in his shed. Other members of the brigade included Tom Saddington, Bill Adkin, John Adkin and Wilf Sheffield. As water from the mains was scarce in war time, the men would practice using the pumps from the brook which ran through the village. The story is told of the enthusiastic firefighters watering each others gardens from the brook. Unfortunately for one young member of the brigade, he had completely forgotten that his mother still had washing on the line.

The Home Guard

During the war Diseworth had an active and efficient Home Guard. Armed with rifles, the band of 20/30 men were ready and able to defend the people of the village. Parades were held each Sunday morning at the little house which stood next to the Plough inn. Two men were required to stand guard at a time and on many occasions the top man from the Local Defence Volunteers (Home Guard) would arrive from Castle Donington. Challenges of 'Halt, who goes there' were met with a typical Captain Mainwaring response but so keen were the guardsmen to defend their territory that they were often reluctant to let him pass.

Training exercises would take them away to Woodhouse Eaves and other rugged locations, often at night. The battalion would travel to the training grounds in an old bus and it is well documented that the enemy would have had ample warning of their approach as the bus trundled up the hill, gears crunching and exhaust backfiring. The men would fill their water bottles with *brown water* from the tap room at the Plough to sustain themselves during the long and arduous night. On arrival at the training venue, they would be expected to sleep on the floor of the village hall and then be roused at 2am to go on exercise. The effects of the brown water would by now have taken effect and memories of the night's manoeuvres were often hazy.

The Comforts Fund

As documented elsewhere in this volume, the people of Diseworth have long been known for the generosity and support they have shown to their fellow citizens. A typical example of this was the formation of the *Diseworth Services Comforts Fund* in October 1942.

The proposal was to send a cash gift for Christmas *To each local member of His Majesty's Forces, without regard to where he or she may be stationed, the husbands of resident Diseworth*

Diseworth War Memorial dedication, with Mr CB Shakespear and Rev Palmer, and the church choir against the church. Circa 1920.

girls to be regarded as local men for this purpose. The committee had decided that an equal amount should be sent to each serviceman or woman, irrespective of rank or status. The Comforts Fund Committee met frequently during the war to arrange fundraising events to augment the fund so that gifts could be sent at regular intervals. These events usually took the form of a combined whist drive and dance and a sub-committee was formed to make the necessary arrangements. Steps had to be taken to avoid duplication of events as occasionally, it was discovered that a similar event was to take place in the neighbouring village of Long Whatton. Emergency meetings would then be convened to make alternative arrangements.

Additional money raisers at these social evenings took the form of a raffle. Even in those days of severe shortages and rationing, the prizes were impressive. They included a cockerel, gloves, postal orders, a box of groceries, a splendid meat-safe made by the treasurer of the committee, a tea cosy and a doll. On one occasion in 1944, the highly desirable prizes of a bed jacket and one pound of chocolate were donated. It was decided to combine these as one prize and tickets were sold at sixpence each. One farmer's daughter, Elizabeth Adkin remembers when five calves were born within seven days which meant an excess of milk. The milk from newly calved cows was too rich for human consumption so they made butter which was wrapped in packs of just under half a pound. The first pack was put up for auction and the rest was then sold for the same price. Small pork pies, (one pounders as they were known), were also sold in the same way.

Miss Rigby, the Headmistress of the school, was a keen supporter of the Comforts Fund. She kept rabbits and would cure the skins and make bedroom slippers for the winners of the whist drives. On many occasions the Women's Institute would assist with the fundraising, including door to door collections. The funds raised would then be shared between the Comforts Fund and the District Nurses of Long Whatton who covered a large area.

As early as 1943, steps were being taken to build up the fund so that *our local men should be given a suitable reception on their perhaps not very far distant welcome home*.

The committee was enormously proud of the people for whom they were raising funds and they continued their efforts for the duration of the war. The vicar, Rev PB Hacker was chairman of the fund and without fail acted as Master of Ceremonies at each whist drive. It was he who proposed a prize for the longest stay at one table and he also suggested spot prizes for dancing. In the absence of French chalk, soap powder would be scattered on the dance floor to create a suitably smooth dancing surface.

The events were for the most part financially successful although there were occasions when the cost of hiring one particular band would seriously erode the profits. On another occasion, the question of an additional payment for use of the school piano was raised after much unpleasant talk in the village. The vicar stepped in to calm the situation and explained that the Education Department had requested the fee. The committee voted that this time the fee be paid but it was decided that at the next event, Mr Dakin should bring his radio.

Gifts averaging £1 per person continued to be posted to servicemen three or four times a year for the duration of the war. There was some anxiety when it was learned that Captain Shakespear of Langley Priory was missing and consternation about the advisability of sending further gifts. The news that he was safe and had returned to England was greeted with relief.

The final meeting of the committee took place on 19th February 1946 when the treasurer declared that all the funds had been distributed and the fund closed on 31st December 1945. A final statement of accounts was posted on the village notice board.

The Royal British Legion

The earliest record comes from a newspaper cutting that noted in 1935: 'A *short service prior to evensong was held near the War Memorial. Mr W Moore said the Act of Homage. The*

Souvent Me Souvient
1914
1918
IN PROUD MEMORY OF THE DISEWORTH MEN WHO FELL IN THE GREAT WAR, AND AS A THANKOFFERING TO GOD FOR THE SAFE RETURN OF SO MANY, THIS TABLET WAS ERECTED: FOUR OF THE CHURCH BELLS WERE RECAST AND REHUNG: A FIFTH BELL WAS ADDED.
R.I.P.
BAINES, C.
BARNETT, S.
BEXON, E.
BEXON, J.
BLACKWELL, T.
BRADLEY, H.
BRADLEY, J.A.
BRISCO, A.
BRISCO, C.H.
BRISCO, C.
BROWN, T.
BURTON, A.
CARTWRIGHT, P.W.
EDWARDS, W.
FERGUSON, W.
HANFORD, W.
HARRIS, A.J.
HARRIS, J.F.
HARRIS, C.
HOWE, D.
HOWE, T.
HOWE, W.
ALLCROFT, J.F.
BARNES, H.
BARNETT, B.
BEXON, F.
FRISBY, G.
HICKLIN, C.N.
HOWE, G.
MAYES, A.
MAYES, W.
MEE, A.
MORGAN, G.
NUNN, S.
ORRIDGE, A.
ORRIDGE, I.H.
ORRIDGE, W.
PALMER, B.
PALMER, W.
SOWTER, A.
THOMPSON, A.
TOMLIN, B.
WAIN, D.
HUBBARD, S.R.
HUDSON, W.
JACKSON, J.
LOCKE, J.K.
LESTER, R.
MASON, J.
MEE, O.W.
MEE, R.
MOORE, E.W.
MOORE, H.R.
MOORE, T.
MOORE, W.
MORGAN, J.V.
ORRIDGE, G.
ORRIDGE, J.
ORRIDGE, S.
ORTON, B.
PADWICK, R.
POXON, A.
POXON, G.
RUSHTON, G.
SCREATON, E.A.

Diseworth War Memorial.

War Memorial was floodlit on Remembrance Day and during the evening. Poppies sold in the village and at Langley Priory raised £6 4s 2d.'

The following year in 1936 another event is reported: '*At 10.45 on Remembrance Day members of the Kegworth British Legion, under the command of ex-Sergeant Major Baxter of Kegworth, paraded at the school and then marched to the War Memorial at the Diseworth Church gates. Mr J King laid a wreath inscribed 'lest we forget' in grateful remembrance of fallen comrades 1914-1918, and the Act of Homage was said by Mr Bernard Smith. The short service was taken by the vicar Rev WJ Wood and an address given by Col Abel-Smith. The Colonel expressed his pleasure at being invited to speak. He urged men to stand firm for the freedom which this country still upholds and for which their comrades gave their lives.*

Mr John Shakespear of Langley Priory was present and had made the arrangements for the presence of the bugler, who with Drummer P Needham of the 5th Leicesters Regiment sounded the Last Post and Reveille. A collection for the Earl Haig Fund came to £2 10s.'

In April 1937 it was reported that the ex-servicemen of Diseworth had a general desire to form a branch of the British Legion.

Alan Yeates recalls the Diseworth Branch being formed in 1955, and prior to then it was the Long Whatton and Diseworth Branch. Mr Moore was the Chairman and about twelve people joined at a shilling per year, many of whom had belonged to other branches. The Diseworth branch met once a month and still do so. A Remembrance Service is always held at the Parish Church War Memorial, and the organisation continues to serve the war widows and ex-servicemen who need help. In recent years, Alan Yeates and Doug Poynton were both presented with the Gold Badge for their work for the Legion. They have also received, together with Rosie Smith, the badge and bars for the very many years of poppy selling.

Peace at Last!

On Victory in Europe day, the vicar ordered the bells to be rung as a thanksgiving for peace in Europe and a special service of thanksgiving was held at 8 o'clock that evening. VE Day celebrations were held in Diseworth on Whit Monday 1945. These commenced with a fancy dress parade in the afternoon followed by a celebration tea in the schools. The fun continued as everyone retired to Cheslyn's field for sports. Other attractions included skittling for a pig, table skittles, a darts match and a hunt for hidden treasure. Diseworth was once more at peace.

CHAPTER FIFTEEN EAST MIDLANDS AIRPORT

In 1916, when the War Office requisitioned a couple of fields between Gimbro Farm and Finger Farm in Diseworth as a Home Defence Landing Ground, surely nobody guessed that it was the very beginning of what was to become a major international airport some seventy years later.

RAF Castle Donington

After the First World War the little airstrip was forgotten until 1941 when the AMWD (Air Ministry Works Directorate) surveyed the area for a three-runway base for an Operational Training Unit for bomber aircrews. On 1st January 1943 RAF Castle Donington opened as a satellite to OTU Wymeswold. In those days there were just three intersecting runways between the two farms and noise problems to persons and livestock were probably ameliorated by 'war time spirit'. This may have been helped, so the story goes, by farmers accepting swill from the cookhouse and possibly a gallon of petrol in exchange for the occasional pig, not to mention the enhanced nightly takings at such places as the Bull and Swan.

After the war the first long distance travel from Diseworth commenced when RAF Castle Donington opened up trunk routes through liberated Europe to the Middle and Far East ferrying troops and supplies, but the station closed to flying in September 1946. A Gliding School was established but did not last long and the airfield was abandoned in 1947 and became derelict for a number of years.

Five Local Authorities Step In

It might never have progressed, but for a survey conducted by the northern division of the Ministry of Civil Aviation on the advantages and disadvantages of Royal Air Force Aerodromes in the early 1960's. At the same time Derby Corporation were considering an alternative site for Burnaston Airport which had a grass runway. But it was not just Derby Council who was keen on a new airport. Nottingham City and Nottinghamshire County Councils, Derbyshire and Leicestershire County Councils were also interested.

It was some time after the five local authorities had joined forces that the chosen site received planning permission in 1963. Castle Donington Airport became a reality and was renamed East Midlands Airport. Derby Aviation, which had used Burnaston Airport, changed its name to British Midland and agreed to move to the new airfield.

Airport Director

An airport director was appointed in March 1964 with the task of completing the airport within fourteen months. The director was Eric Dyer, a former Air Force pilot who brought with him the experience of having set up Southampton Airport. In the one year allocated to him Eric Dyer was expected to transform the flat airstrip into a fully operational civilian airport. He recalls that when he commenced work he had no office and no direct employees!

It is interesting to note that the Airport Director considered Diseworth a pleasant place as Eric Dyer brought his wife and family to live in the village for many years.

There were five task masters to assist Eric:

Derby Council handled Administration and Law
Derbyshire County Council provided the Civil Engineers
Leicestershire County Council became the Land Agents
Nottingham City Council took responsibility for Finances
Nottinghamshire County Council supplied the Architects

Building Commenced

Thus construction began with many site workers. This was happening at the same time as the M1 was being built and a huge area of land in and around Diseworth must have appeared as a vast building site. But the director knew what he was doing and, in persuading the local authorities to purchase as much land around the proposed airport as they could, the future East Midlands Airport took shape. In the months left the 5,850 foot long runway was constructed, the terminal building begun, hangar floor and aprons created as well as parking for the very many cars coming on to the airfield. And of course the job of finding business from European-wide airlines.

The deadline was reached and in July 1965 the official opening by Prince Philip took place.

The Building Continued

By 1970 both the runway and the terminal were extended, and not long after a campaign was launched calling for EMA to be made the regional airport for central England. Further growth continued and ten years on the Airport became a public limited company. In 1993 EMA became the first regional airport to enter the private sector when it was purchased by National Express.

Thirty-five years after its opening the Airport sees over two million passengers through the terminal each year in addition to providing one third of the amount of the United Kingdom's freight traffic.

Gimbro Farm and Finger Farm are now just names in the old Census returns and the vast, busy complex of East Midlands Airport is a part of Diseworth life.

CHAPTER SIXTEEN IN LIVING MEMORY

Florence Ada Measey nee Bee

Florence Bee was born in a little cottage at the end of Hall Gate in 1905. When she was two Ada's parents moved, with the little girl to the house in Hall Gate where Ada has lived ever since, and where her brother Maurice was born. Ada grew up in a home without electricity, with oil lamps and candles, and where the water was pumped from the well outside the house. In winter when the water in the well froze, she would be sent to the farm for water. Her father worked on the railway at Castle Donington and her brother obtained an apprenticeship with Shields when he was fourteen years old.

The young Ada attended the village school and remembers the teachers Mr and Mrs Taylor. She loved her school days, her great friend was Kitty Fletcher, and the friendship has continued with Kitty's daughter Janet. She was taught reading and writing and recalls the anxious moments when the inspectors called at the school. It was a happy childhood in Diseworth, and Ada has a strong memory of running to the gate to see the sheep being driven through Hall Gate to the sheepwash. She also recalls that one could set the clock at 5.30 when the milk buckets were placed on the cart at Marshalls. At school the girls were taught sewing and made all their own underclothes. The sewing stood her in good stead when she left school and began to help her mother with the traditional hose 'chevenning'. This was embroidering 'clox' on men's hose. Ada would sometimes work all day at this in order to have the work ready for the Adkin carrier cart to collect the hose to go to Loughborough.

Sometimes she would travel on the morning cart to Loughborough for an outing, but rarely for food shopping, as you could buy all you needed in the village. There was always a pig in the sty in the garden, which was slaughtered at the right time and the meat hung in the cellar. Various carts came round selling produce, butter and eggs were bought from Marshall's farm across the road and milk was collected from Mrs Hutchinson who lived against the Methodist Chapel.

The Methodist Chapel has featured strongly in Ada'a life, her family were staunch Methodists, two cousins were ministers, one of whom worked abroad with leper colonies for a number of years. Through an uncle Ada Bee was introduced to Philip Measey who also worked on the railway, and they were married in the late 1920's. Ada brought her husband back to the family home where they all lived in harmony.

Annie Fletcher nee Branson

Catherine Ann Fletcher was born on 25th July 1905 in Castle Donington. Her grandparents, Richard and Emma Corbett lived in Longmere Lane in Diseworth and her parents ran the butcher's shop in Clapgun Street in Castle Donington. Her father delivered meat to Diseworth twice a week on his horse and cart, often taking the little girl

Ada Measey's wedding day.

with him. It was a busy task with as many as sixty-three customers in the village to visit. Annie remembers best steak at a shilling a pound. She attended Castle Donington Church School and at the age of seven was taught the piano, an interest and ability she has kept throughout her busy life. Annie recalls getting up at 6.30 am to practice on the piano for an hour, then she set off to deliver meat locally until school time. Twice a week after school, she would walk to Cavendish Bridge in Shardlow to collect the meat order from the convalescent home. At the age of thirteen Annie's father died and her mother was left with the business to run and two daughters to bring up. This she managed and Annie as she grew older taught music to young people. One of her pupils was Miss Roseia Shakespear from Langley Hall. One of her memories is the Castle Donington Picture House where it was 3d for the matinee performance and 6d for the evening one. One night the resident pianist was taken ill, and Annie was asked to step in. It was the era of the silent films, and the pianist had to watch the film and play appropriate music. Annie recalls the film was Charlie Chaplin in 'The Kid' and for a week she played at the piano, for which she was paid the princely sum of 15s.

During her visits to Diseworth she met a young man, Joseph William Fletcher, son of Frederick Joseph Fletcher, the village wheelwright, joiner and undertaker. Will Fletcher was soon travelling to Castle Donington to court Annie, but only when he could borrow his father's bicycle, and never on Thursdays, which was bell ringing night, a practice he maintained all his life and is followed by his eldest son Arthur. Will and Annie's courtship took place around the old windmill in Diseworth Lane in Castle Donington, now part of the airport runway.

They were married at Castle Donington Church on 2nd June 1924 and came to live in Longmere Lane in Annie's grandparents house. It was there that the first four of her thirteen children were born. From there they moved to Hall Gate where they lived for thirty-one years, and where the other children were born. Annie makes light of having thirteen children at home, with no running water, no electricity, and no medical help. *'You just got on with it'* she smiles. A woman in the village, a Mrs Poxon, came to help, and of course the family were around. For the latter births a nurse in the village was available. When 'Granny Fletcher' died, Annie and her husband moved into the family house at the Woodyard to carry on the family business of wheelwrights and joiners. Annie remembers oil lamps being lit in the church, and the stove being stoked for the 8am communion service. One of her children, Alma, died at the age of four years. The little girl had been a member of the Sunday School, and the collection for Alma provided a vase in her memory. For the next twenty-nine years, every week, Annie would fill the vase with flowers and place it on the font.

Annie, her husband, and all but one of the children have been baptised in the Parish Church. The exception is Rosemary, the youngest, who was very ill after her birth in 1947, and was baptised firstly at home and subsequently in the church.

A village resident who has lived through two world wars, and remembers the effect they had on village life, seen piped water and electricity come to Diseworth, Annie Fletcher is one of a number of nonagenarians who is truly a child of almost the whole of the twentieth century.

Elizabeth Adkin

Nellie Elizabeth Adkin was born in 1908 at Isley Farm in Ladygate. Her parents, John and Mary Ellen kept the farm; they had two other children, Steven Robert, older than Elizabeth, and Charles William the youngest of the three. One of her earliest memories was going to school at the age of three years. In those days, when one's mother had to go to Loughborough it meant a day's journey by carrier or horse and trap, and the school was willing to take the three-year-old in for the time. Elizabeth recalls being sat on a bench, where there were things to play with, as she was looked after by some of the older girls. One year later, in 1912, it was school proper, and Elizabeth's teacher was Mrs Taylor, wife of the Head Teacher, Mr Samuel Taylor. The Taylors had two daughters, Connie and Hattie. Connie helped in the school and Hattie kept house. Mrs Moore was the school caretaker, and each morning she lit the large stove to ensure the school was warm. Thereafter, it was the task of the older boys to keep the fire going with shovels full of coal from the coalhouse. Elizabeth remembers her classmates, Chris Fletcher, Annie Morris, Kenneth Barnett, Annie Allen, Stanley Hine, Victor Buckley and Elsie Lester among others. She also recalls the vicar, Rev Palmer coming in to school and they were all told to be very quiet, as he was studying for his doctorate.

Soon it was the First World War, the school was blacked out, and all the children were issued with small circular badges. Before leaving school in the afternoon, the badges were warmed in front of the fire till they glowed, they were then pinned on the child's clothes, and body heat kept them glowing on the journey home. Elizabeth's older brother Steve left school at twelve. This was permitted, as it was wartime and his father had need of him on the farm.

As she grew older, Elizabeth attended the senior school at Castle Donington for one day a week for one year, and then two days a week for the final year. The classes were cookery and laundry, and the pupils, after having registered at the Diseworth School in the morning, then walked across the fields to Castle Donington and back again in the afternoon. If in winter it was snowing, they had to keep to the roads, which meant arriving home much later. And when school finished for the day, the farm work began. Elizabeth recalls at the age of five being given a pan of chicken feed to distribute to the fowls, and a bottle for suckling calves.

School finished for Elizabeth at the age of fourteen and she worked full time on the farm. She had already learned a great deal and this was to be very useful, as her mother became ill shortly after, and the young girl had to care for her and take her share on the farm. Another concern arose when her younger brother had appendicitis, and after an emergency operation, had to be nursed for six weeks at home, before resuming work.

In 1939, the Second World War broke out and in the same year Mary Ellen Adkin died. Elizabeth was now 31 years old keeping house and working on the farm. However she still had to go to Castle Donington when her age group was called up for war effort. "*You are down as housekeeper for your father*" she was told. "*An older woman could do that*". "*Yes*" the young woman replied. "*But could she go out and help with calving at the same time!*" So

Elizabeth stayed on the farm and did the same work as the men. This involved helping in the fields with the growing of wheat, barley, oats, and beans and harvesting. A tough job was shocking. Shocking was putting together eight sheaves or shocks and getting them to stand up in the field. Vegetables were grown, fowls and pigs and sheep were kept, and always the regular attention to the cows. Elizabeth's tasks included getting them to their fields, and bringing them down for milking, washing the udders in readiness, and shifting the churns full of milk.

She recalls one day when she went to collect the cows and seeing a heifer in a field about half a mile further on. With the heifer was a small exhausted calf. Elizabeth carried the calf for $1\frac{1}{2}$ miles as she brought the cows back. When she could carry it no longer she laid the animal down safely, took the cows home and one of the workers went back for it. Having up to twenty-four cows incurred the work of making butter and curd cheese. Butter called for a strong wrist to turn the churn and then to pat the butter to exclude all the water.

Pigs were also reared on the farm and after slaughter, another of Elizabeth's tasks involved cutting the joints, curing the bacon, and making sausages, faggots, pork pies and brawn. Making the brawn meant no part of the pig was wasted. The joints and bacon, after salting and curing were hung in storage. These were days of no refrigeration, and yet a well-cured bacon flitch could be kept for up to two years.

Elizabeth Adkin has always been a member of the Baptist Church in Diseworth, and in addition to all the work on her father's farm, she was a scholar at the Sunday school, then pupil teacher, then teacher and finally superintendent of the Baptist School. She also collected the rents from the two cottages, which used to abut the Church.

Minnie Louisa Hutchinson nee Orton

As related elsewhere in this volume, Bertram Orton was the youngest son of Henry Orton. Bert and his wife had one daughter Minnie and she has fond memories of them both. Minnie Hutchinson tells the romantic story of how her parents met. Bertram had joined the 5th Leicester regiment and was based at the Wigston barracks where he met the young Louisa Rastall. When he was posted to India he asked her to wait for him until he returned. This she did and they were married at Diseworth church in 1907. Minnie was born in 1912 and was just two years old when Bert was called up again for the First World War. She and her mother lived during this time in a cottage in Ladygate, an area that was susceptible to flooding. During one flood, Minnie remembers that they had to remove the drawers from a dresser and when they opened the dresser door, an Eskimo doll floated out. Bert survived the battles of the First World War and when he was demobbed he took his wife and young daughter to live in the middle one of three cottages (now combined as one house) on Clements Gate which was also known as Church Street. He was known in the village as the *Enemy of all weeds and friend of churchyard paths*.

There were two cottages in Clements Gate (known as The Old Homestead) where Henry lived and Minnie tells of being sent with her cousins down to the potato store in the cellar. Halfway down the steps there was a large nail sticking out of the wall. Grandma Orton used to say that a lady had hanged herself on this nail, a story that frightened the children so much they would argue among themselves over who would be the last back up the steps.

The church played a large part in the lives of the Orton family and both Minnie and her father were christened, confirmed and married at Diseworth church. Bert was a dedicated bell ringer and became captain of tower and would often ring hymns on the bells. The present captain of tower, Arthur Fletcher remembers that the ringing team would assemble for the Sunday morning service and if they were a person short, several rings on one bell would bring Bert Orton padding down the street in his slippers to make up the numbers.

Minnie was a member of the church choir in her younger days and after choir practice, she and her cousins would climb over the stile and walk across Hall Close Field to see the Dakin family at Wartoft Grange. One twilight evening they were confronted by two lads with sheets over their heads pretending to be ghosts and hoping to frighten the young girls. One of the culprits was none other than Cyril Wood, son of the vicar at that time.

A particularly poignant memory is of the gypsies who often came to Diseworth. The travellers had a regular campsite in Green Lane and would visit the village selling their wares. During one of their brief stays in Diseworth, a gypsy baby died and was buried in the churchyard under the trees. Each time the travelling community visited, they would place flowers in the pretty pots that covered the grave.

Jessie Wooldridge nee Clarke
Jessie was born in 1917, and started at Diseworth School in 1921

At the age of eight or nine her mother decided she should attend the school at Castle Donington. "*There were no buses, we had to bike it, just me and my brother Martin*" Jessie remembers. It was often dark when they set off in the morning and Jessie recalls being frightened as they cycled along the lanes.

At Castle Donington she learned the usual lessons, and also cookery and laundry. Garments were washed and ironed. One day, Mr Weston, the Headmaster called for her to go into his study. Jessie was terrified, thinking she was in trouble. But he said to her "*You cycle to school. How would you like a Bus Pass?*" Jessie says she jumped up and replied "*Oh Yes Sir, Yes*".

At the age of fourteen years Jessie left school and went into service in Loughborough at the home of Mrs Hibbens who owned the shoe shop. She was given a uniform, a white apron and small head band and was left each day to run the house. This entailed cleaning throughout, cooking, laundering and serving the meals of Mrs Hibbens and her daughter. Her meals were eaten in the kitchen. Each week she had two afternoons and evenings for herself.

After marriage to Bill Wooldridge, Jessie came back to Diseworth and the young couple needed somewhere to live. Next to the Baptist Chapel in Lady Gate were two cottages. "*Mr Adkin came and said to me, you can live in one of them if you clean the chapel*". And so they set up home there, the first of a number of houses they were to occupy in Diseworth. In later years as her children grew Jessie hired a Griswold machine, and like so many of her contemporaries in the village knitted socks for the Fullers and Hambly factory in Hathern.

Bessie Poynton nee Howe
Bessie was born in Reading in 1922 and moved to Diseworth five years later, attending the village school. She recalls her teacher Miss Grimley as a very kind and gentle person. At fourteen years Bessie left school to work at Gibsons on Station Road in Castle Donington where she was trained to make socks. Bessie's weekly wage was 8s 6d (42½p) Soon after she moved to Dakins on Packington Hill in Kegworth where the pay was much better, £1 per week. Bessie cycled to work with her village contemporaries, Hilda and Dot Winfield, and Renee and Joyce Crossland. Her father had given her a new bicycle, costing about £4, and Bessie was so pleased she immediately rode out on it. She remembers cycling all round and returning home later than expected, presumably worrying her parents because her father took the bicycle off her and kept it in his bedroom for a week!

Bessie Howe with her new bicycle, 1936.

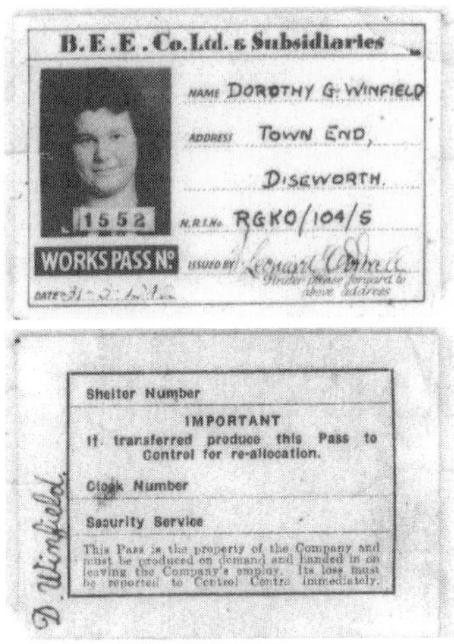

Dot Winfield's Works Pass, 1942

After many years Bessie moved on to Fullër and Hambly's in Hathern. These were the war years and the Diseworth workers cycled to work, but cycle batteries were virtually unobtainable in those times. Bessie recalls an event when the cyclists were stopped by PC Huffer, for having no lights. A well known local policeman, PC Huffer proceeded to ask their names. "*Well, after a while, someone started singing 'We'll meet again', and others joined in.*" she said. "*Yes we will*" replied the irate constable "*See you in court*".

Dorothy Yeates nee Winfield

Dot Yeates was born in 1922, in Diseworth. She attended school four years later and remembers Miss Shaw as her teacher. Dot walked to and from school with Bessie (Poynton) and the two friends still live close to each other in the village. At the age of fourteen Dot worked at Dakins Hosiery factory on Packington Hill in Kegworth along with others from the village. But at the onset of the Second World War women were needed to work at the Brush Factory in Loughborough and Dot joined them. She recalls:

"*Wheildons buses dropped us off at Clarence Street and we worked long hours. The bus picked us up at Town End at 6.55am each day and sometimes we had to work seven days a week. We drove cranes, five, ten and fifteen ton trucks lifting tanks and transformers. These tanks were sent wherever in the world they were needed.*" Other work included making winders for transformers and small electrical components. Despite gaining so much experience, when the war ended there was no place for her at the Brush. "*You are taking a man's job*" Dot was informed.

Harriet Catherine Lockett

Kate Lockett arrived in Diseworth as a post war bride in 1948. Diseworth was a lively agricultural village then, with five herds of cattle moving up and down Ladygate, twice daily to fields up Long Mere Lane. Horses and handmilking were still being used, but tractors and modern machinery were taking over.

The Church and the two Chapels were at the centre of village life. The church was a large part of the school life, while bell ringing, choir and Mother's Union all played their part in the activities of the village. The two chapels were well attended, with the Baptist Ladies Guild and Mr Sutton's Sunshine Club, young children and adults joined in each other's festivals, particularly the Anniversary services.

Kate recalls that the arrival of the sewerage system in the 1950's was gladly welcomed, as was mains water instead of pump water, though many people still had a well.

The Village Hall, gained by much fund raising, was another centre of village social life. It sheltered the Women's Institute, The Co-op Guild, Retired Residents, music hall socials by the Church, pantomimes and events by the school, whist drives and dances, and the well supported Flower Show.

Council houses were built in Page Lane and Clements Gate for the people returning from the war. The aerodrome land was returned to its previous owners.

Doctor's surgeries were held in Diseworth in those days. On Tuesdays and Fridays, Drs Montford and Carmichael, and in latter years Dr Beauchamp would come to Miss Moore's front room in Grimes Gate at the house still named 'The Old Surgery'.

Kate recalls those years after the war when one did not have to travel far for shopping.

The Co-op at Long Whatton collected grocery orders on Mondays and delivered them the following Friday. Butchers, bakers, coalmen, and a travelling ironmonger from Worthington selling paraffin etc. all appeared on different days. Many salesmen selling cattle food, farm seeds etc. also called regularly.

The village had two shops then, Miss Howe's containing the Post Office and Miss M Adkin's in Grimes Gate. Miss Adkin, her brother William and his wife had a big milk round in Castle Donington for many years.

Kate believes that as peacetime became the norm, industry quickly advanced, men left the farms, and young people were not content with the old ways. The construction of the motorways meant big business, goods and people could move far more quickly. With more money to spend people began to take holidays, something Kate had not heard of in her youth. In the 1960's she noted, that despite objections, the aerodrome was revived to meet needs for travel by air. Progress continued in Diseworth, new houses were built in the Woodcroft and Shakespear Close and the buildings in Orchard Close followed these in later years. Old barns and outbuildings became converted into houses, thus bringing in new generations with new ideas. Kate does not think this is a bad thing and she sees some old ways returning as well.

Rosalyn Edwards

Rosalyn Edwards was born in 1932 at Wartoft Grange. Her paternal grandparents, Edwards, farmed at Cross Farm, and her maternal grandparents, Dakin, farmed at Wartoft Grange. When Vera Dakin married Thomas Edwards he moved to Wartoft Grange and the family stayed there until 1964. The children were all born there, Joe (Herbert) in 1929, Gladys in 1931, Rosalyn in 1932, and Jennifer in 1940.

Rosalyn's memories are of a happy childhood, in a large farm with so many places for play and exploration. The children and their friends would spend hours playing in the fields, climbing trees and making bridges and dams in the brook. When there were races at Donington Park Race Track, the children would climb on haystacks to see the traffic pass. One memory was waiting all day to see the Duke of Kent go by.

Sadness came when she was just six years old and her sister suffered appendicitis. This turned to peritonitis, the other children were whisked away to an aunt, and on Christmas Eve, Gladys died. Two years later Rosalyn saw the family pram brought out and cleaned up which was the nearest anyone got to inform her of a new arrival. Then she was taken upstairs to see her new baby sister, Jennifer. This was wartime, and Diseworth was bombed when the baby was just a couple of months old. Rosalyn recalls her father in the passageway with the baby in the pram, and the rest of the family under the dining room table. Incendiaries were falling around the farmhouse and the children were terrified, as the night sky was lit up. For the parents the fear was that the hay barn would catch fire. Many years later one could still dig up the incendiary bombshells. The family was supplied with a Morrison shelter, a steel table under which they could shelter.

Rosalyn attended Diseworth school and recalls the various teachers, and going to Kegworth School to sit the examination for the High School. Kegworth School seemed such a big place after Diseworth and was rather daunting. However, she passed the tests, and with her cousin Nancy Moore attended Loughborough High School. But again tragedy was to hit the family, when Rosalyn was thirteen years old her mother died. Teenage life was hard for the young girl, who then had to look after her father. At that time Rosalyn recalls Father Hacker summoning three girls, one of them herself, to help teach the Sunday School. The girls were fourteen years old, and they had a large group of small children. Rosalyn stayed for fifty years teaching in the Sunday School. She is now a sacristan and has seen the changes in style of eight vicars in her time at the Church.

A woman who was very much known and loved in Diseworth, Doris Moore, had been Rosalyn's Sunday School teacher. Doris Moore had been born and brought up at the 'Old Surgery' on Grimes Gate. She was an extremely small woman, who did not venture much beyond the village because of her size, but who worked tirelessly for people in Diseworth. Rosalyn recalls when Doris was at the end of her life, living on her own in the house, how villagers brought her meals, and cared for her.

In 1964, Mr Edwards and his daughter left Wartoft Grange and moved to a house on The Green. When Mr Edwards died in 1980, Rosalyn decided to move to Long Whatton, to a house that had once been in her family. However she is still 'from Diseworth' and supports the Church, and many village organisations.

Andrew Crowe
Andrew Crowe came to live in Diseworth, in 1939, at the age of four years, and apart from National Service years, Diseworth has been his home ever since, most of his life having been spent in Clements Gate. Andrew's earliest memories are naturally wartime, and living at 7, Clements Gate, where his father had purchased a canning machine for the Women's Institute. The ladies would arrive with fruit and vegetables to preserve and there would always seem to be a lot of boiling water around. Sometimes the cans would be incorrectly sealed and one would explode causing much consternation. But it is probably the air raids that stay strongest in his mind.

'Mrs Webster lived next door, and her husband was away in the Army, and the siren sounded. My mother and I went to sit with her, and we were in the little front Parlour when the bombs fell on Cheslyns (the cricket field). We heard three loud bangs; Mrs Webster threw herself on top of me and we all went down on the floor. When I looked up there was a huge crack across the ceiling. The next day, Brian and Tony Howe and I went up the jitty to see the craters and look for shrapnel, which was highly collectable then.

'My father was an air raid warden, he had a narrow escape, he was walking towards Iron Farm when it got hit, he dived to the ground and was unhurt

'Another time we were at school, and there was a day raid, and the teacher shouted, "under the desks", I was little and an older boy was under the same desk, and he terrified me with war stories'

Andrew suffered many childhood illnesses, along with other children of his time, and he can recall many weeks off school first with pneumonia and then with scarlet fever. Scarlet fever was a serious illness, and the children were sent to Markfield Isolation

Hospital, where parents were only allowed to look at them through windows in the wards. But there were many good times, and the young boys could play safely in the village and beyond. They used to get together for long walks. These were the 'Green Lane' walks, the 'Fairy Glen' walks (near Wartoft Grange) and the brook walks. The brook walks involved a starting point in a brook, usually in the village and then setting off, staying in the brook and seeing how far one could travel before having to get out. His great companion of those days was David Cherry.

As he grew older and the war ended, Andrew watched as his mother worked hard for the Women's Institute. He recalls her helping to make the curtains for the new Village Hall, out of parachute silk. Entertainment was the village Youth Club and the cinema in Loughborough. The cinema was a weekly outing for the young people. Every Sunday there was a double bill from 6pm until 9pm. The problem was that Mr Lester's last bus left 'The Rushes' just after 9pm. Andrew recalls the group of friends, all needing the Long Whatton and Diseworth bus, standing in the aisles of the cinema, desperate to see the end of the film, until one would make the move and the dash to the bus stop would begin. If they were early they would rush into the fish and chip shop for 3d worth of chips and race for the bus. Many a time they would jump on as it was moving, and as they alighted, Mr Lester would say, *"I'll not wait for you next time"*.

Andrew loved sports, and excelled at cricket. He formed his 'Boy's Own' cricket team, arranged the fixtures and the travel, often on foot or by bicycle, and kept an accurate record of the results. The team were aged between 11 and 14 years, and such was their enthusiasm, they would take on any group and offered handicaps, such as playing left-handed.

The Youth Clubs at Diseworth and Long Whatton were popular with the young people, each village attending the other's venue as well as their own. Andrew recalls his friends, among whom were Raymond Allen, David, Gordon and Dick Fletcher, Kenneth and Brenda Lakin, the Linthwaite family; Christopher, Robert and Pauline, Jennifer Edwards and Ruth Barnett. But the one who made the biggest impression was Maureen Kelham, from Long Whatton. They were subsequently married and have lived in Clements Gate ever since, bringing up their four children in Diseworth.

Gordon Fletcher

Gordon was born in 1938 at 16, Clements Gate and moved next door to number 18 when he married in 1961. He has a wealth of memories of village life, with fond ones of the village school in general and of Miss Rigby in particular. This indomitable lady had a reputation for being strict but very fair and children knew their boundaries. She was very fond of her cats and one; a long-haired black and white called Patch would wander into the classroom and sit on Gordons desk. Health problems meant that he missed a part of his early education. However with the help of his mother who taught him to read and Miss Rigby's support he soon caught up. Miss Rigby encouraged the children to listen to schools programmes on the radio and also taught the children to weave on a loom in the schoolhouse. After leaving Diseworth at the age of eleven he went on to Castle Donington school for two years before moving to Loughborough College where he took a course in building.

The vicar during the 1940s was the Rev PB Hacker, known as Percy Bernard or 'squeaky brakes and bucket'. This good man used to ride a moped, the brakes of which had a particularly troublesome squeak and the vicar would frequently oil the brakes in an attempt to overcome this annoying problem. Legend has it that following one particular lubrication, the revving Rev found himself riding apace down Mill Hill and finding that he could not stop, careered, unannounced into Cross Farm. It is not known whether he was wearing his cassock at the time but it is to be hoped that he found sanctuary in a bale of hay! His other nickname of bucket referred to his receipt of scraps from the school kitchen for his chickens. Any boy who had not behaved in class would, as punishment, have the task of taking the slop bucket to the vicarage.

The vicar began a bible class, which many local boys attended, and his wife often gave extra tuition at the vicarage for those who required it. Mrs Hacker is remembered as a very houseproud lady. On wet days she would lay sheets of newspaper at strategic intervals on her tantalisingly spotless hall floor and the young Gordon would ache to place muddy footprints on the pristine surface. An annual treat was when the Bible class had an outing on Ascension Day to such places as Bradgate Park and Dovedale.

When Percy Hacker left the village his replacement was Nigel Turner and on his very first Sunday he was approached by the boys and told of the bible class. Without hesitation he held a class that very afternoon. Rev Turner proved to be a very popular cleric. Percy Bernard had been high church and did not attract large congregations but the Rev Nigel Turner was low church and much more approachable. He appeared to fill the church effortlessly and a congregation of 40-50 was not unusual. In addition to his village duties, he lectured on theology in Derby.

With the guidance and support of an adult committee, Gordon helped to start the first youth club in Diseworth with Raymond Allen. (Ray Allen was a keen magician who went on to become a redcoat and a member of the Magic Circle. He subsequently turned professional adopting the stage name Ray King)

The youth club was for 10-13 year old boys and girls and was held in the village hall. A married couple used to come from East Leake to teach ballroom dancing to the boys and girls and a dancing club was later formed. Dances were usually held once a month and club members would often travel to dances in neighbouring villages. There was little in the way of entertainment for young people in Diseworth apart from the youth club and visits to the cinema. The youth club attracted young men and women from Long Whatton and it brought many couples together who subsequently married. Gordon remembers that travel to Castle Donington was more direct in those days. The bus route was via Swan Rivers, across what is now the runway of East Midlands Airport and down Diseworth Lane to the Nags Head.

Gordon inherited a love of music from his mother and from an early age was a member of various choirs. His tutor at Loughborough College encouraged him to join the lunchtime choir and gave him private singing lessons. He was also persuaded to sing as a tenor rather than bass. He sang with the Kegworth male voice choir, the Loughborough College choir and has been a member of local Operatic Societies for thirty years. He remembers going carol singing round the village with the church group. Seats were placed on a trailer hitched to a tractor and the group toured the village in style. The evening came to an end at Langley Priory for refreshments, with the men in one room (where the whisky flowed freely), while the ladies and children enjoyed tea, coffee and soft drinks in the drawing room

An enthusiastic member of the amateur dramatic group, Gordon appeared in many plays. The group lapsed when Miss Rigby retired. It was later revived for a short time before sadly folding completely.

Gordon's connections with the church go back for several generations, his father was a churchwarden and his mother was the organist. She loved the organ and would practice for long hours. The church had a large choir and they would sing an anthem at least once a month and on one occasion they performed Stainers Crucifixion. As a fitting sequel to the tale of *The Organist and the Bellows Boy*, Gordon remembers having to pump the organ when his mother practised. As he was in the choir, the task of pumping the organ during services fell to his cousin Arthur Fletcher. Arthur often said that he had to pump twice as hard when Mrs Fletcher played as she used more stops than anyone else.

At one time there were 18 farms in the village, each having a herd of cows that had to be walked through the village twice daily for milking. This involved fairly intricate timing so that each of the herds could be easily identified and arrive at their home farms. Clements Gate alone had three herds of cows. Life was good in those days with plenty of fresh fruit, vegetables and home produced eggs and no apparent sign of the post-war shortages suffered nationally.

Gordon continues to work for the church, carrying out as much of the day to day maintenance as possible. In addition he undertakes the role of auctioneer at the annual flower and produce show. Taking up his position at the front of the village hall stage and leaning on an upended sweeping brush, he begins the auction of exhibits, often sold in multiple groups. Gently but firmly and with great good humour, he skilfully persuades those present to pay considerable sums of money for egg and chips: (six eggs in a basket and five potatoes) or a cream tea: (teatime scones, a jar of home made jam and a pot of cream). All proceeds go, of course, to local organisations.

Rosemary Smith nee Fletcher

'It started like an ordinary day at school, I always left home at a quarter to nine and walked to the top of the lane to meet my friends. We would walk to school together. The bell would ring at 9am and we all marched into school. After register we would start our lessons. I remember that morning we all had to go to the front of the classroom to collect something from the table. I remember leaving my desk and going up to the front and standing at the table. The next thing I can remember is sitting on the playground at the front of the school, propped up against the wall with my brother John leaning over asking if I was alright. Dr Carmichael looked at us all in the playground and said we must all go home. I cannot remember how we got home because there were few cars in the village then. I do remember being at home, lying on the settee with a terrible pain in my chest and stomach'

The Day the Children Fainted November 7th 1957

Miss Rigby recorded the event in the school logbook. She had come into school at 8.30am and found the place was full of smoke. All the doors and windows were opened and the children kept outside until 9.15am. The opening assembly was taken as usual and the infants went to their room. The older children were working when at 10.15 Miss Rigby saw one of them sink down under her desk. She lifted her up and thinking her faint, put her head between her knees and sent a child for water and another for Mrs Watson-Walker. By the time the assistant teacher arrived, two, then three, then four other children were falling over and two of them getting cut and bruised. The Headmistress rushed to phone for the doctor and to get more help. The children were told to get outside as quickly as possible.

The doctor arrived and said the children must go home and no one was to return to the room that day. The children were driven home *'after they had come round and been given weak tea as advocated.'*

Thomas John Jarrom

John Jarrom is the eldest son of Frank and Grace Jarrom. He was born at his grandmothers home in Castle Donington and brought to live on Page Lane in Diseworth with his family. He has lived all his life in the village and has followed the family line into farming. He attended Miss Coles school in Long Whatton and Loughborough Grammar School and considers that from an early age he knew he was going to be a farmer. As children the young boys were expected to help out on the family farm, and like most young lads going on the tractor was an exciting event. John attended college courses where the curriculum involved learning about machinery maintenance, crop husbandry and the feeding of farm livestock. But he claims he was really trained through the family, especially by his father. He recalls planting crops, kale and mangols in Spring and hand hoeing, using the baler and making hay in June and July and spreading muck and ploughing in August. In the Autumn the winter wheat was drilled and winter barley sown. His tasks included milking and rearing of the cows. It is now only the rearing of the cattle in which the farm is involved and he and his brother William farm 400 acres between Ladygate and Longmere Farms. This means having 25 milking cows for the calves which are bought in at 2-3weeks. They are kept four to a pen and can be nursed by one cow. The calves are sold at 30 months, all with cow passports. John recalls the different farmers in the village and his contemporaries who grew up with him and still live in Diseworth. He is one of a large family who have farmed in the village for hundreds of years.

Dave and Jackie Adcock - A Village Romance

Dennis and May Adcock moved to Page Lane when they were married in 1949. Their son Dave was born in January 1961. Four days later Jackie Pass was born to Reg and Doreen Pass who lived next door to the Adcocks. The two children grew up together, and went to Diseworth School, Castle Donington School and Burleigh Community together, always in the same classes.

They both have fond memories of the village school, of Miss Knight, '*the best teacher one could have*', and who was firm but fair. If you were ill, you went to the Surgery, opposite the school, to see Dr Carmichael, and it seemed however bad you felt, after he had seen you, off you were sent across the road to school.

An event, which occurred frequently as they recall, was the flooding of the brook.

In the early sixties, the Diseworth brook ran through the village without the high banks we have today, and after heavy rain the brook could rise by up to two feet virtually cutting the village in half. The usual passing places, at the bottom of Page Lane, or the Bowley, or Ladygate, were impassable. At such times Uncle John Fletcher would arrive with his taxi and pick up the children and drive beyond Wartoft Grange, round the airport and come down Grimes Gate to the school. Jackie and Dave both attended the old village school, which was demolished to make room for the one which stands today. The brook was re-coursed in parts, and the banks built up in the early seventies.

Dave and Jackie Adcock's wedding day.

In January 1982, at the Parish Church, Jackie and Dave were married, and the reception was held in Diseworth Village Hall. Their wedding was conducted by Rev Greaves and was the last marriage he solemnised before emigrating to Australia. They left Diseworth for a few years, but have returned to Page Lane, to the house where Dave was brought up, and live there with their three children. They are both much involved in village life, Jackie with the Youth Club, the Guides, the Village Hall, and the school, and Dave with cricket, football, dominoes matches and the annual fun runs.

CONCLUSION

Diseworth entered the third millennium with a bang. Fireworks and champagne corks exploded at midnight followed by the joyful peal of the bells at mid-day as the village gathered in the parish church for CELEBRATION 2000.

The thundering tones of the old one hundredth as the congregation sang 'All People Who On Earth Do Dwell' were succeeded by the beautiful words and haunting melody of 'Make Me A Channel Of Your Peace', sung by a churchwarden. The celebrations continued with lunch.

Diseworth has had its share of troubles in the past and not a few in recent years. It will though, remain a delightful place to live, with a strong sense of community sustaining it as the population continues to support and encourage each other.

PANTULF

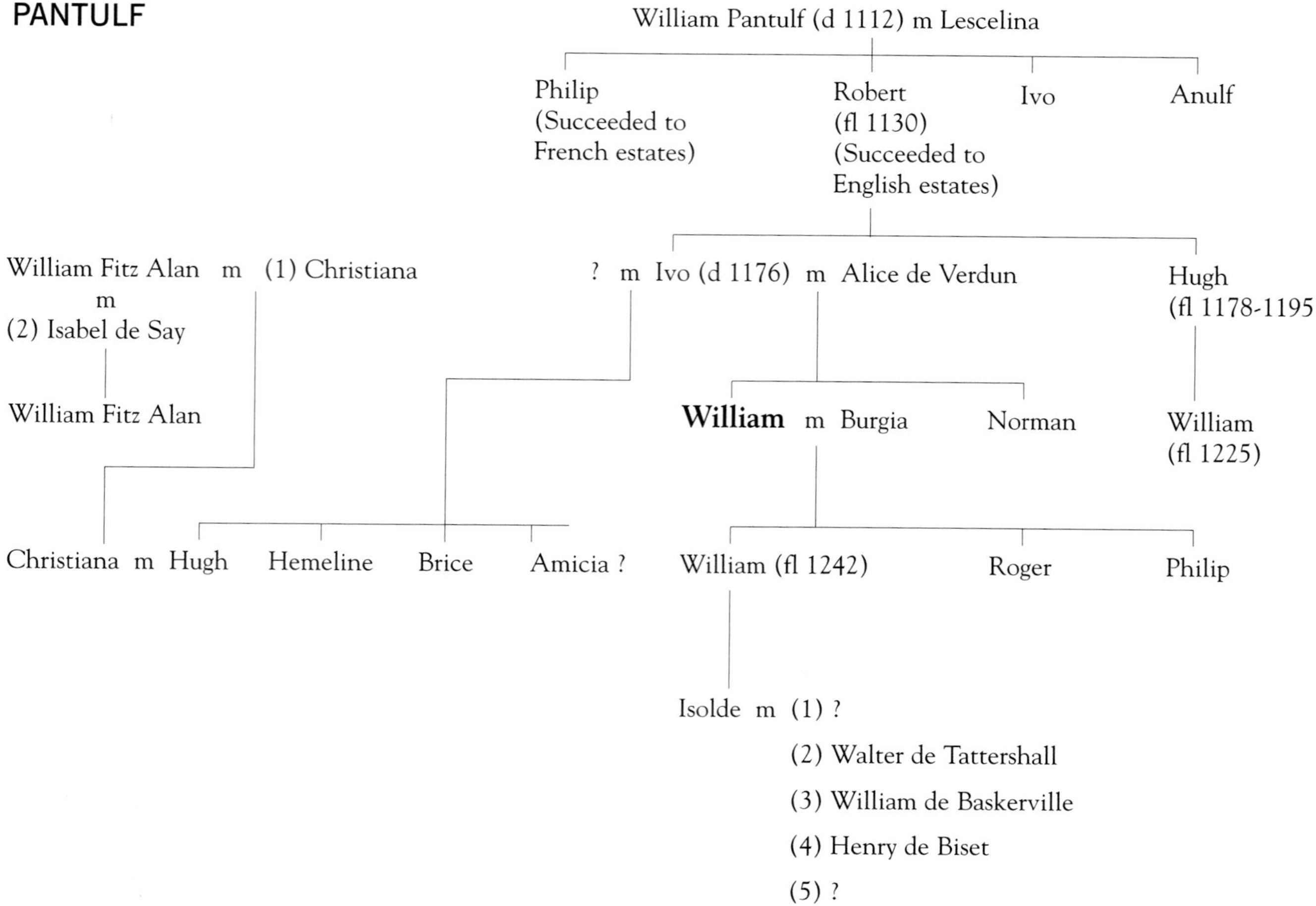
William Pantulf (d 1112) m Lescelina
Philip (Succeeded to French estates)
Robert (fl 1130) (Succeeded to English estates)
Ivo
Anulf
William Fitz Alan m (1) Christiana
m
(2) Isabel de Say
William Fitz Alan
? m Ivo (d 1176) m Alice de Verdun
Hugh (fl 1178-1195)
William m Burgia
Norman
William (fl 1225)
Christiana m Hugh
Hemeline
Brice
Amicia ?
William (fl 1242)
Roger
Philip
Isolde m (1) ?
(2) Walter de Tattershall
(3) William de Baskerville
(4) Henry de Biset
(5) ?

DE VERDUN

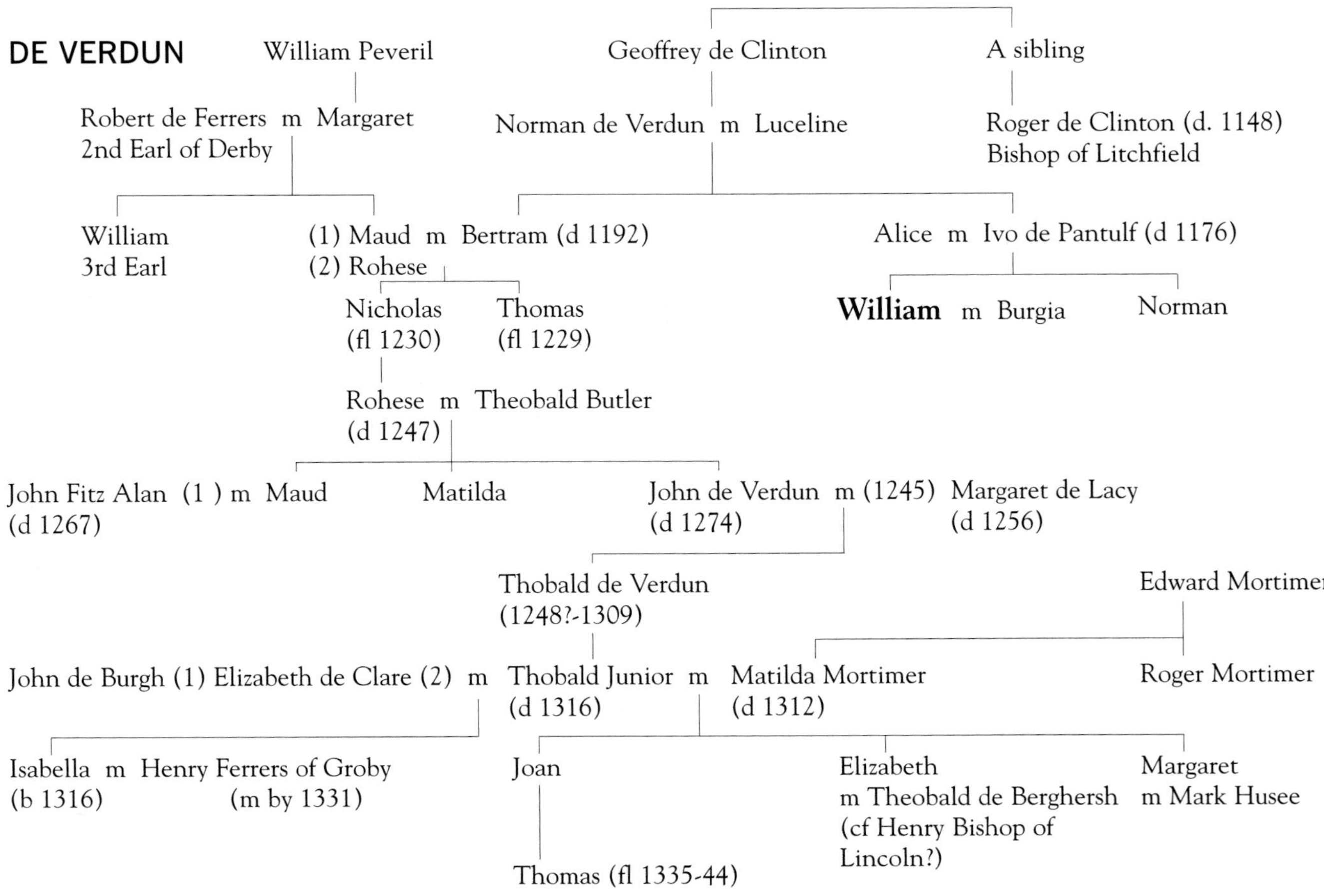

William Peveril
Robert de Ferrers m Margaret
2nd Earl of Derby
Geoffrey de Clinton
A sibling
Norman de Verdun m Luceline
Roger de Clinton (d. 1148)
Bishop of Litchfield
William
3rd Earl
(1) Maud m Bertram (d 1192)
(2) Rohese
Alice m Ivo de Pantulf (d 1176)
Nicholas
(fl 1230)
Thomas
(fl 1229)
William m Burgia
Norman
Rohese m Theobald Butler
(d 1247)
John Fitz Alan (1) m Maud
(d 1267)
Matilda
John de Verdun m (1245) Margaret de Lacy
(d 1274)
(d 1256)
Thobald de Verdun
(1248?-1309)
Edward Mortimer
John de Burgh (1) Elizabeth de Clare (2) m Thobald Junior m Matilda Mortimer
(d 1316)
(d 1312)
Roger Mortimer
Isabella m Henry Ferrers of Groby
(b 1316)
(m by 1331)
Joan
Elizabeth
m Theobald de Berghersh
(cf Henry Bishop of
Lincoln?)
Margaret
m Mark Husee
Thomas (fl 1335-44)

DE FERRERS EARLS OF DERBY

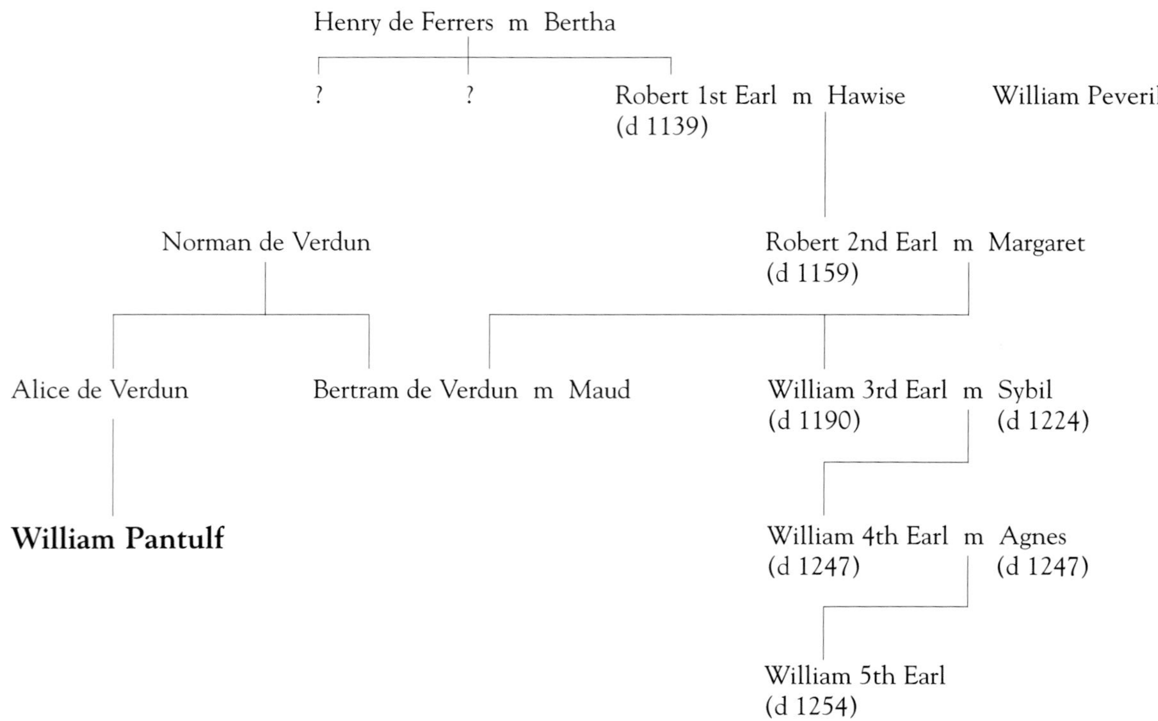
Henry de Ferrers m Bertha
?
?
Robert 1st Earl m Hawise
(d 1139)
William Peveril
Norman de Verdun
Robert 2nd Earl m Margaret
(d 1159)
Alice de Verdun
Bertram de Verdun m Maud
William 3rd Earl m Sybil
(d 1190)
(d 1224)
William Pantulf
William 4th Earl m Agnes
(d 1247)
(d 1247)
William 5th Earl
(d 1254)

TATTERSHALL

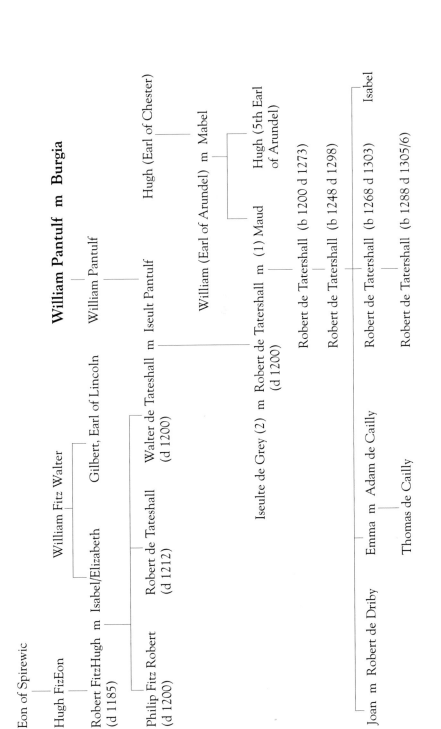

Eon of Spirewic

Hugh FizEon | William Fitz Walter | **William Pantulf m Burgia**

Robert FitzHugh m Isabel/Elizabeth (d 1185) | Gilbert, Earl of Lincoln | William Pantulf

Philip Fitz Robert (d 1200) | Robert de Tateshall (d 1212) | Walter de Tateshall m Iseult Pantulf (d 1200) | Hugh (Earl of Chester)

William (Earl of Arundel) m Mabel

Iseulte de Grey (2) m Robert de Tatershall m (1) Maud (d 1200) | Hugh (5th Earl of Arundel)

Robert de Tatershall (b 1200 d 1273)

Robert de Tatershall (b 1248 d 1298)

Joan m Robert de Driby | Emma m Adam de Cailly | Robert de Tatershall (b 1268 d 1303) | Isabel

Thomas de Cailly | Robert de Tatershall (b 1288 d 1305/6)

CHESLYN FAMILY

Oliver Cheslyn of Exall Hall Warwick married Jane Sweeting.

Richard 1634 - 1717 married:
1 Blake
2 Fazakerly

3 Elizabeth Nodes :	William 1660 - 1708 m Sarah Flaxney	
	Richard 1669 - 1693 m Elizabeth Rock	John Nicholas-schoolteacher Thomas
	John 1674 - 1759 m Martha Eales	John Martha William
4 Sarah Flaxney:	Charles 1684 - 1716 m Barbara Bate	
	Robert 1691 - 1750 m Cave King	**Richard** Ten daughters Four more Sons **Thomas**

Richard 1715 - 1787	m Katherine Bainbrigge	
Thomas 1736 - 1814	m Sarah Webster	**Richard** m Anne Barber Five more boys Five girls
	m Mary Baker	Six Boys Four girls
Richard 1770 - 1843	m Anne Barber	Anne Sophia **Richard** Sarah

From Parish Church Memorial	Born	Died	Buried
Richard Cheslyn	1634	1717	Diseworth
Sarah, widow of above	1648	1720	
William Cheslyn	1660	1708	Bath
Sarah, widow of above	1676	1734	
Sarah Flaxney Cheslyn		1720	
Richard Cheslyn	1669	1693	Tottenham
Elizabeth Cheslyn nee Rock			
John Cheslyn	1674	1769	Diseworth
Martha Cheslyn, widow of above		1754	
Charles Cheslyn	1684	1716	Jamaica
Barbara Cheslyn, widow of above		1722	Scropton, Derbys
Elizabeth, infant	1688	1689	St Sepuchres, London
Robert Cheslyn	1691	1750	Diseworth
Cave Cheslyn, widow of above	1680	1763	
Richard Cheslyn	1715	1787	
Katharine Bainbrigge, widow of above			Lockington
Cave Cheslyn	1716	1769	Diseworth
Sarah Cheslyn	1717	1808	
Mary Cheslyn	1719	1740	
Eleanor Cheslyn m Edward King	1720	1783	Coventry
Elizabeth Sweeting	1664	1721	Diseworth
Anne Cheslyn	1722	1787	
Francis Cheslyn	1722	1792	
Penelope Cheslyn	1723	1801	
William Cheslyn	1725	1758	
Robert Cheslyn, child	1726	1727	
Martha Cheslyn	1728	1761	
Robert Cheslyn, child	1729	1730	
Robert Cheslyn	1731	1772	Malton, Yorks
Harriot Cheslyn	1732	1744	Diseworth
Elizabeth Cheslyn	1734	1760	
Thomas Cheslyn	1736	1814	
Sarah Cheslyn nee Webster, wife of above	1747	1786	Woolston, Warcs
		(removed to Diseworth 1792)	

NB Not all the Cheslyns made it to the family vault. In the Parish churchyard a tombstone records one Thomas Cheslyn who died January 9th 1891 aged 76 years, and Mary Cheslyn, shopkeeper, who died on August 22nd 1880 aged 77 years.

SHAKESPEAR FAMILY

John 1739 - 1786 married Martha 1752 - 1828

John born 14th August		1861 purchased Langley Priory
Samuel	born	1775
Joseph	born	1776
Thomas	born	1779
William	born	1783
Jabez	born	1786

Charles 1811 - 1899 married Elizabeth 1831 - 1916

Martha Elizabeth	born	1861
Constance	born	1862
Emily	born	1863 died April 1898
Gertrude	born	1866 married William Gross 1st June 1899
Selina	born	1867
John	born	1869 died September 1886
Charles	born	1871 died 1959 married Mary Jane Foster
		John Hornby 1911 - 1970
		Margeret Roseia 1912 - 1943

Tombstones in Breedon churchyard give some history of the Shakespear family.

John Shakespear died 3rd April 1786 aged 47 years.
Martha, his wife died 31st January 1828 aged 76 years.

Samuel Shakespear, son of John and Martha, from Staunton Harrold died at Tonge 14th January 1833 aged 58 years.

Joseph Shakespear died 24th October 1800 aged 24 years.

Thomas Shakespear, fourth son of John and Martha died 30th September 1849 aged 70 years.

William Shakespear (born Staunton Harrold) died 20th September 1815 aged 32 years.

Jabez Shakespear - youngest son of John and Martha died 3rd September 1846 aged 70 years.

Hepzibah Shakespear, widow of Samuel Shakespear. Youngest daughter of John and Hepzibah Hall of Tonge died 12th November 1849 aged 74 years.

From the headstones in Diseworth Parish Churchyard

John Shakespear, eldest son of
Charles and Elizabeth Shakespear died 16th 1886 aged 17 years.

Emily sister of above
Died April 14th 1898 aged 34 years.

Charles Shakespear
Died April 25th 1899 aged 88 years.

His wife Elizabeth
Died December 17th 1916 aged 85 years.

Margaret Roseia, only daughter of
Charles Bowles and Mary Jane Shakespear, died April 28th 1943 aged 31 years.

Charles Bowles Shakespear
Died February 16th 1959 aged 88 years.

John Hornby Shakespear
Died May 10th 1970.

GLOSSARY

Advowson	Right of appointing a priest to a benefice. Held by a patron, either an individual or an institution.
Bovate	An eighth of a carucate. Approximately 15 acres. As much land as one ox could plough in a year.
Carucate	Measure of land varying in size according to condition of soil. As much land as could be ploughed in one year by eight oxen. Eight oxgangs or 120 acres.
Cartulary	Collection of charters or records. Place where these are kept.
Cordwainer	Shoemaker
Corrody	Pension. Traditional mediaeval right to demand an allowance of food and clothing from a monastery.
Cottar	Lowest of the peasant hierarchy at the time of the Domesday Survey. A cottager with 4 acres or less.
Croft	Small field near a dwelling house used for pasture.
De Banco Roll	Court of Common Pleas.
Demesne	Land belonging to the lord of the manor and worked by peasants for the lord's profit.
Dorter	Bedroom or dormitory, especially in a monastery or nunnery.
Esquire	Attendant who carried the shield of a knight and who ranked immediately below him. Title of gentleman of noble birth but considered of higher rank than a gentleman. (Lat) Scutarius - shield bearer.
Estovers	Necessaries allowed by law to tenant of land, especially wood for fuel and repairs.
Extra-Parochial	Licensed for worship but not ministering to a parish.
Fee	Freehold property which could be inherited.
Fine	Sum of money paid by an incoming tenant in consideration of a small rent.
Frater	Refectory
Freeman	A tenant holding land at a fixed rent but free of feudal service.
Gentleman	Man of good breeding and chivalrous manners and good social position. In the middle ages - of status between esquire and yeoman.
Glebe	Portion of land attached to a clergyman's benefice.
Hereditament	Inheritance. Property which can be inherited.
Hide	Measure of land - normally 100 acres. Amount of land necessary to support a peasant household.
Hundred	Sub-division of county or shire and having its own court. Unit of 100 taxable hides.

Ibid	Following.
Ichabod	Exclamation of regret - "the glory has departed".
Knight's fee	System of military service. Obligation to the king to do battle when called upon in return for occupation of land.
Manor	An estate with jurisdiction over tenants.
Messuage	Dwelling house with outbuildings and surrounding land.
Moiety	Half. One of two parts.
Mortuary	An ecclesiastical payment or customary gift claimed by and due to a minister.
Oblation	Offering.
Octaves of St Martin	Seventh day after a festival, in this case St Martin's day. Period of eight days including a festival and its octave
Oxgang	Bovate. Between ten and eighteen acres.
Plough	Amount of arable land on an estate. As much land as could be ploughed by one team of oxen in a year.
Quitclaim	Renunciation of right to land.
Seise	Legal possession of land by freehold rather than ownership.
S.P. *Sine Prole*	Childless (*Died* S.P. Died without issue.)
Tenement	Any rented land or dwelling.
Terrier	A register of landed property describing site, boundaries, acreage etc.
Toft	Homestead. Site of house and outbuildings. Elongated plot of land set at right angles to the road and originally provided for tenants to cultivate.
Villein	Feudal serf and highest class of peasantry, frequently holding 30 - 100 acres. Of superior status to a slave but below that of sokeman and freeman.
Virgate	Area of land between 20 and 30 acres. A quarter of a hide.
Warrant	Written authority to supply or receive goods or money. Also to carry out a search or arrest.
Yardland	Area of land, usually 30 acres or one fourth of a hide.
Yeoman	Man holding and cultivating a small landed estate. Historically a person qualifying to possess free land of annual value of forty shillings, serve on juries and vote for knight of the shire etc. Often known as a forty shilling freeholder.

ACKNOWLEDGEMENTS

Awards for All, National Lottery Heritage Fund, for sponsorship.
Master, Fellows and Scholars, Christ's College, Cambridge, for permission to use copies of documents belonging to Christ's College.
Professor Geoffrey Martin, Keeper of the Muniment Room, Christ's College, for his valuable assistance, encouragement and time on behalf of our research.
Record Office for Leicestershire, Leicester and Rutland
Record Office for Derbyshire
Local Studies Dept, Loughborough Library.
Pat Guy, Archivist, Diseworth Local History Society
Head Teacher and Governors, Diseworth CE School
Eric Dyer and Peter Beddoe for information on East Midlands Airport
Malcolm and Nancy Cowley for contributions to 20th century Diseworth
Mary Gidlow - for proof reading the bulk of the book
Minnie Hutchinson for information on the Orton Family
Christopher Loveday - for research on Langley Priory
Liz Jarrom for information on the Jarrom Family
Woolley, Beardsley and Bosworth, Solicitors
The Local History Press Ltd for information and advice.

Ken Brompton
Martin Hening
Dave and Jackie Adcock
Elizabeth Adkin
Andrew Crowe
Rosalyn Edwards
Annie Fletcher
Arthur Fletcher
Gordon Fletcher
John Jarrom
Catherine Lockett
Mrs D Matthews
Ada Measey
Bessie Poynton
Mike Shaw
Karen Sims
Rosemary Smith
Bill Tollington
Jill Wagstaffe
Alan and Dot Yeates
Villagers of Diseworth

BIBLIOGRAPHY

Aspects of Kegworth, Kegworth Museum
Barker H - Circle of Trees
Beckett JV - East Midlands from AD1000
Charity Commissioners Report 32nd edition
Curtis - History of Leicestershire 1830
Dictionary of National Biography
Diseworth Baptist Church Two Hundred Years of Christian Witness
Diseworth Churchwardens Accounts
Diseworth Local History Society documents and booklets
English Historical Documents
Farnham GF - Leicestershire Medieval Village Notes
Jack S - The Last Days of the Smaller Monasteries
Jack S - Monastic Lands in Leicestershire and their Administration on the eve of the Dissolution
Kellys Directory
Leicestershire Archaeological Transactions
Leicestershire Architectural Society
Mee A - Leicestershire and Rutland
Methodism in Diseworth - Public Library
Nichols - History and Antiquities of Leicestershire 1804
Palmer M - Framework Knitting
Peile J - Cambridge University College Histories Christ's College
Simon B - Education in Leicestershire 1540 - 1940
Shardlow Union - Guardians Minute Books
Victoria County Histories, Leicestershire
Victoria County Histories, Staffordshire
Whites Directory of Leicestershire and Rutland
Wrights Directories